Catholics For A Free Choice EXPOSED

BRIAN CLOWES, PhD

HUMAN LIFE INTERNATIONAL™
Front Royal, Virginia
©2001

© 2001 HUMAN LIFE INTERNATIONAL™

HUMAN LIFE INTERNATIONAL™
4 FAMILY LIFE
FRONT ROYAL, VIRGINIA 22630
PHONE: 540/635-7884 ❖ FAX: 540/636-7363
WEB: WWW.HLI.ORG ❖ E-MAIL: HLI@HLI.ORG

Library of Congress Catalogue Card Number Application Submitted
ISBN 1-55922-047-3

Printed in the United States of America

Dedication

This book is dedicated to the great work of *Vida Humana Internacional*, which has been battling Catholics for a Free Choice and the Culture of Death in Latin America for more than a decade. In a special way, we would like to honor Magaly Llaguno, who has led VHI in defending the rights of preborn children everywhere for many years, and is now also fighting for her own life against cancer. If all pro-lifers would fight with the determination and zeal of Magaly and VHI, the world would be safe for our preborn brothers and sisters.

"Therefore, my beloved brethren, be steadfast, immovable, always abounding in the work of the Lord, knowing that in the Lord your labor is not in vain." — 1 Corinthians 15:58.

Acknowledgements

The author would like to express his sincere thanks to Adolfo J. Castañeda of *Vida Humana Internacional*, whose theological work provided the foundation for the latter section of the book, Magaly Llaguno and the late James Miller, upon whose work he built.

Table
of
Contents

Introduction

Who and What Are We Fighting? Centuries ago, the great Chinese general and strategist Sun Tzu wrote in his classic *The Art of War* that "All warfare is based primarily on the deception of an enemy. Fighting on a battlefield is the most primitive way of making war. There is no art higher than to destroy your enemy without a fight — by subverting anything of value in your enemy's country."[1]

Pro-abortionists know full well that their agenda is repugnant to the majority of thinking individuals. Public opinion polls repeatedly show that Americans believe that the vast majority of abortions should be banned.[2] Because of this, pro-abortionists cannot rely upon the democratic system. They must instead force their agenda on the nation by gaining control of society's organs of power and influence through a tactic called "infiltration and subversion," so ably described by General Sun.

The general strategy of the leaders of the Culture of Death is to place talented people in the leadership positions of the sources of influence in society, which are;

* The **executive branches** of the national governments, regions and states;
* The **courts**, particularly the national court systems;
* The **legislatures** at the national, regional and state levels;
* The leaders and boards of **associations** with relevant missions, including organized medical and legal professionals, foundations, non-governmental organizations (NGOs) and public interest groups;
* The **media**, particularly the entertainment industry (motion pictures, television, radio), the print and news media (newspapers, magazines, book authors and publishers and newscasters) and the arts;
* **School leaders**, from grade school board members to the policymakers at medical and legal colleges; and
* The leadership of the **churches**, particularly the Catholic Church.

Once they accomplish this objective, the new leaders can introduce their agendas, stonewall pro-life initiatives, and subvert the organization so that its voice is added to the ranks of those prestigious groups loudly chorusing for "progress" and "change."

Regarding the field of strategy and tactics, the Catholic Church is identical to other organizations in many important ways. For example, the Church is actually *strengthened* by an overt attack carried out by a visible enemy.

However, the Church is extremely vulnerable to a long-term and persistent program of infiltration and subversion, because the visible results of such an attack take place slowly and in increments small enough to escape attention. Since it is always easier to defend against an enemy that presents a *visible* threat, the infiltrators escape the determined and concentrated counterattack that would beat back an external assault. As the pro-abortion extremist group Population Institute brags, "The biggest organizations are difficult to beat, but they are the easiest to infiltrate and exploit."[3]

In an address before the Roman Senate, Cicero described how infiltration and subversion works;

> A nation can survive its fools and even the ambitious. But it cannot survive treason from within. An enemy at the gates is less formidable, for he is known and he carries his banners openly against the city. But the traitor moves among those within the gates freely, his sly whispers rustling through all the alleys, heard in the very halls of government itself. For the traitor appears no traitor; he speaks in the accents familiar to his victims, and he wears their face and their garments and he appeals to the baseness that lies deep in the hearts of all men.[4]

This is the role played by Catholics for a Free Choice.

They are the traitors whose sly whispers are couched in terms familiar to real Catholics. They actively work to look and sound like real Catholics. And they most certainly appeal to our fallen nature — the weakness and baseness that lies deep in the hearts of all men and women.

CFFC occupies a vital niche in the worldwide pro-abortion movement. The Catholic Church has always been the most powerful opponent of abortion in the world. The primary objective of CFFC is to paralyze effective action by the Catholic Church against the Culture of Death by sowing confusion and discord among its members. By doing so, CFFC shows that it is being influenced by the

Devil, whom Jesus Christ described in the following terms;

> If God were your Father, you would love Me ... You are of your father the devil, and your will is to do your father's desires. He was a murderer from the beginning, and has nothing to do with the truth, because there is no truth in him. When he lies, he speaks according to his own nature, for he is a liar and the father of lies [John 8:42,44].

The Purpose of This Book

The writers and speakers associated with Catholics for a Free Choice are masters of smooth speech and soothing words. To anyone who picks up a copy of CFFC's journal *Conscience* and reads it straight through, or listens to a few tapes produced by the organization, its ideology seems reasonable, its theologians orthodox and its sources of information unimpeachable.

However, CFFC subscribes to a morally relativistic ideology. As described in the encyclical *Veritatis Splendor* ["The Splendor of Truth"], it is literally impossible for moral relativists to be consistent in their thinking or in their actions, because their morality is always shifting in order to justify their activities and accomplish their objectives.

As a researcher delves more deeply into CFFC's materials, it becomes obvious that its ideology is extreme and hypocritical, its reasoning inconsistent and contradictory, and its sources of information distorted or deliberately misrepresented.

This book highlights the many deficiencies in CFFC's deadly ideology and describes its history, its funding, and the wide range of its anti-life activities. Thus armed, real Catholics can expose Catholics for a Free Choice for what it is —craven traitors to the Faith and a pseudo-religious facade for the international population control and pro-abortion movement.

Strategies of Catholics for a Free Choice

How CFFC Describes Itself. According to the *Encyclopedia of Associations*, Catholics For a Free Choice (CFFC) is an association of "Catholics within the Roman Catholic Church who support the right to legal reproductive health care, especially to family planning and abortion." The *Encyclopedia* says that CFFC's goal is to "preserve the right of women's choices in childbearing and child rearing." CFFC "advocates social and economic programs for women, families and children" by engaging in "public education on being Catholic and pro-choice."

In order to accomplish its ultimate goal of abortion on demand through all nine months of pregnancy worldwide, CFFC pursues three primary supporting strategies.

CFFC's First Strategy. CFFC's first strategy is to create confusion, discord and dissent among Catholics regarding what the Catholic Church teaches on abortion. CFFC strategists know that if they can plant a seed of doubt in people's minds about the traditional Catholic response to abortion by asserting that the Church did not *always* oppose prenatal baby-killing, then the Church will appear inconsistent and punitive when it *does* oppose abortion.

Former CFFC Board member Marjorie Reiley Maguire tries to make dissent sound like altruism when she says that

> God wills dissent to reach the blindness and hardness of heart of many Church leaders. Dissent is a constructive not a destructive activity in the religious community. ... Dissent with laws and rules of the Church does not mean that I have put myself outside Church membership. It is simply an indication that the rules and laws must be examined anew by all the members of the Church to determine whether they have ceased to serve the whole Church.

CFFC's Second Strategy. CFFC's second strategy is to persuade people that the unrestricted availability of abortion is necessary in order for them to enjoy full religious freedom. CFFC asserts that, if abortion is restricted in any way, religious freedom is being unacceptable compromised. CFFC says that if abortion is criminalized, a particular religious belief about when life begins is being forced upon the people. Of course, CFFC never mentions that the particular religious belief that life begins *at birth* is being enforced by governments in many nations right now.

CFFC's Third Strategy. CFFC's third strategy is to persuade people that they can be good Catholics and still kill their preborn children with clear consciences. In fact, CFFC insists people cannot be good Catholics *unless* they support abortion! This is in line with its insistence that every Catholic hospital must commit abortions, and every insurance plan must pay for them, even if the hospital or insurance plan is operated by a church to whom abortion is morally repugnant.

Conclusion. Discerning CFFC's overall strategies is an essential step towards understanding its rhetoric. Once we recognize that CFFC seeks to undermine Church teachings regarding abortion through an aggressive program of infiltration and subversion, and once we see that its ultimate goal is the legalization of abortion worldwide, the organization's unsavory history and its alliances make more sense.

Additionally, we can comprehend the true magnitude of the threat that CFFC represents.

Part 1

The History of Catholics for a Free Choice

"Because of its opposition to the human rights of some of the most defenseless members of the human race, and because its purposes and activities deliberately contradict essential teachings of the Catholic faith. ... Catholics for a Free Choice merits no recognition or support as a Catholic organization."
— United States National Council of Catholic Bishops.[5]

The 1970s: The Pro-Abortion Movement Finds Its `Catholic' Voice.

The Beginnings. Three members of the extremist feminist group National Organization for Women (NOW) organized Catholics for a Free Choice in 1970 in order to protest the Catholic Church's staunch opposition to New York's permissive abortion laws.

CFFC's three founders were Joan Harriman, Meta Mulcahy and Patricia Fogarty McQuillan. Showing its disrespect for the Catholic Faith right from the beginning, the group's first public act was to crown McQuillan "Pope Joan I" on the steps of St. Patrick's Cathedral in New York City.[6]

CFFC's first office was located in the New York suite of the Planned Parenthood Federation of America (PPFA), owner of the largest chain of abortion mills in North America. From the beginning, CFFC and PPFA have shared not only office space, but ideologies and objectives.

For example, former PPFA president Pamela Maraldo claimed that

> I go to church on Sunday but do not subscribe to many of the basic tenets of the Church. That does not mean I am any less a Catholic. ... Jesus has little to say about sexuality, so it is

1

impossible to cite Gospel text to support efforts to direct human sexual behavior ... To my mind, the church would do well to follow Christ's example of compassion, respect for women, and silence on questions of human sexuality and reproduction. ... *Humanae Vitae* will take its place with other embarrassing teachings in the annals of Vatican, curiosities for generations to come.[7]

In other words, Maraldo ran the largest chain of abortion mills in North America for several years, and considered this no impediment to being a "good Catholic."

As we will see, this is an example of the mentality that Catholics for a Free Choice promotes all over the world.

After the United States Supreme Court legalized abortion in 1973, CFFC affiliated with the newly organized Religious Coalition for Abortion Rights (now RCRC). CFFC described itself as "a national educational organization that supports the right to legal reproductive health care, especially family planning and abortion."

CFFC's Early Leaders. Former Jesuit Joseph O'Rourke held the post of CFFC president until 1979. In 1974, O'Rourke, then a CFFC Board member, challenged Boston Archbishop Humberto Cardinal Madeiros' ban on the baptism of babies of publicly pro-abortion mothers and was dismissed from the Jesuits for his disobedience.[8]

O'Rourke acknowledged that CFFC's primary function was to provide an allegedly Catholic voice at pro-abortion press conferences when he said that "CFFC really was just kept alive for years because the mainline pro-choice movement wanted a Catholic voice."[9] This was a cunning move by the pro-abortion movement — a gaggle of self-described 'Catholic' traitors could get away with activities that would get any other group plastered with an "anti-Catholic" label.

In 1979, Pat McMahon became the executive director of CFFC and the organization's emphasis shifted from lobbying to education. CFFC began to more clearly define its mission as defending the "right" of Catholics to be pro-abortion, and it began to publicly challenge Church doctrine on abortion.

The Sunnen Foundation gave CFFC a $75,000 grant to fund its first publications, a series of booklets entitled "Abortion in Good Faith." The most popular of this series, "The History of Abortion in the Catholic Church," remains a core CFFC publication.

In the late 1970s, pro-life groups strongly supported several Human Life Amendments (HLAs) to the United States Constitution. During Pope John Paul II's visit to the United States in 1979, CFFC sponsored an advertisement in the *Washington Post* claiming that a Human Life Amendment would "establish as the law of the land the religious views of a minority of Americans."

In 1979, CFFC had little visibility and an annual budget of about $65,000, almost two-thirds of which was provided by grants from a Unitarian Universalist church in New York.[10]

The Early 1980s: CFFC Refines Its Mission.

Kissling Takes Over. In 1980, Frances Kissling took over the leadership of CFFC. She had been a co-founder and president of the National Abortion Federation (NAF), a trade association of abortion mills. CFFC maintained close ties with NAF, whose member abortuaries opened their doors to CFFC in 1981 so it could conduct a survey of Catholic women having abortions. The two groups also shared some funding sources.[11]

In 1981, CFFC began to claim that it had more than 5,000 members. However, it received a total of only about $5,000 annually from membership dues. In fiscal year 1983, this figure comprised less than 3 percent of CFFC's $221,900 income. The balance was from private foundations and other tax-exempt groups. This was a result of Kissling's emphasis on obtaining funding from foundations whose philosophies are hostile to Catholic teachings on sexual ethics.

For example, CFFC received $10,000 from the Playboy Foundation in each of the years 1982 and 1983. During these same years, Playboy also funded the Religious Coalition for Abortion Rights (RCAR), to which CFFC belongs.[12]

Onlookers frequently remarked that it was curious indeed that two allegedly "religious" groups that boast of "standing up for women's rights" would accept money from Hugh Hefner, whose entire life and fortune are based upon exploiting and degrading women. Yet perhaps we should not be so hasty in condemning CFFC and RCAR for accepting money from pornographers. After all, there is more consistency here than first meets the eye. Does not abortion exploit and degrade women as well? Abortion fits into the "playboy philosophy" perfectly, and enables unscrupulous men to exploit women in even more damaging ways than pornography.

When questioned about her group's Playboy funding, Frances Kissling said that "I've never felt that by taking money from someone indicates that we support them." However, she stated that CFFC would never accept money from *Hustler* magazine, because, as she put it, "There are boundaries of good taste."[13]

CFFC finally disassociated itself from Playboy because of the criticism it was receiving from both friend and foe. Kissling said much later that "At that time, we viewed it [the funding] as reparation for the magazine's sexism."[14]

Some astute observers asked that, if *Playboy* Magazine was so "sexist," and CFFC took funding from it for "reparations," why did it suddenly decide to stop receiving the funding? We can be sure it wasn't because *Playboy* Magazine suddenly stopped being sexist!

One of CFFC's largest sources of funding in the early 1980s was the Sunnen Foundation (see Appendix D). The Sunnen Foundation was founded on the profits from Emko contraceptive foam, and it funded the litigation that led to the Supreme Court's 1973 *Roe v. Wade* and *Doe v. Bolton* rulings legalizing abortion. Sunnen has been involved in pro-abortion projects ever since.

Sunnen also helped fund a 1979 newspaper ad that blamed the church's teaching on birth control for world hunger and urged Catholics who wanted the teaching changed to donate money to the Population Institute.[15] Finally, Sunnen's director has called the Catholic Church "detrimental to the world," and has demanded that the Church be *forced by law* to change Her teachings on abortion![16]

If agitation doesn't work for pro-abortionists, they never hesitate to use force.

CFFC Confronts the Catholic Bishops. On November 5, 1981, CFFC held a press conference at the United States Senate Building to protest the testimony of the Catholic bishops favoring legal protection of preborn children. Claiming the bishop's stance was unrepresentative of Catholic opinion and behavior, CFFC released a study of Catholic women having abortions. The results of the study were deliberately skewed because it did not survey Catholic women who practiced their Faith; it instead focused on women describing themselves as "non-practicing Catholics" or as "ex-Catholics."

On August 30, 1982, CFFC filed a brief with other members of the Religious Coalition for Abortion Rights in the Supreme Court case *City of Akron v. Akron*

Center for Reproductive Health. The RCAR brief argued that *all* restrictions on abortion are based on a purely theological opinion regarding the beginning of life, and thus violate the First Amendment's guarantee of freedom of religion. The brief, of course, ignored the fact that abortion on demand is *also* based on a theological opinion — that human life begins at birth.

RCAR and CFFC also claimed in their *Akron* brief that factual descriptions of fetal development should not be made available to women seeking abortions because they constitute a "propaganda tool for the anti-abortion position." Finally, the brief condemned a one-day waiting period to give women time to think over the abortion decision as "intolerable," because abortion is "a moral decision sacred to dissenting faiths."[17]

In September 1982, CFFC conducted a briefing for Catholic members of the House of Representatives. This meeting was sponsored by three self-described "pro-choice Catholic" members of Congress, including failed vice-presidential candidate Geraldine Ferraro (D-NY). CFFC published the proceedings in a booklet entitled "The Abortion Issue in the Political Process." Mrs. Ferraro's introduction claimed that the presentations by pro-abortion theologian Daniel Maguire and others disproved the existence of a "monolithic" Catholic stance on abortion.

In January 1983, CFFC held a similar press conference at the United States Senate and announced that Catholic social justice principles *require* Catholic members of Congress to vote for funding of elective abortions for poor women, regardless of their beliefs on the issue. Frances Kissling predicted that CFFC would have "an opportunity to affect not only the public policy positions of the church but also the internal treatment of the subject of abortion." This event also marked the first public release of CFFC's "Statement on Abortion and Catholicism" that was to be the basis for its subsequent *New York Times* ad.[18]

In September 1983, CFFC began to openly contradict Catholic teaching regarding the formation of conscience by publishing a booklet entitled "Abortion: A Guide to Making Ethical Choices." Daniel and Marjorie Reiley Maguire, drafters of the "Statement on Abortion and Catholicism," authored this publication.

CFFC distributed this booklet to abortion mills and student health services nationwide. Its supposed purpose was to help guide decisionmaking on abortion for young Catholic women and others. According to the preface by Kissling, its guiding principle was that "the decision to abort can be a moral decision justified by many circumstances." It also claimed that "abortion must be legal for women to even begin to make a moral choice with real freedom."

The basic message of the booklet was that abortion can be right or wrong depending upon motive or circumstances. Naturally, the booklet framed the issue so that abortion is never really "wrong," and it was very effective at salving the consciences of Catholic women considering abortion.

The 1984 *New York Times* Advertisement. In March 1984, CFFC organized a "Catholic Committee on Pluralism and Abortion," which revised the "Statement on Abortion and Catholicism" and renamed it the "Catholic Statement on Pluralism and Abortion." The Committee distributed this Statement to members of various theological societies along with a questionnaire on their abortion views. Although this was a project of CFFC, the statement and questionnaire did not mention its name; responses were to be sent to "CFFC" at the organization's Washington address. There was also no indication that this statement would become an advertisement in a secular newspaper.[19]

The Day Arrives. The Catholic bishops of the United States designated October 7, 1984 as Respect Life Sunday. On this date, CFFC took the opportunity to publish a deliberate slap in the face to the bishops and to all real Catholics: A full-page advertisement in the *New York Times* entitled "A Catholic Statement on Pluralism and Abortion." The ad's primary thesis was that "A diversity of opinions regarding abortion exists among committed Catholics."

CFFC sponsored the ad and gathered the signatures. It was designed and placed through Planned Parenthood's New York ad agency. The agency's president said he accepted the task of designing the ad as "a favor to Planned Parenthood."[20]

The controversy generated by the ad catapulted CFFC into national prominence in the pro-abortion movement, which for the first time realized the full potential value of sowing dissent, discord and confusion among Catholics. After all, an uncertain and confused opponent is much weaker than one which holds to one true philosophy and speaks with one voice.

Surveying the Theologians. CFFC's claim that the majority of the American laity reject the Church's teaching on abortion is unfortunately accurate. This is primarily because most Catholics are confused and/or uninformed about the issues due to silence from the pulpit and confusion deliberately sowed by many dissenting groups, including CFFC. However, CFFC failed to mention that those

6

Catholics who actually *practice* their Faith are overwhelmingly pro-life.

The *New York Times* ad also asserted that there were diverse "legitimate Catholic positions" on abortion. There certainly are *diverse* beliefs among nominal Catholics regarding abortion; yet only one of these is *legitimate*.

CFFC's claim that "a large number of Catholic theologians" believe that direct abortion "can sometimes be a moral choice" is demonstrably false. To begin with, not *one* of the nation's prominent Catholic moral theologians signed the ad — only those who were either CFFC's "house theologians" or those whose writings placed them on the extreme fringe of theology, far removed from authentic Catholic teaching. The ad's claim was also strongly disputed by famous liberal theologians who were asked to sign but refused. One of these was Father Richard McBrien, Chairman of the University of Notre Dame's Theology Department and author of the book *Catholicism*, who observed that "very, very few Catholic theologians support the pro-choice position."[21]

A survey conducted by the sponsors of the *New York Times* ad confirms the fact that only a tiny minority of renegade theologians support unlimited access to abortion. Shortly after the ad appeared, CFFC published the responses to the questionnaire it had sent out to the members of various professional societies, including the Catholic Theological Society of America (CTSA). CFFC deliberately excluded from its survey groups that *supported* the Vatican's policies, presumably targeting organizations with a history of dissent from Catholic teachings on sexual ethics or criticism of the Vatican. Despite this fact, more than 75 percent of the survey's recipients did not return the questionnaire.

Among those theologians who *did* respond, a slim majority (51 percent) said that abortion should never be "left to the conscience of the pregnant woman," while only 6 percent favored the current legal policy permitting abortion until birth. Regarding the Supreme Court's *Roe v. Wade* decision legalizing abortion, 58 percent described it as "completely unacceptable" and another 16 percent said it was "too permissive."

The questionnaire also asked when "human life becomes a person." Among respondents,

*   47 percent said that human life becomes a person at conception;
*   19 percent said that human life becomes a person at some time between conception and birth;
*   21 percent said the answer cannot be determined;
*   12 percent said it was an irrelevant question; and

* only 1 percent supported CFFC's opinion that personhood begins at birth.[22]

Surveying the Laity. CFFC's *New York Times* ad also claimed that the National Opinion Research Center (NORC) found that "only 11 percent of Catholic laity surveyed disapproved of abortion in all circumstances."

However, the NORC poll referenced by CFFC was concerned only with legal policy. Even the most committed pro-life activists favor leeway in the law for cases such as danger to the mother's life.

A Gallup poll conducted at about the same time as the *New York Times* was released showed that;

* 21 percent of the general public favors making abortion illegal in all circumstances;
* 55 percent want it to be legal only under certain limited circum stances, including for the life of the mother, for rape and incest, and for severe birth defects; and
* only 21 percent favor CFFC's official position, which is no restrictions whatever.

The NORC and Gallup polls show that support for restricting abortion is higher among Catholics than among the general population, and certainly would be higher still among *practicing* Catholics.[23]

Fallout From the Ad. CFFC's *New York Times* ad concluded with vague calls for "dialogue" in the Church and demands for acknowledgement of the complexity of sexual ethics, the right to dissent, and the necessity of opposing legislation that would curtail "freedom of religion" or discriminate against poor women. Those who agreed with the ad were urged to contribute to CFFC.

About 2,000 people had received the March 1984 mailing mentioned above, but only 95 signed the *New York Times* ad. 65 of these possessed academic degrees in theology or religious studies. 27 of the signers were members of religious orders.

The Vatican's Congregation for Religious and Secular Institutes (CRIS) informed the members of religious orders that they would be disciplined unless they retracted their false statement that there were diverse "*legitimate* Catholic positions" on abortion. The drafters of the "Catholic Statement on Pluralism and

Abortion" reacted by publishing a second ad expressing solidarity with the first statement's signers and protesting what it called the "repression of freedom of speech" within the Church.

CFFC took advantage of the controversy it initiated with the ads and stepped up its cooperative efforts with other pro-abortionists. Events since 1984 prove that the *New York Times* ad was part of a purely political strategy designed to undermine the Catholic Church's efforts against the abortion industry, and not "a serious contribution to the theological discussion within the church" as the ad drafters claimed.

Even the liberal *National Catholic Reporter* accused CFFC of taking the abortion issue "from the level of serious religious commitment and theological discussion to that of a mere political sign-up campaign." *NCR* also urged its readers not to sign the ad. Kissling responded that *NCR*'s criticism was based on a "gross misunderstanding" of her organization's agenda, but of course did not elaborate.[24]

The Late 1980s: CFFC Joins Forces with Other Pro-Abortion Groups.

CFFC Capitalizes on the Publicity From the *New York Times* Ad. The 1984 *New York Times* ad was the most direct and well-publicized challenge to Church teaching authority and doctrine that had ever been launched by a pro-abortion group. CFFC used its newfound status and notoriety by stepping up its cooperative efforts with other pro-abortionists.

The Bishops' Committee for Pro-Life Activities responded to the *New York Times* ad on November 25 by reaffirming the Church's 20-century-old condemnation of abortion, and by pointing out that CFFC had no status in the Church (Appendix A includes the Bishop's statement). The bishops also stated that they did not doubt CFFC's sincerity, and urged its members to study the Church's teaching on the obligation to protect human life as proclaimed by the Second Vatican Council.

In March of 1985, CFFC demonstrated that it was not interested in listening to the bishops or in dialoguing with them when it joined the Unitarian Universalist Association and other RCAR affiliates in filing a pro-abortion brief in the *Kendrick v. Heckler* case, claiming that the Federal Adolescent Family Life program violated the First Amendment by forbidding most abortion counseling and referral by grantees. The signers of the brief claimed that they counseled adolescents "individually and through the Clergy Counseling Network of the Religious Coalition for Abortion Rights" and were "among the many religious denominations foreclosed from participating in [this program] because they cannot conscientiously counsel adolescents on pregnancy and cannot discuss the option of abortion."

CFFC repeated these arguments in the *City of Akron v. Akron Center for Reproductive Health* case, objecting to informed consent and parental notification provisions and requirements that all abortions must be performed in a hospital and that the remains of aborted babies must be disposed of in a "humane and sanitary manner."

These legal briefs revealed several facets of CFFC's evolving ideology and tactics. First, they demonstrated that CFFC is truly *pro*-abortion, because its official position is that it is unreasonable to place any restrictions whatever on abortion, and that the act of abortion can be morally justified in virtually any circumstance. Second, CFFC's financial and other ties with secular pro-abortion and population control groups seem much stronger than its links with other dissenting organizations. Third, although it publicly and repeatedly claims to favor "dialogue" within the Church, CFFC has studiously avoided opportunities for dialogue in favor of forthrightly confrontational tactics. Many of CFFC's activities are designed to counteract the Catholic Church's public policy impact by presenting itself as something akin to an alternative religious denomination, a claim it actually made in the *Kendrick v. Heckler* brief described above.

National and International Cooperation. CFFC's crusade against life and the family has naturally led it to join organizations and coalitions both nationally and internationally in order to promote the legalization of abortion, euthanasia, divorce, population control and ersatz homosexual "marriage."

CFFC works closely with other anti-life groups, including the International Women's Health Coalition, the Women's Global Network for Reproductive Rights, the Women-Church Convergence, the Unitarian Universalist Association, Planned Parenthood, the National Organization for Women, the Religious Coalition for Reproductive Choice (formerly RCAR), the National Abortion Federation and the National Abortion and Reproductive Rights Action League (NARRAL).

CFFC also works with dissenting self-described "Catholic" groups, including Catholics Speak Out, Chicago Catholic Women, Institute of Women Today, Loretto Women's Network, National Coalition of American Nuns (NCAN), Women in Spirit of Colorado Task Force, the Women's Alliance for Theology, Ethics and Ritual (WATER), and the Women's Ordination Conference.[25]

CFFC Board members Mary Hunt and Rosemary Ruether spoke at the 1994 Call to Action National Conference in Chicago. Both also sat on the Board of the "We Are Church Coalition." According to CFFC's *Conscience* magazine, "Catholic Organizations for Renewal and the Women Church Convergence have asked CFFC and the Women's Ordination Conference (WOC) to act as a bridge between them in order to keep each coalition informed of the other's activities and facilitate collaboration."[26]

In 1987, CFFC joined other anti-life feminist organizations in South America to establish the Latin American Women's Health Network, whose objective is to promote "reproductive health" and "reproductive rights," which are code words for unlimited free contraception, sterilization and abortion. The Network publishes a newsletter in Spanish titled *Revista de la Red de Salud/Isis Internacional* ("Magazine of the Health Network/Isis International") in Santiago, Chile, and distributes it in Latin America through its information service, Isis International, the most visible Latin American anti-life feminist organization.[27]

The 1990s: CFFC Finds a Global Forum.

Overview. Since Catholics for a Free Choice obtained United Nations nongovernmental organization (NGO) status, it has aggressively exploited its standing to pursue an anti-life agenda at the global level.

CFFC gathered about forty anti-life and feminist groups in preparation for the United Nations' International Conference on Population and Development (ICPD), which took place in September 1994 in Cairo, Egypt. The key agenda issues of this coalition were to redefine family and gender and establish abortion as a universal "human right."[28]

During the United Nation's Fourth World Conference on Women in Beijing in 1995, Frances Kissling presented a speech entitled "Responding to Religious Conservatism," in which she complained that "conservatism often expresses itself in ways that are intolerant, violent, silencing and provocative," but of course she provided no concrete examples. CFFC also lobbied to gain support for its plans to deny the Vatican special observer status at UN gatherings.

In 1996 CFFC came to the defense of the United Nations International Children's Emergency Fund (UNICEF) when the Vatican withheld its annual contribution because of UNICEF's promotion of contraceptives and abortifacients. Frances Kissling raved that the Vatican was engaging in "intimidation" and "strong arm tactics," and was conducting a "dirty little war" against "every good thing."[29] CFFC could have quietly made up the $2,000 the Vatican withheld, but instead launched a public relations blitz to condemn the Holy See, which was presumably just "following its conscience" when it decided not to donate to UNICEF. In CFFC's eyes, it seems that only "pro-choice Catholics" may follow their consciences.

Frances Kissling once again tried to divert attention from the topic of abortion as she bleated that "It's time we sent a clear signal to the church hierarchy that we are sick and tired of this single-minded obsession with abortion and family planning. We want to get on with the church's mission to feed the hungry, clothe the naked, comfort the sick, and shelter the homeless. Especially the children."[30]

It is interesting that CFFC tries to portray the bishops of the Catholic Church as "obsessed" with sexual issues. Daniel C. Maguire, for instance, in his comments on the encyclical *Veritatis Splendor*, said that "Many others light on the references to the pelvic issues that have so consumed this and previous pontificates and remains a preoccupation here."[31]

We must ask *who* has a "preoccupation" with the "pelvic issues." A study of the documents of the Church and the homilies of Pope John Paul II shows that about five percent address the so-called "pelvic issues." As for CFFC — well, a careful look at its literature shows that it talks about little else. CFFC is by *any* definition (including its own) *totally obsessed* with these issues.

As for Kissling's allegation that CFFC wanted "to get on with the church's mission to feed the hungry, clothe the naked, comfort the sick, and shelter the homeless," we have seen no evidence that CFFC has actually *done* any of these activities. All it *has* done is push abortion.

"We Are [0.06 Percent of the] Church." In 1996, CFFC enthusiastically promoted the "We Are Church" Referendum organized by dissenting Sister Maureen Fiedler, co-director of the Quixote Center and Catholics Speak Out (CSO). Fiedler directed the effort in the United States, confidently predicting that it would garner more than one million signatures.

CFFC ran a full-page ad promoting the Referendum in the Summer 1996 issue of its *Conscience* magazine, and claimed that "Similar movements in Austria and Germany have already gathered 2.3 million signatories."

Signature collecting in the United States was originally scheduled for Pentecost 1996 to Pentecost 1997, then extended into the Fall of 1997. Fiedler finally gave up after only 37,000 signatures had been collected, and, after admitting that "we really gave it everything we had" (including offering schoolchildren a dollar for each signature collected), offered a variety of excuses as to why the referendum flopped so spectacularly.[32]

Perhaps it was the extremist agenda spelled out in the Referendum, which called for ordination of women as priests and deacons; lay participation in the selection of bishops and pastors; making priestly celibacy optional and reinstating married priests to active ministry; promoting homosexual rights; allowing divorced and remarried Catholics to return to all the Sacraments; and acknowledging "primacy of conscience" on questions of sexual morality.

Or maybe it was the disreputable and extreme nature of the groups working on the Referendum. In addition to CFFC, other organizations pushing the Referendum included Call to Action; the Association for the Rights of Catholics in the Church (which has drawn up a grandiose manifesto for reorganizing the Church called the "Catholic Constitution"); the National Association for a Married Priesthood; Dignity USA (a group of unrepentant 'Catholic' homosexuals); New Ways Ministries; and Priests for Equality.

The "See Change" Sees No Change.

What is the Purpose of the Campaign? Catholics for a Free Choice and all of the other pro-abortion groups at the United Nations frequently brag about their "inclusiveness" and "tolerance" of all viewpoints — except, of course, those viewpoints that happen to disagree with their ideology. The pro-abortionists at the United Nations would like to eliminate all opposition so that they might enact their agendas in an efficient and dissent-free atmosphere.

Hypocritically, CFFC, which so staunchly defends the rights of "dissenters" in the Catholic Church, works hard to silence the voices of pro-life "dissenters" in the United Nations.

The Campaign Kicks Off. In March 1999, CFFC launched the "See Change" campaign. Its purported objective is to influence the United Nations to downgrade the status of the Vatican from permanent observer status to that of non-governmental organization, or NGO, like CFFC itself. Frances Kissling has remarked that "Some of us have been wondering whether or not Euro-Disney had as many qualifications for permanent observer status as the Vatican State."[33]

According to its Web site, the See Change Campaign began with seventy participating pro-abortion organizations, including the International Planned Parenthood Federation (IPPF), the National Abortion Federation, the Center of Reproductive Law and Policy, Equality Now, Marie Stopes International, the Feminist Majority, the Sierra Club, Population Concern, the Center for Research on Population and Security, the American Humanist Association, Atheists United and the National Organization for Women (NOW).

Mission Impossible — Fortunately. Questions regarding the statehood of the Holy See have long been settled by the international community. The Holy See, as the government of the Catholic Church, is recognized by the whole world as a state. She has sent diplomatic legations to other nations since the middle of the fourth century. This is 1,650 years longer than a hundred member states of the United Nations General Assembly have even existed.

Currently, 177 nations have diplomats permanently attached to the Holy See, including the United States. All of these recognize the Holy See as a district sovereign personality for all functions of state, including entering into treaties.[34]

The Holy See joined the United Nations in 1964 as a permanent observer by agreement between U.N. Secretary-General U Thant and Pope Paul VI. Like Switzerland, the Holy See chose permanent observer status in order to remain neutral during armed conflicts, and so that it would not have to contribute financially to United Nations military efforts. The Holy See could apply for regular United Nations membership at any time, and no one (of any importance) doubts that it would be unanimously accepted.

Why Push This Campaign in the First Place? In light of the above facts, the leaders of CFFC must have known from the beginning that the "See Change" campaign would fail to achieve its stated objective. What, then, was CFFC trying to accomplish?

The real intent of the See Change campaign is purely tactical and political. Its purposes are to isolate and intimidate the Holy See's delegates to the United

Nations and to frighten away its sometimes-nervous allies.[35]

A United Nations conference is very intimidating, especially when a delegation challenges the reigning anti-family ethos. The United Nations works not by voting but by consensus. This means that every delegation must agree to every word, and means that a small coalition of states can stop almost any language from being incorporated into a UN document. All they need do is dig in their heels and speak out.

The world is a dangerous place, and many governments rely upon foreign aid, industrial development and military protection. The Holy See neither gives nor receives this kind of country-to-country assistance, and therefore it cannot be controlled or intimidated by nations willing to use foreign aid as a club in order to impose their agendas.

Kissling and her pro-abortion cronies want the Holy See to stay in its foxhole and would like to isolate it from its potential allies. Time and time again, the Holy See has stood virtually alone at United Nations conferences, opposing population control programs that are promoted through deceit, trickery, intimidation and manipulation of language. The Holy See's unique status and financial independence from the wealthy nations frees it from the kind of intimidation UN critics say is routinely employed against the developing world, thus enabling it to speak without fear of retribution when issues of human dignity and morality are at stake.[36]

Since the Cairo conference in 1994, a coalition has jelled around the life and family issues. This *ad hoc* alliance, which includes the Holy See and other Catholic and Muslim states, has stopped the United Nations from transforming abortion into an international human "right." The pro-family alliance has also stopped the UN from redefining the family to include homosexual `couples.' It has also stopped the attempt to expand the number of natural genders by defining new categories, such as homosexuals and those who call themselves the "transgendered."[37]

The See Change Campaign Flops. The See Change Campaign was doomed from the beginning. A year after it was launched, only 350 groups had signed on, and 2-1/2 years after its beginning, it had the endorsement of 653 organizations, most of them tiny local groups with no national or international stature, such as individual abortion mills or groups such as the "Alliance of Lucent and AT&T Atheists and Secularists."[38]

By vivid contrast, the Catholic Family and Human Rights Institute (C-FAM)

15

launched a counteroffensive named the "Holy See Campaign" in January 2000. It garnered 1,015 signatures in only two months, and had an impressive total of 4,207 signatures as of September 2001.[39]

Many influential persons and official agencies spoke out in favor of the Holy See. For example, the President of the European Union and President of Finland, Martti Ahtisaari, said that the Holy See "represents a special forum, as it has invaluable knowledge of events in the world, promotes peace, solidarity and tolerance, values to which we attach much importance."[40]

On July 11, 2000, the United States House of Representatives voted by a lopsided margin of 416 to one to condemn CFFC's move to end the Vatican's permanent observer status at the United Nations. The resolution commended the Holy See for its commitment to fundamental human rights; voiced objections to any effort to change its permanent observer status; and suggested that degrading its status would damage the credibility of the United Nations with countries that see the Vatican as a moral and ethical presence in the world body.[41]

Despite the near-unanimous vote of *416 to one*, Frances Kissling implied that Congressional objections were coming only from a small minority of what she described as "Republican anti-choice" representatives. Kissling continued to demonstrate how out of touch with reality she was when she claimed that the absence of support among national governments for the anti-Holy See campaign was a *positive* sign. Their "silence" was a "victory," she said.[42] It never occurred to Kissling that her "See Change" campaign was simply beneath their notice.

By contrast, the only people speaking in favor of the "See Change" campaign were pro-abortionists with no stature on the international scene.

On May 10, 2000, the National Conference of Catholic Bishops used exceptionally strong language to condemn CFFC, calling it an "arm of the abortion lobby" and publicizing the fact that "It is funded by a number of powerful and wealthy private foundations, mostly American, to promote abortion as a method of population control." The statement concluded by saying that "Catholics for a Free Choice merits no recognition or support as a Catholic organization."

Appendix A contains the full text of the NCCB statement.

The New Millennium: CFFC's Current Activities.

The Current Situation. CFFC has expanded its range of advocacy far beyond simply agitating for contraception, sterilization and abortion. CFFC's current activities show that it joins other activist pro-abortion groups on the extreme fringe of public opinion.

As described in detail later in this book, CFFC supports *all* abortions, no matter how hideous or unjustified. It seeks to compel Catholic hospitals to violate Church doctrine by distributing contraceptives and performing sterilizations. It wants to force pro-life Americans to pay for abortions, not only in the United States, but in developing countries. It even fights the most certain remedy to sexually transmitted diseases and the "unwanted pregnancies" it claims to abhor — chastity education. CFFC also demands an "inclusive" priesthood (open to women and the married), and homosexual rights, including gay "marriage."

CFFC Wants to Force Catholic Hospitals to Violate Church Doctrine. CFFC would like to force Catholic hospitals to violate Catholic sexual ethics by compelling them to offer contraceptives and sterilization services.

During the 1990s, there were 159 mergers between Catholic and non-Catholic hospitals in the United States, and Catholic hospitals now constitute the largest single group of nonprofit hospitals in the country. CFFC has been tracking these mergers since the early 1980s, and frets that "Reproductive health care is severely limited by Catholic hospitals and when Catholic hospitals merge with non-Catholic facilities."

Frances Kissling justifies CFFC's actions, saying that "Health care is not like every other business. This is not your corner candy store or K-Mart. Health care is a public trust, and as such, it is regulated by the government in ways that other businesses are not."[43]

With this statement, Kissling once again flaunted the glaring hypocrisy of her group. After all, CFFC believes that abortion is *also* "health care," yet bitterly opposes any government regulation of it whatsoever. In the *City of Akron v. Akron Center for Reproductive Health* litigation, CFFC joined in the Religious Coalition for Abortion Rights brief, which argued that *all* restrictions on abortion are based on a purely theological opinion regarding the beginning of life, and thus violate the First Amendment's guarantee of freedom of religion.

> **No matter how long or how strenuously CFFC and other dis-
> senters agitate, this silly "Woman of Cloth" doll, a popular
> sale item at Call to Action conferences, is as close as they will
> ever get to women's ordination.**

In other words, CFFC believes that Catholic hospitals should be closely regulated by the government because they are health care organizations, but that the
same government has absolutely no business regulating abortion in any way.

In summary, if CFFC can compel Catholic hospitals to violate Catholic teachings against contraception and sterilization, it can then rail against such "inconsistencies" between Catholic teachings and practice, and will gain a great public
relations victory. CFFC will also point to these hospitals as "proof" that the
Catholic Church can "change" its teachings on contraception and sterilization —
a situation it would have forced through civil litigation in the first place![44]

CFFC is a great advocate of the separation of church and state — except when
it uses the state#s power to force the church to bend to its will. In CFFC's mind,
"separation of church and state" means that whenever the state advances, the
church must retreat.

CFFC Supports Partial-Birth Abortions. Dilation and extraction (partial-
birth) abortion involves delivering all of a preborn child except for the head, and
then, instead of completing the delivery, puncturing the child's head and suctioning out his brains. It would be simple to complete the delivery of the head,
but this cruel procedure is designed for one reason: To make sure the child is
dead beyond a shadow of a doubt.

Thousands of second-trimester and third-trimester partial-birth abortions are
committed in the United States every year. These are not all done in extreme situations, contrary to what pro-abortion groups claim; abortionist Martin Haskell,
who invented the method, says that about 80 percent of all partial-birth abortions
are committed purely for convenience purposes. He also stated that he did abortions right up until the moment of birth for "maternal depression."[45]

Nothing betrays CFFC's extremism more than its wholehearted support of
partial-birth abortions. CFFC aggressively promotes *every* abortion decision as
a moral choice, even if it is a grisly third-trimester abortion committed for pure
convenience. Naturally, CFFC studiously avoids talking about the bloody reality of the killing of *viable and healthy* preborn babies. Instead, it tries to divert
the public's attention to tangential issues.

CFFC ran a full-page ad in the *National Journal Convention Daily* at the 1993 National Republican Convention, attacking the American bishops for being "single-issue" on the PBA. In a letter to the editor in the *Washington Times*, Frances Kissling criticized the bishops' postcard campaign against President Clinton's veto of the Partial-Birth Abortion Ban Act. She said "By exhorting Catholics attending church services on Sunday to sign postcards asking Congress to override President Clinton's veto during an election year, the bishops once again are using the Mass in a highly politicized and inappropriate way."[46]

Here we have yet another example of CFFC's hypocrisy. CFFC, which claims to represent the Catholic Church, gets directly involved in the politics of the United States and several other nations, but denies this same right to the *leaders* of the Catholic Church — the bishops — because this is, in its view, a "violation of the principle of the separation of church and state."

CFFC Supports Forced Funding of Abortion. The average issue of CFFC's magazine *Conscience* is generously larded with at least a dozen references to public opinion polls supporting CFFC's positions on one issue or another. This seems to imply that CFFC somehow respects the results of these polls or uses them to help guide the formation of its ideology.

This is another example of CFFC's hypocrisy, because it simply ignores the results of polls it does not agree with when the outcome is unfavorable to its goals.

Every national public opinion poll taken on the subject shows that Americans do not want their tax dollars paying for abortions. This is true even of most Americans who refer to themselves as "pro-choice."

Yet for years, CFFC has worked *against* public opinion by supporting the so-called "Justice Campaign" since its beginnings in 1986.[47] The goal of the Campaign is to demand Federal funding of *all* abortions for poor women. CFFC boasted that it "... helped to lead the 1993 campaign against the Hyde Amendment, which bars federal Medicaid funding of abortions. ... CFFC helped to coordinate press events, design and place print ads, and bring women from all socioeconomic levels to lobby on Capital Hill." CFFC has also filed amicus briefs in federal cases in support of forced funding of abortion.[48]

In 1988 CFFC also supported the "Michigan Campaign," which demanded tax-funded abortions in that state, by conducting a speaking tour and organizing pro-abortion "Catholics."[49]

CFFC Supports Population Control. Most Americans do not want their tax dollars used to suppress the fertility of women in developing nations.

Once again, CFFC ignores public opinion polls that do not support its ideology. CFFC works against government restrictions on international "family planning" assistance programs. These limitations are based on the conviction that taxpayer funds should not be used to pay for abortions or advocate abortion, either in the United States or abroad.

On June 22, 2001, President George W. Bush reinstated the Mexico City Policy — originally instituted by President Ronald Reagan in 1984 — that denies aid to organizations that engage in abortion-related activities overseas. CFFC denounced the President's decision, characterizing it as "an astonishing and unconscionable disregard of the most basic principles of democracy and respect for national sovereignty."[50]

Strangely, CFFC did not protest when President Bill Clinton also "disregarded the most basic principles of democracy" by *eliminating* the Mexico City Policy with an executive order on January 22, 1993. Additionally, CFFC apparently has no sense of irony whatsoever, or is completely ignorant of the fact that the millions of population control dollars pumped into the developing world by the richest nations undermine the national sovereignty of these countries.

CFFC also signed a February 7, 2001 statement that denounced the President's "callous disregard for the plight faced by women throughout the world," and said that the "gag rule" would "violate medical ethics by denying women access to the full range of information about reproductive health services, including safe abortion."[51]

These statements reflect the curious pro-abortion view that governments *must* support abortion and *must* fund abortion, regardless of their religious views or the beliefs or attitudes of their people. This all fits into CFFC's idea that the only "rights" that pro-life Catholics have regarding abortion is the "right" to open their wallets and pay for it. As Argument #12 in the latter section of this book shows, CFFC believes that pro-life Catholics *must* violate their consciences while sitting on the sidelines and doing nothing about what they know to be child murder.

CFFC Supports Destructive Embryonic Stem Cell Research. CFFC supports unlimited stem cell research on embryonic stem cells. Despite the fact that the majority of Americans oppose such research, CFFC treats all preborn children as mere commodities to be exploited and used in whatever way researchers deem "necessary."

Just as the promoters of the abortion pill RU-486 did, researchers who engage in embryonic stem cell research have made many promises about hypothetical miracle cures while ignoring a constant principle of morality — that we may never accomplish good by committing evil.

CFFC is silent about other promising areas of stem cell research. Stem cells derived from adult tissue and from placentas after childbirth have produced concrete results, even as the use of embryonic cells to treat Parkinson's disease patients has proven disappointing and even disastrous. These non-embryonic stem cells can be acquired through entirely moral means, yet CFFC refuses to support or even mention them.[52]

CFFC Opposes Chastity Education. CFFC fights abstinence-only sexuality education, which teaches that sexual activity exclusively within marriage is the expected standard for school-age children. CFFC claims it defends the rights of teenagers to prevent sexually transmitted diseases and to avoid unwanted pregnancies without "renouncing their sexuality."[53]

Once again, CFFC betrays its gross ignorance of the most basic aspects of human sexuality. In CFFC's view, sexuality is not part of what a person *is*, but what a person *does*. Therefore, the more sex a person *has*, the more "sexual" he is. If this bizarre belief were true, it would mean that a promiscuous person has more "sexuality" than a virgin, and anyone who chooses a celibate life is "renouncing their sexuality."

By contrast, the *Catechism* says that "Chastity means the integration of sexuality within the person. It includes an apprenticeship in self-mastery. Among the sins gravely contrary to chastity are masturbation, fornication, pornography, and homosexual practices" [¶2395-2396].

CFFC even elevates the act of sex itself to the status of a sacrament. In *Conscience* Magazine, Maggie Hume writes that "Good sex — sex which is as pleasurable as possible on as many levels as possible — operates as a channel of grace. ... A marriage license does not endow sex with new power. Sex *itself* has a sacramental power. I propose that sexual pleasure is good for its own sake."[54]

Like everyone else, CFFC is aware of the undeniable fact that *all* STDs and *all* "unwanted pregnancies" can be avoided by women and men who remain chaste before marriage. So while CFFC claims that it wants to reduce the incidence of abortion, it fights the most effective way of doing so.

CFFC's European Activities.

Introduction. CFFC uses much of the money it raises from United States foundations to promote abortion in many other countries, primarily those with predominantly Catholic populations and beliefs.

CFFC is a member of the European Network/Church on the Move (EN), a network of dissenting Catholic groups, which itself works closely with the International We Are Church Movement. It also cooperates with *Wir Sind Kirche* ["We Are Church"], Jubilee People, *Droits et Libertas dans les Eglises* ["Rights and Liberties in the Churches"] and *Initiative Chritennrechte in der Kirche* ["Initiative for the Rights of Christians in the Church"].[55]

Catholics for a Free Choice has partners in Spain, Canada, Chile, Colombia, Bolivia, Brazil, Mexico and Argentina.

The United Kingdom. Frances Kissling took part in an English campaign to oppose Member of Parliament David Alton's 1988 bill to lower the time limit on abortion to 18 weeks.[56]

In January 1996, Kissling addressed the House of Commons in London. CFFC subsequently produced two publications on the activities of Opus Dei and the Vatican's influence on reproductive policies in the European Union. The latter booklet was an anti-Catholic conspiracy theorist's delight. It warned darkly that "The growing ranks of academics, doctors, parliamentarians, government ministers, judges, and journalists give the Vatican a powerful, hidden force that toils to impose its moral code not just on members, or even only on Catholics, but on the population at large."[57]

In March 1998, CFFC submitted to the government commission examining Irish abortion law a paper entitled "Catholic Options in the Abortion Debate: Reforming Irish Law," offering input "from a pro-choice Catholic perspective." In this document, CFFC favored Option Seven of those laid out by "the Green Paper on Abortion." This Option would permit abortion for economic or social reasons; on request where there was congenital malformation; in rape and incest cases; and where there was risk to the physical or mental health of the woman. As American pro-lifers well know, this is a formula for abortion on demand throughout all nine months of pregnancy.[58] CFFC also expressed disappointment that the Green Paper "did not more strongly address the need for separation of church and state in Ireland on this as well as other issues." CFFC repeated its desire that the Catholic Church be sidelined and marginalized, fretting about "the undue influence of the current church leadership in this matter."

In July 2000, Kissling, CFFC vice-president Jon O'Brien, and board member Eileen Moran attended a meeting with the All-Party Qireachtas Committee on the Constitution. The American National Conference of Catholic Bishops contacted the Committee and pointed out that CFFC does not speak for the Catholic Church and that it distorts Catholic teaching on the rights of the preborn. Subsequently, on the final day of the abortion hearings Chairman of the Committee Brian Lenihan questioned the status of CFFC.[59]

Poland. CFFC boasts that Poland is now "home to a new Federation for Women and Planned Parenthood, whose creation and funding were facilitated by CFFC and the International Planned Parenthood Federation."[60]

CFFC sponsored a Polish study by the national Planned Parenthood affiliate (the Polish Federation for Women and Family Planning), and distributed it to Polish Parliamentarians.[61] CFFC has also written and produced several publications in Polish that promote abortion, contraception and "reproductive choice" from an allegedly "Catholic" perspective. CFFC sent letters to fifteen Polish parliamentarians and government officials to support legislation that would relax that country's so-called "harsh" abortion ban.[62]

The Philippines. CFFC is even agitating in the most Catholic and pro-life nation in the world, the Philippines. The group is collaborating with a Benedictine nun there in its efforts to undermine Church teachings on abortion.[63]

In 1990 at the International Women and Health Conference in Manila, CFFC helped form a group called the International Network for Feminists Interested in Reproductive Health and Ethics (IN/FIRE), which "serves as a clearinghouse and information center for feminists." IN/FIRE's secretariat is located at CFFC's office in Washington, D.C.[64]

CFFC's Hispanic and Latin American Activities.

"Latinos are the great brown hope of the Vatican, which is counting on them to set the church back on course by bringing their fervent piety and ethic of machismo into the mainstream of American Catholicism."
— *Conscience* Magazine.[65]

Introduction. The population of Latin America [Central America, the Caribbean and South America] is about 525 million. Of this number, 460 million, or 87 percent, of the population of Latin America consider themselves Catholics, nearly half of the total number of Catholics in the world. Abortion is illegal in 28 of the 35 nations of Latin America.

Since Latin America is the most Catholic region in the world, CFFC is hard at work there undermining and misrepresenting Catholic teaching on sexual ethics.

CFFC paints a sensational caricature of the Latin American Church fanatically defending the traditional family and male domination while showing absolutely no mercy towards a woman's right to pleasurable sexuality. CFFC alleges that the Church's objective is to maintain men's domination over women and [church]men's domination over all of society.

As CFFC so vividly claims, "Motherhood and servitude is the only possible redemption for women; the gate to hell is knowledge and power."[66]

Who has the answer to this awful situation?

Why, CFFC, of course, which "proposes a *different* concept of motherhood from the sacrificial model of the Catholic church."[67]

Católicas por el Derecho a Decidir [*CDD*, or "Catholics for the Right to Decide"], which is CFFC's Hispanic outreach, says that "Only a feminist perspective can begin to restore the relevance, particularly to the bodies of women, of the violent imposition of Catholic moral doctrine." *CDD* loftily proclaims that it "defends the possibility of dissenting from the pope's positions and teachings without having to leave the church. ... The justice awaited by Latin American women is rooted in their renewed consciousness of dignity and power. It is a longed-for justice only they themselves can give."[68]

Notice how CFFC pretends to speak for *all* Latin American women. It completely ignores the possibility that many or most of them may find solace and comfort in the Church.

The History of *CDD*. Catholics for a Free Choice was present at the Fifth International Meeting on Women and Health held in 1987 in Costa Rica. There CFFC established *Católicas por el Derecho a Decidir*, whose stated goal was to contribute "to the rise of sexual ethics and procreation based on justice."[69]

In 1989 CFFC established a regional office of *CDD* in Montevideo, Uruguay. Cristina Grela, CFFC's Regional Coordinator for Latin America, claimed that her "turning point came in 1986 at an ecumenical encounter of Christian women meeting in Argentina on new forms of spirituality for women," hosted by the Women's Alliance for Theology, Ethics and Ritual, or WATER.[70]

The feelings-based "New Age" spirituality common to groups like WATER seems to be the vehicle by which Grela and many other Latin American women have become incorporated into Catholics for a Free Choice. Grela bought into the CFFC ideology that one can be pro-abortion and remain in good standing in the Church. In an article published in Argentina, she stated that "every woman who continues being Catholic, going to church and using family planning methods is a Catholic for a Free Choice member because these women have opted for this, with a clear conscience, disobeying the position of the hierarchy."[71]

At the Fifth Latin American Feminist Encounter in Argentina in 1991, CFFC was instrumental in establishing the coordinating committee for the promotion of the right to abortion in Latin America and the Caribbean, which is now actively working for this objective in these Hispanic countries.[72] CFFC's regional office for Latin American is located in Córdoba, Argentina.

CFFC's Latin American Publications. CFFC has published several books in Spanish for general circulation in Latin America.

Of these, the book that best summarizes CFFC's ideology is entitled *Mujeres e Iglesia: Sexualidad y Aborto en América Latina* [*Women and the Church: Sexuality and Abortion in Latin America*].[73] The authors of this anthology closely follow in the footsteps of American anti-life feminists, attacking the Catholic Church and promoting the "rights" to contraception, abortion and lesbianism.

Contributor Sylvia Marcos praises the pre-Colombian Aztec women priestesses of early "American sexual spirituality," whom she calls "privileged celebrants." She also claims that pre-Colombian pagan rites are "a source of inspiration for those of us who question the morals we received and believe that the experience of pleasure brings union with the divinity."

It is not surprising that people who approve of the brutal partial-birth abor-

25

tion procedure would also admire a religion whose practitioners cut the still-beating hearts out of thousands of screaming victims.

In the book, Cristina Grela denounces "the myth of heterosexuality" and laments that women are forced to "fall in love with the good looking man. What freedom do you have to fall in love with a woman?" Ana María Portugal condemns what she calls "forced heterosexuality" as "an oppression of all women." María Ladi Londoño states that the Vatican condemns abortion not as the result of a "doctrine of love," but in order to control the lives of women. She also trots out an old bit of discredited anti-Catholic bigotry when she says that "as a consequence of a definite misogyny and discrimination against women, who they do not accept as an equal and of whom it taught, up until the Council of Trent, that she had no soul."

Mujeres e Iglesia presents a "new ethic" beyond the right to abortion and contraception to "give ourselves permission to live out, without guilt, the desire, the pleasure and the enjoyment of the body... without obligations or commitments." This is an eerie echo of Margaret Sanger's credo, which was "unlimited sexual gratification without the burden of unwanted children ... The Right to be lazy. The Right to be an unmarried mother. The Right to destroy. The Right to create. The Right to love. The Right to live."[74]

Finally, the book promotes Women-Church communities "to question the plan that God supposedly had for us." In the Epilogue, Frances Kissling urges that "we [women] unite in the Women-Church movement to celebrate our lives, to study and work toward change in the institutional Church. This book came out of this movement."[75]

The CFFC-Chiapas Connection. For more than a decade, CFFC has been actively involved in organizing the pro-abortion movement in the Mexican state of Chiapas.

Its efforts led to success with the legalization of abortion in Chiapas in October 1990. Since that time, the pro-life movement has led a legal battle that has kept it from going into effect.

At the beginning of the pro-life counteroffensive, CFFC called on readers to "send letters and telegrams demanding the de-penalization and legalization of abortion in the State of Chiapas and in all of Mexico."

In 1996, CFFC gave $5,000 to six women's groups in Chiapas, and twenty CFFC board members held a retreat there "to visit and learn from progressive movements." Rosemary Radford Ruether, who attended the retreat, claims support from the local bishop, Samuel Ruiz García. María Consuelo Mejías, CFFC's Mexico director, boasted at the 20th Anniversary gathering of the Call to Action Conference in Detroit in 1996, that Bishop García has "close ties" with CFFC in Mexico.[76]

CFFC's Spanish newsletter *Consciencia* contradicts these claims. Marta Lamas decried the fact that Bishop García called a protest march against abortion which was attended by over 3,000 Catholics from the parishes in his diocese. She also called the Bishop's stance on abortion "antiquated."

The Bishops of Chiapas, in a July 1, 1991 pastoral letter entitled "The New Campaign Against Life," condemned in detail the arguments advanced by CFFC. The letter denounced abortion as "cowardly," and rebuked CFFC directly:

> On the occasion of the so-called "National Forum on Voluntary Motherhood and the Decriminalization of Abortion" held in the city of Tuxla Gutierrez, Chiapas, we, the Bishops of Chiapas, proclaim the following: ...
>
> 7. To this Forum was invited a group of foreigners that call itself "Catholic Women for Choice," that is, women who say they support legalized abortion. If this be true, we have to affirm with utmost clarity that such a position nullified their claims to be Catholics. They have excommunicated themselves; they have placed themselves outside the Church. A truly Catholic woman is one who accepts the Church's doctrines. If she does not accept them, she is free to change her religion or to lose it; but she has no right to use the word "Catholic" because she is not a Catholic. Such manipulation of this word is deplorable, for only confusion results. Could it be a ploy by the organizers of the Forum to make people believe that within the Church there is no unanimity on this point? The Devil works that way.

CFFC's "Hispanic Project." In 1939, Margaret Sanger's American Birth Control League (later Planned Parenthood) launched the "Negro Project." This project persuaded influential American Blacks to accept birth control, and urged them to convince their followers and admirers to use it as well. The overall objective of the Negro Project was to reduce the birth rate of Blacks in support

27

of a program of negative eugenics carried out in cooperation with the American Eugenics Society.[77]

In August 1991, CFFC launched its "Hispanic Project" in terms eerily reminiscent of the "Negro Project." The "Hispanic Project" is designed to reach Hispanic organizations in the United States in order to "educate" Hispanics on "reproductive health care" (this was also the objective of Sanger's "Negro Project").

Among the organizations working with CFFC are LULAC (League of United Latin American Citizens), MANA (Mexican American National Association), NACOPRW (the National Conference of Puerto Rican Women), *La Raza*, Hispanic Women's Council, Hispanic Health Council, COSSMHO (National Coalition of Hispanic Health and Human Services Organizations), and *Mujeres Latinas en Acción* (Latin Women in Action).[78]

In 1992, CFFC followed up with the "Latina Initiative" in order "to provide information on reproductive health care and public policy to Hispanic organizations in the U.S." The "Latina Initiative" convinced several major Hispanic organizations to join CFFC in publicly demanding that Medicaid cover abortion services. Among these organizations are MALDEF (Mexican American Legal Defense and Education Fund); New York's National Latina Council; The Coalition of Women in Trade Unions (a branch of the AFL-CIO), NACOPRW; the Puerto Rican Education and Legal Defense Fund; and *Promujer* (Pro Women) of Puerto Rico.[79]

CFFC has published a comic book in Spanish and has distributed it in Latin America. It is entitled "*Y Maria fue Consultada para ser Madre de Dios*" ["Mary Was Asked if She Wanted to be God's Mother"]. It depicts a young mother on its cover asking the Virgin Mary what she can do about her unwanted pregnancy. The comic book claims that, since God gave *Mary* the choice to say 'yes' or 'no,' *every* woman should have that choice.

This comic book is a perfect example of what CFFC does best: Use the deeply-held Faith of Hispanics against them in order to undermine their beliefs in the sanctity of human life. This is a reprehensible and dishonest tactic that does not seem to bother CFFC in the least.

The comic book makes the same discredited claims CFFC makes in the United States, and has the same function as its pamphlet entitled "Abortion: A Guide to Making Ethical Choices," whose purposes are to deceive Catholic women about authentic Catholic teachings and to salve their consciences as they decide to abort.

Some of the deceptions in the comic book include;

* that abortion is not always a sin, but that it depends on each case [of course, the language in the comic book makes certain that women can justify *all* abortions];
* that many bishops agree that contraception is a decision that should be left up to the couple [naturally, the comic book does not name any of these bishops];
* that, since the Pope has not made a formal infallible pronouncement on abortion, it is a matter left to the individual's conscience;
* that, if a person has a doubt concerning when personhood begins, there is freedom of conscience when deciding whether or not to have an abortion; and the hideous assertion that
* since God gave the Virgin Mary the freedom to choose whether or not to be the Mother of God, that He gives every woman the freedom to decide whether or not to have an abortion.[80] Naturally, CFFC does not mention that God asked Our Lady to be the Mother of God *before* she conceived by the Holy Spirit.

CFFC also produced a video in Spanish entitled "*Católicas por el Derecho a Decidir*" ["Catholics for the Right to Decide"], in which it distorts the teaching of the Church on human sexuality, abortion and contraception. The video begins by showing a procession in which women are carrying a statue of the Virgin Mary, and includes interviews of very poor women who lament their economic inability to take care of their many children. CFFC cleverly manipulates the situation of extreme poverty of Latin America in its attempts to "justify" abortion in all circumstances.[81]

CFFC knows full well that it could never convince Latin American women to accept contraception, sterilization and abortion through any means but a distortion of the teachings of the Catholic Church. The use of faith as a weapon against an entire people is a despicable tactic worthy of the unprincipled propagandists of an age gone by.

CFFC's Push for Abortion Legalization in Brazil. CFFC has been agitating for legalized abortion in Brazil since 1988. In May of that year, Frances Kissling addressed legislators, aides, journalists and pro-abortion activists on "pro-choice Catholic" ethics and reproductive health politics at the Brazilian Parliament.[82]

CFFC joined other pro-abortion organizations in producing a film promoting the legalization of abortion, and showed it at the Federal Senate in Brazil during public debate over a bill that proposed decriminalizing abortion.[83]

CFFC grossly exaggerates statistics in its drive to obtain legalized abortion by any means possible. It said that "Four million abortions are performed annually in Brazil. ... Most significantly, ten percent, or 400,000 of the abortions, result in the death of women, because of poorly performed procedures."[84]

Pro-abortion groups often "cook the numbers" to make their point (recall that reformed abortionist Bernard Nathanson tried the same tactic in the United States by claiming that 5,000 to 10,000 American women died of illegal abortions each year). But CFFC has committed the wildest exaggeration any pro-abortion group has ever dared print. The *Instituto Brasileiro de Geografia e Estatistica* (IBGE, or Brazilian Institute of Geography and Statistics) showed that only 55,066 Brazilian women between the ages of 14 and 50 died *of all causes* in 1980. The IBGE figures were confirmed by World Health Organization statistics showing that 41,685 Brazilian women between the ages of 15 and 41 died in 1986 and, of these, 241 died of complications due to both legal *and* illegal abortions.

This means that CFFC is inflating the actual number of illegal abortion deaths by *166 thousand percent!*[85]

CFFC also published and distributed a Brazilian pamphlet in Portuguese entitled "An Untold Story," which distorts Church teachings on abortion throughout history.[86]

Why CFFC is Not a Catholic Organization.

Nothing in Common With Catholicism. Catholics for a Free Choice presents itself as an authentically Catholic social justice organization in order to deceive uninformed people into believing that it is an authoritative voice on the teachings and ethics of the Catholic Church.

However, CFFC's ideology and its actions are in direct opposition to the doctrine of the Catholic Church;

* CFFC does not recognize the authority of the Catholic Church to teach on sexuality, nor does it recognize the authority of the Pope (see Argument #4, below).

* Instead of engaging in respectful dialogue with the leaders of the Church it claims to represent, CFFC viciously attacks them (for examples of some of the names CFFC has called the Pope and Catholic bishops, see Argument #12, below).

* CFFC has never *once* agreed with the Catholic bishops on any aspect of Church teaching on sexual ethics. Once again, CFFC has never offered to dialogue on such issues; rather, it is an opportunistic organization that publicly attacks Church teaching at every possible occasion.

* CFFC even denies the core beliefs of Christianity and rejects the Sacraments of the Catholic Church, as described later in this book.

CFFC has been condemned repeatedly by the Catholic bishops of several nations, who have unanimously agreed that CFFC is not Catholic in any way;

* In the United States, the National Conference of Catholic Bishops (NCCB) issued statements in 1984 and 1993 denying that CFFC is a Catholic organization. The 1993 statement said that "Many people may be led to believe that it is an authentic Catholic organization. It is not. It has no affiliation, formal or otherwise, with the Catholic Church." The bishops stated that CFFC "... has rejected unity with the Church and holds positions that deliberately contradict essential teachings of the Catholic Faith." The statement concluded that "Catholics for a Free

31

Choice merits no recognition or support as a Catholic organiza
tion." The texts of both the 1984 and 1993 NCCB statements are
in Appendix A.

* In March of 1996, Bishop Fabian Bruskewitz of Lincoln, Nebraska
  issued a statement condemning CFFC and other anti-Catholic groups.
  He warned that their members would be excommunicate if they contin
  ued their associations in these organizations, which hold beliefs that are
  incompatible with Catholic Faith. Indeed, the Diocese of Lincoln,
  Nebraska has condemned CFFC as being "virulently anti-Catholic."[87]

* Latin American Bishops have also condemned CFFC's activities. In a
  statement regarding CFFC, the Mexican Episcopal Conference affirmed
  that "... no group which promotes abortion can legitimately call itself
  "Catholic"." The Conference quoted Canons 215 & 216, saying that
  "no initiative, however, can lay claim to the title `catholic' without the
  consent of the competent ecclesiastical authority" [March 23, 1995].

* The Permanent Episcopal Conference of Uruguay stated that "We find
  ourselves obligated to strongly reiterate that the organization `Catholics
  for a Free Choice' hasn't any formal affiliation with the Catholic
  Church and expressly contradicts the Church's genuine teachings"
  ["Declaration of the Permanent Episcopal Conference of Uruguay,"
  March 24, 1995].

* On May 10, 2000, the National Conference of Catholic Bishops used
  exceptionally strong language condemning CFFC in reaction to its "See
  Change" campaign. The text of this statement is in Appendix A.

* In summary, despite CFFC's occasional claims to the contrary, no
  Catholic bishop, no matter how liberal his leanings, has *ever* endorsed
  the organization, its tactics, or its objectives.

The person who can best describe the anti-Catholic and un-Catholic character of Catholics for a Free Choice is former Board member Marjorie Reiley
Maguire, who said that

> CFFC does not deserve [United Nations] accreditation because
> it has actually become an anti-woman organization. Various
> personal experiences with CFFC have led me to believe that its
> agenda is no longer simply to defend the *legality* of a woman's
> abortion choice against efforts to recriminalize that choice.

Instead, I now see CFFC's agenda as the promotion of abortion, the defense of every abortion decision as a good, moral choice and the related agenda of persuading society to cast off any moral constraints about sexual behavior. I don't think this is a Catholic or pro-woman agenda whether you are liberal or conservative, pro-life or pro-choice. ... CFFC's claim to the name "Catholic" is very questionable. Even if most of its dues-paying members were baptized Catholics, that does not necessarily make them "Catholic" today. Only an outdated, legalistic, zap theology, which CFFC adherents reject in every other respect, would call people Catholic simply because they were baptized. ... Additionally, I think that the label "Catholic" is proper only for a person who participates in the sacramental life of the church. Thus, regular attendance at Mass (except for the elderly and invalids) seems to be the minimum sign of membership in the church. When I was involved with CFFC, I was never aware that any of its leaders attended Mass. Furthermore, various conversations and experiences convinced me they did not. I myself did not. Today I see this failure as proof that I was not actually a *Catholic* for a Free Choice.[88]

A Parallel. CFFC members claim with straight faces that they are "Catholics in good standing," while simultaneously ignoring and ridiculing the teachings of the Church that do not happen to accommodate their lifestyles.

Imagine, if you will, a person who joins the Army and then chooses which regulations to follow (only the easy ones) and which he will not follow (because they are personally distasteful to him). This person does not wear the uniform (too conformist) and will not salute officers (too slavish). He detests manual labor and work details. This person also refuses to even *touch* a weapon because he is a pacifist. He also loudly criticizes every decision made by his officers, and publicly questions their fitness and competence at every opportunity.

How long would this person last in the Army?

Not very long, because he would be immediately court-martialled and discharged!

We should apply the same parallel to the members of Catholics for a Free Choice.

Every organization, whether secular or religious, should have the right to formulate its own dogma and doctrine. It should be allowed to teach these beliefs to those willing to listen and should be permitted to compete in the marketplace of ideas.

Those who disagree with the teachings of the Catholic Church certainly have the right to criticize them. But they do *not* have the right to aggressively undermine these teachings with underhanded and dishonest tactics. They do *not* have the right to deliberately misrepresent and distort Church teachings and history in order to achieve their own goals. They do *not* have the right to whip up hatred against the Church. And they certainly do *not* have the right to proclaim themselves "members in good standing."

But members of CFFC and other dissenting groups do not have the courage to simply get out of the Church and let those who want to embrace true Catholicism do so in peace.

Why don't the dissenters simply *leave?*

Because, as long as the Roman Catholic Church exists in Her current form, and as long as Her teachings on moral issues remain inviolate, Her very existence will be a rebuke to those committing immoral acts and will cause them to feel guilty, whether they are inside or outside of the Church. So CFFC's members emphasize not personal repentance and sanctification, but the removal of the *sensation* of guilt while continuing and rationalizing their own sinful behaviors. They can only do this by changing the teachings of the Church to support their lifestyles.

After a person begins to sin, he must rationalize his own behavior in order to live with himself. What better way to do this than to band together with those who think and act like him? CFFC and its supporters can praise one another for being "courageous," stroke one another, denounce authentic Catholics together, and make plans to entice (or coerce) everyone else into being just like them.

The only way the members of CFFC can be free of their burden of guilt is if everyone in the Church accepts and applauds their immoral acts. And the only way to achieve this is to drain the Church of Her vitality, in the same way a host of tiny spiders drains the vital fluids from a beautiful butterfly.

Frances Kissling: The "Cardinal of Death."

Frances Kissling is the longtime director of `Catholics' for a Free Choice, and this position suits her morality and theology perfectly. There is no more ideal person to run CFFC.

Kissling likes to mention her background as a nun (conveniently not mentioning that she quit the Sisters of St. Joseph after only six months). Kissling basks in the title "The Flying Nun," but is no more a nun than a person who drops out of medical school after six months is a doctor.[89] We would also question the honesty of a man who strutted around calling himself "Father" after making it only halfway through his first year of seminary.

She boasts about shacking up with men, says that she would have an abortion if she got pregnant, and says she was sterilized in 1978 (the Catholic Church teaches that sterilization is a mortal sin).[90]

She co-founded the National Abortion Federation (NAF), the abortionists' trade association, and worked as a highly-placed official of the International Projects Assistant Services (IPAS), which specializes in subverting the law in foreign countries and setting up illegal abortion mills in contravention to local beliefs and customs.[91] Kissling herself smuggled illegal abortion equipment into Mexico, and says that "I have no problem in helping women get illegal abortions."[92]

Kissling's system of "ethics" appears to transcend national statutes as easily as it does Church teachings.

Kissling also helped set up illegal abortion mills in Mexico and Italy, and ran two New York aborturaries: The Eastern Women's Center and the Pelham Medical Group, which, she boasts, killed more than 50,000 preborn babies during the time period 1970 to 1973.[93] This activity is a source of pride to Kissling and to CFFC, which bragged that

> A cardinal caught running an illegal abortion clinic in Rome is the stuff of papal nightmares. But Frances Kissling, president of the American lobby group, Catholics for a Free Choice, is no ordinary prince of the church. Nicknamed "The Cardinal" by friends and foes for her determined opposition to the Catholic hierarchy's teaching on abortion, she actually went so far as to defiantly found an abortion clinic within sight of the Vatican's walls.[94]

Kissling has boasted about a wide range of pro-abortion acts which represent enough grave sin to excommunicate her a thousand times. She revealed her totally pro-abortion worldview and her stark hatred of the Church she claims as her own when she raved, "The Catholic religion makes the fetus into an icon, a figure of religious veneration, which I think is sick, really sick."[95]

Despite Scripture mentioning sexual behavior scores of times, Kissling blandly asserts, "I don't think God cares very much about our sexual activity."[96]

CFFC's Connections to the Radical Feminist and New Age Movements.

"See to it that no one makes a prey of you by philosophy and empty deceit, according to human tradition, according to the elemental spirits of the universe, and not according to Christ."
— The Letter of St. Paul to the Colossians [2:8].

Overview. CFFC is intimately connected to the Women-Church and New Age movements which have deeply infiltrated many dioceses in the Catholic Church. Pope John Paul II is keenly aware of this danger and has said that "New Age ideas sometimes make inroads into [Church] preaching, catechesis, conferences and retreats, and in this way come to influence even practicing Catholics, who may not be conscious of the incompatibility of such ideas with the faith of the Church. New Age ideas propose a pantheistic concept of God which is incompatible with Sacred Scripture and Tradition."[97]

Real Catholics must be made aware of the fact that occult or "New Age" feminists are literally trying to replace Catholicism with a Goddess-centered faith under the disguise of dissent. They are striving to eliminate any trace of the Father and of the Son, to include a reworking of the Sacraments and an overhauling of Church language.

In short, they are attempting to perform a Godectomy on the Roman Catholic Church.

The founder of the Women-Church movement is pro-abortion feminist Rosemary Radford Ruether, a self-styled "Catholic theologian" who is also a board member of CFFC. Ruether was instrumental in uniting many feminist groups into a coalition called the "Women-Church Convergence."[98]

In general, feminist theologians now refer to the feminist crusade in religion as "women-church," a "movement of `self-identified women and women-identified men' from all denominations whose common goal is to reinterpret the Gospel from the perspective of women's liberation."[99]

Ruether claims that Women-Church is a movement of "radical Christianity" that "tends to see the traditional religion as false or fallen," and that "anticipates the New Age, expecting it soon to dawn upon the earth and seeking to pattern itself after what it believes to be the social order of redemption."[100] Ruether admits that "Women-Church is rooted in creation-based spirituality, which is the occult, the New Age teachings of Matthew Fox, who was expelled from the

37

Dominican Order."[101]

We must acknowledge that Fox certainly has original ideas. He said in his book *Creation Spirituality* that "I say 'thank you' for the orange that dies for me this morning when I drink a glass of orange juice by promising to be as succulent and round and radiant as an orange throughout the day." In his book, Fox also praises a friend who "liberates" ice cubes from freezers at gas stations by throwing them into nearby ponds.

Strangely, Fox, who cares so deeply for the welfare of fruit and ice cubes, does not seem to have any room left in his heart for preborn human babies.

This is the kind of "theologian" that CFFC finds credible.

Ruether fully intends to completely destroy Catholicism and replace it with a "New Age" construct. She says that

> As Women-Church we repudiate the idol of patriarchy ... Our God and Goddess, who is mother and father, friend, lover and helper, did not create this idol and is not represented by this idol ... this idol blasphemes by claiming to speak in the name of Jesus and to carry out his redemptive mission, while crushing and turning to its opposite all that he came to teach ... all social reforms superimposed upon our sick civilization can be no more effective than a bandage on a gaping and putrefying wound. Only the complete and total demolition of the social body will cure the fatal sickness. Only the overthrow of the three-thousand-year-old beast of masculist materialism will save the race. ... No token accommodations will satisfy us. What is required is the *total reconstruction* of God, Christ, human nature, and society ... we know we will die unless a WomanChrist pops up (like a rabbit out of a hat) between breasted mountains ...[102]

CFFC shows that it is much more than just ideologically aligned with the New Age movement by enthusiastically promoting its rituals. "Led by ... Ruether ... women have created their own life-cycle ceremonies. They include rituals to mark the start of menopause, the union of a lesbian couple, mourning for a still-birth and recovery from abortion."[103]

Ruether has not just attempted to graft New Age beliefs onto Christianity, but has rejected the core tenet of Christianity itself: That Jesus Christ is our Savior and Redeemer. Ruether says that

> Redemption does not mean sending down the divine from some higher spiritual world where God is located, into a bodily world we find is alien to God, but rather perhaps it means the welling up of authentic life in a true creation transforming us from death-dealing to life-giving relations. It is to say `Flesh became Word,' not `Word became Flesh.' ... Some theologians, such as womanist Delores Williams, have answered this question by the decisive rejection of the idea that the cross, or Christ's suffering, is redemptive. It is not Jesus' suffering and death but His life as a praxis of protest against injustice in solidarity in His life, it is this praxis that is redemptive.[104]

What CFFC has done is turn the story of the Prodigal Son on its head. With all their talk about "patriarchy" and "victimization," they parody Luke 15:21 by saying "Father, You have sinned against us, and are no longer worthy of being called our Father."

CFFC's Pro-Abortion Rituals. In keeping with its rigidly pro-abortion ideology and its desire to reconstruct the Catholic Church, CFFC has formulated rituals to encourage and celebrate abortion — but none to advocate or honor choosing life for a preborn child.

In 1992, CFFC published a pamphlet entitled "Liturgies for Responsible Reproduction," which included two ceremonies that conspicuously direct a woman's decision towards one choice only: Abortion. These "liturgies" supposedly "celebrate women's spirituality by affirming the integrity and holiness of their decisions," but focus solely on approval of the abortion decision.[105]

The first of these is the "Liturgy of Affirmation for Making a Difficult Decision," formulated by Diann Neu, co-director of WATER, the Women's Alliance for Theology, Ethics and Ritual. Neu describes herself as a "feminist liberation theologian," and her "Liturgy" has five steps;

(1)   Gathering and singing "A favorite, comforting song, one that the woman likes;"

(2)   Prayer: "Praised be you, Mother and Father God, that you have given your people the power of choice. We are saddened that the life circumstances of (_____ woman's name or, if

appropriate, woman's name and her partner's name) are such that she has had to choose to terminate her pregnancy. Such a choice is never simple. It is filled with pain and hurt, with anger and questions, but also with integrity and strength. We rejoice in her attention to choice;"

(3)   Read a poem or Scripture verse;

(4)   Blessing with oil, "As a sign of our affirmation of you and of your choice;" and

(5)   Closing or "blessing" song.

The second ceremony is entitled a "Liturgy for Seeking Wisdom," also consisting of five phases:

(1)   Play soothing background music;

(2)   "Light a candle, absorb its power, and pray;"

(3)   "Visualization:" Imagine yourself in ten years (a) with a child and (b) without a child. Find a "cozy room with a comfortable chair" and sit in it for a while;

(4)   Sing a song entitled "i found god in myself;" and

(5)   "... do something comforting, for example, drink a cup of tea or take a warm shower."

Neu also agitates relentlessly for a complete "makeover" of the Mass into a feminist construct, including the substitution of a whole cafeteria of elements for the bread and wine that, in a *real* Mass, would be transubstantiated into the Body and Blood of Jesus Christ. Among her recommendations are harvest bread ("for the harvest season"), cranberry bread, walnut-raisin bread, tortillas ("to celebrate Latin Americans"), nut bread ("for dreamers and prophets"), champagne ("celebrating festivity"), corn bread ("Native Americans and African Americans"), apple juice ("to reclaim women as holy — Eve got a bad rap"), rice cakes (for Asian culture), milk (to celebrate nursing mothers), shortbread (for children), water ("women's lifegiving powers") and saltines (for the "salty elders" among us).[106]

Worshipping False God[ess]es. CFFC board member Mary Hunt was one of the most popular speakers at the "Re-Imagining Conference" held November 4-7, 1993, in Minneapolis, Minnesota.

At this conference, radical feminists literally worshipped the "goddess of Wisdom" Sophia with prayers such as: "Our maker Sophia, we are women in your image ... Sophia, Creator God, Our mother Sophia, we celebrate your life-giving energy ... we celebrate the sensual life you give us ... We celebrate our bodyliness, our physicality, the sensations of pleasure, our oneness with earth and water."[107]

One conference participant claimed that "Sophia is the divine energy in women being unlocked by the goddess rituals." Another said "Sophia is the wisdom within me." And the conference program's introduction read: "Sophia is the place in you where the entire universe resides." As one critic of the conference said in reference to the cult of Sophia: "These extreme feminists have made for themselves an idol and they call that idol God. Without knowing it, they are worshiping themselves."[108]

CFFC leaders also heartily endorse this cult of the "Wisdom goddess." As Donna Steichen reports, "[Rosemary] Ruether made several references [at a synod of Women-Church], as she had in her Women-Church book, to Wisdom as God the Mother. She spoke of 'the inner voice of Mother Wisdom' and 'the source of life and new life which we call Mother Wisdom'."[109]

Ruether goes far beyond paying tribute to the mythical feminist goddesses. She even sings praises to the pagan god Ba'al, committing the same idolatry that caused God to punish the Israelites so many times;

> "... we see the death of Baal, overwhelmed by the forces of drought and death ... [the goddess Anath] buries him with rites of mourning ... From her sowing of the new wheat in the ground, Baal rises. With a cry of exaltation, we rejoice at the close of the drama: The Lord has arisen, is seated again on the throne. He reigns! Alleluia!"[110]

It takes one's breath away to imagine that a person who calls herself a "Catholic theologian" can possibly praise pagan gods with such abandon. Ruether has obviously forgotten the confrontation between Elijah and the 450 priests of Ba'al [1 Kings 18:18-40]. The best response to Ruether might be to follow the lead of the prophet Elijah and mock her, saying "Cry aloud, for he is a god; either he is musing, or he has gone aside, or he is on a journey, or perhaps he is asleep and must be awakened" [1 Kings 18:27].

But even paying tribute to Ba'al does not define the limit of CFFC's folly. It goes so far as to publish poems praising Lucifer in its *Conscience* Magazine. One of these short poems reads;

> "Lucifer, each note sounds like
> your sweet name, lyrical, holy.
> It bursts over heaven
> while you break your long
> back over the world.
> Brother, first of us,
> you never heard songs
> like these. They shine
> in heaven's edges.
> For you, all
> the angels are dancing."[111]

Conclusions. We have seen that Catholics for a Free Choice rejects Catholic teachings regarding sexual morality.

But CFFC goes much further than that.

It denies the *authority* of the Catholic Church to teach in God's name.

It worships pagan gods and goddesses, even the bloody Old Testament Ba'al.

It even glorifies Satan.

No thinking person can possibly believe that Catholics for a Free Choice even *remotely* resembles anything Christian or Catholic, despite all of its protestations to the contrary.

CFFC's Interesting Financial History.

Where CFFC Gets Its Money. CFFC often claims that it represents the majority of Catholics. Yet according to its income tax returns, CFFC has not received a dime from private donors in years (see Table 1). If CFFC is so popular, why doesn't it receive any funding from individual Catholics?

Perhaps CFFC just doesn't *need* the support of the people. After all, it is backed by foundations with combined assets of more than forty *billion* dollars.

During the time period 1979 to 2000, CFFC received more than 25 million dollars in donations from private foundations, and lately this number has been increasing rapidly. Table 2 shows how CFFC's annual foundation funding has increased nearly sixty fold, from a paltry $65,500 in 1979 to $3.9 million in 1999.

Table 1

Summary of 1998-2000 Annual Revenues and Expenses, Catholics for a Free Choice

Annual Revenues	1998	1999	2000
Direct public support (line 1a, Form 990)	4,005,876	4,323,656	4,233,781
Indirect public support (line 1b)	27,224	29,404	25,936
Program service revenue (line 2)	5,612	7,300	8,748
Membership dues and assessments (line 3)	0	0	0
Interest on savings (line 4)	112,811	143,731	299,799
Other revenue (line 11)	1,000	0	0
Total Annual Revenue (line 12)	**4,152,523**	**4,504,091**	**4,568,264**
Annual Expenditures			
Program services (line 13)	2,171,961	2,361,786	2,487,924
Management and general (line 14)	107,265	72,174	93,441
Fundraising (line 15)	160,042	159,290	162,766
Total Annual Expenses (line 17)	**2,439,268**	**2,593,250**	**2 ,744,131**

Annual Excess Revenue and Net Assets			
	1998	1999	2000
Excess for the year (line 18)	1,713,255	1,910,841	1,824,133
Net assets at end of year (line 74)*	4,902,841	6,984,499	9,209,679

* CFFC's 1998 Form 990 shows that its net assets at the end of 1997 were $2,951,465.

Table 2

Foundation Grants Given to
Catholics for a Free Choice by Year, 1979-2000

Year	Total Grants	Year	Total Grants
1979	$ 65,500	1990	$ 707,000
1980	158,750	1991	1,539,483
1981	222,550	1992	899,230
1982	208,060	1993	1,447,500
1983	247,500	1994	1,993,200
1984	182,000	1995	1,475,350
1985	280,000	1996	3,228,000
1986	200,500	1997	640,000
1987	348,200	1998	4,163,300
1988	518,000	1999	3,892,500
1989	309,625	2000	2,283,335 (incomplete)

**Total Foundation Funding of Catholics for a Free Choice,
1979-2000: $25,009,583**

NOTE: Appendix D shows details of all CFFC foundation funding available in the *Foundation Grants Index* and *Taft Foundation Reporter*. The information in this table is not complete, since the section of the IRS forms 990 for non-profit organizations like Catholics for a Free Choice, which lists foundation income, is not open to public inspection. The information in this table must be compiled by examining records from the individual foundations themselves, or by examining annual editions of the *Foundation Grants Index* and the *Taft Foundation Reporter*, which are themselves incomplete.

Table 3

Foundation Grants Given to
Catholics for a Free Choice, Ranked by Donor
1979-2000

Ranking	Grants to CFFC	Name of Foundation
(1)	$6,380,760	Ford Foundation
(2)	5,095,800	David & Lucile Packard Foundation
(3)	2,199,500	John & Catherine MacArthur Foundation
(4)	1,066,700	Sunnen Foundation
(5)	1,050,000	William & Flora Hewlett Foundation
(6)	887,900	Educational Foundation of America
(7)	781,208	George Gund Foundation
(8)	692,635	General Service Foundation
(9)	675,000	Buffett Foundation
(10)	590,000	Public Welfare Foundation
(11)	545,000	Huber Foundation
(12)	535,000	Scherman Foundation
(13)	457,000	Robert Sterling Clark Foundation
(14)	400,000	Wallace Alexander Gerbode Foundation
(15)	350,000	Richard & Rhoda Goldman Fund
(16)	310,000	Compton Foundation
(17)	268,775	John Merck Fund
(18)	250,000	Leland Fikes Foundation
(19)	250,000	Open Society Institute
(20)	250,000	Wallace Global Fund
(21)	248,850	Albert A. List Foundation
(22)	190,000	Moriah Fund
(23)	173,500	Nathan Cummings Foundation
(24)	164,853	Brush Foundation
(25)	140,000	Weeden Foundation
(26)	115,000	Alfred Jurzykowski Foundation
(27)	110,000	Turner Foundation
(28)	95,000	Jessie Smith Noyes Foundation
(29)	94,500	Prospect Hill Foundation
(30)	82,500	North Shore Unitarian Veatch Program
(31)	75,000	Esther A. & Joseph Klingenstein Fund

Ranking	Grants to CFFC	Name of Foundation
(32)	60,000	Mary Reynolds Babcock Foundation
(34)	50,000	Geraldine R. Dodge Foundation
(35)	50,000	Summit Charitable Foundation
(36)	50,000	Tides Foundation
(33)	60,000	Rockefeller Foundation
(37)	35,000	S.H. Cowell Foundation
(38)	27,500	Norman Foundation
(39)	24,625	Ruth Mott Fund
(40)	20,000	Playboy Foundation
(41)	15,500	Ms. Foundation
(42)	15,000	Field Foundation
(43)	15,000	Global Fund for Women
(44)	10,000	C.S. Fund
(45)	10,000	Dyson Foundation
(46)	10,000	J. Roderick MacArthur Foundation
(47)	9,947	Alida Rockefeller Dayton Fund
(48)	7,530	Cabot Family Charitable Trust
(49)	5,000	Louise L. Ottinger Foundation

Total Foundation Funding of Catholics for a Free Choice, 1979-2000: <u>$25,009,583</u>

NOTE: Appendix D shows details of all CFFC foundation funding available in the *Foundation Grants Index* and *Taft Foundation Reporter*. The information in this table is not complete, since the section of the IRS forms 990 for non-profit organizations like Catholics for a Free Choice, which lists foundation income, is not open to public inspection. The information in this table must be compiled by examining records from the individual foundations themselves, or by examining annual editions of the *Foundation Grants Index* and the *Taft Foundation Reporter*, which are themselves incomplete.

CFFC may be unique among non-profit groups in that its income is entirely derived from donations from private foundations.

The motivations of the primary funders of CFFC are glaringly obvious in the descriptions of the purposes of their grants.

Some examples:

* "for projects in Central/South America — reproductive rights," "for projects in Latin America," and "for projects in Mexico and general support" [Leland Fikes Foundation].
* "general support for work with their Latin American partners - *Católicas por el Derecho a Decidir*. CFFC is the leading Catholic-based critic of the Church's contraception and abortion positions. Funds will help them maintain a strong media presence in Mexico, counter the efforts of Human Life International in Bolivia, and support their publications and technical assistance services" [Weeden Foundation].
* "for continued support for public education and dissemination of Catholic pro-choice values [in Mexico and Brazil];" "to promote public discussion among Catholics in Mexico on sexual and reproductive health;" and "for consolidation of pro-choice Catholic groups in four Latin American countries: Argentina, Chile, Colombia and Peru" [Ford Foundation].
* "to raise awareness of Catholic support for reproductive health care and to counter the Catholic Church's attempts to undermine reproductive freedom;" "for the organization's work to counter efforts of the Roman Catholic Church to limit legal access to reproductive health care [in Latin America];" "to fund the Chiapas Initiative, a public education campaign in Mexico, to assure participation of pro-choice women's organizations in the debate regarding expansion of legal abortion;" and "to support Latin American Program which utilizes ethical and theological perspectives and service-oriented methods to assist Latin American Catholics with issue of reproductive choice" [General Service Foundation].
* Most incredibly, "for [a] program to educate American Catholics about [the] wide diversity of opinion that exists within [the] Church on [the] issue of reproductive freedom, and to provide Catholic citizens with a *rational* alternative to Church doctrine" and "for continued support of

CFFC's research on the Catholic Right, mergers of Catholic and non-Catholic hospitals, and a new initiative challenging the Vatican's obstruction of the United Nation's delivery of reproductive health care internationally" [Robert Sterling Clark Foundation].

* CFFC has also received more than $100,000 from the Turner Foundation. Ted Turner has called Christians "bozos," and has referred to Christianity as "a religion for losers." He has also proposed "Ten Voluntary Initiatives" as a replacement for the Ten Commandments. The third of these is "I promise to have no more than two children, *or no more than my nation suggests*." He has also said that "What we need to have for 100 years is a one-child policy ... If everybody voluntarily had one child for 100 years, we'd basically be back to 2 billion people, and we could do it without a mass die-off and the kind of misery you see on TV in Rwanda ... "Increase and multiply," that's what is says in the Bible, right? Now scratch that out and say, "Multiply in a very limited way, because there's too many people."[112] The fact that CFFC can accept money from a foundation that was initiated by such an outspoken anti-Christian bigot shows that it is not at all selective about where it gets its money from [remember *Playboy*?]

We must ask ourselves why these foundations give tens of millions of dollars to an organization that is so patently and obviously anti-Catholic.

The foundations aren't intrinsically evil. Most of them don't hate the Catholic Church. They simply perceive it as an obstacle to doing what they see as good and altruistic work. And, to many of these foundations, "good works" includes donating tens of millions of dollars yearly to groups supporting "reproductive rights."

Why do foundations give so much money to Catholics for a Free Choice? Their utilitarian thinking is simplistic and based upon unchecked and politically correct assumptions. It goes something like this;

(1) There is poverty in Latin America.
(2) Overpopulation causes poverty.
(3) Therefore, we must reduce the population of Latin America in order to reduce poverty.
(4) This can only be done through "family planning" programs.
(5) But the vast majority of Latin Americans are Catholic.

(6) The Catholic Church condemns abortion and contraception.

(7) Therefore, we must convince Latin Americans to stop listening to the Church.

(8) Let's fund CFFC, which accomplishes this under the cover of being "Catholic." If we attempted to subvert and undermine the teachings of the Catholic Church *ourselves*, people would call us "anti-Catholic." So let's leave the dirty work to Catholics for a Free Choice, because they can get away with it under the guise of being "Catholic" them selves.

How CFFC Spends Its Money. Just as interesting as its funding sources is how CFFC disposes of its income.

Table 4 shows that nearly 90 percent of the $1.5 million in direct grants CFFC has distributed over the past three years have been to pro-abortion organizations in Latin America. Nearly 99 percent of its Latin American grants, or about $1.3 million, has gone to its own affiliates in Argentina, Bolivia, Brazil and Mexico.

Table 5 shows the allocation of CFFC's program expenditures over the time period 1998-2000. This table is a concise summary of CFFC's primary activities.

* Item IIIa, "Education and Communications," makes up about one-fifth of CFFC's program expenditures, and represents the costs of the group's publications and public events, primarily in the United States and Europe. These activities are designed to misrepresent Catholic teaching on abortion in order to influence politics and judicial decisions regarding abortion and to help raise funds for CFFC's activities in Latin America.

* Item IIIb, "Constituency Building," comprises a little more than one-tenth of CFFC's annual program expenditures. This money is spent in support of crucial collaboration with other pro-abortion and dissenting organizations.

* Item IIIc, "Research," also a little more than ten percent of expenses, focuses primarily on watching Catholic hospital mergers and keeping an eye on the Catholic bishops.

* Item IIId, "International Program," represents a little less than one-tenth of CFFC's expenses. The group uses these funds to support its activities in Europe, including coordination with the thriving dissent move-

ment on that continent.

* Item IIIe, "Latin America Program," consumes nearly one-third of all of CFFC's program expenditures, and helps undermine Catholic teaching on reproductive issues in this most Catholic of continents, as already described. The primary objective of these expenses is to legalize abortion on demand through all nine months of pregnancy throughout Latin America.

* Item IIIe, "Religion and the United Nations," comprises about one-tenth of CFFC's expenditures, which go towards presenting an "alternative Catholic" viewpoint on abortion, contraception and population control at major United Nations conferences.

It is apparent that CFFC is stockpiling capital to serve as either a stable source of income or as funding for an ambitious project or series of projects, most likely in Latin America. Its net assets at the beginning of 1998 were $2,951,465, and its net assets at the beginning of 2001 were $9,209,679, an average increase of about $2.1 million per year, or nearly half of its $13.2 million total revenue over this period (see Table 1). Such a large amount of money would allow CFFC to exert a major influence on abortion-related legislation in Latin America over a period of several years, and perhaps would even allow it to play a decisive role.

Table 4

**Grants and Allocations Given by
Catholics for a Free Choice, 1998-2000**

	1998	1999	2000	Total
Ambasa Constance Rose (Kenya, research)	—	—	5,000	5,000
Beijing+5 Host Committee (New York City)	—	—	2,000	2,000
Bella Abzug Memorial Fund (New York City)	100	—	—	100
Body Politic (Binghampton, New York)	50	—	—	50
Casa de la Mujer (Oaxala, Mexico)	2,000	—	—	2,000
Catholics Speak Out (CSO, Hyattsville, Maryland)	100	—	—	100
CDD/Argentina	45,595	46,432	2,573	94,600
CDD/Bolivia	46,750	84,264	60,715	191,729
CDD/Brazil	99,427	66,623	50,000	216,050
CDD/Mexico	292,281	214,717	297,427	804,425
CDD/Spain	—	5,000	—	5,000
CFFC/Canada	—	—	2,500	2,500
CFFC/Oregon	—	1,500	—	1,500
Choice USA	100,000	—	—	100,000
Christians for Human Rights (London, England)	150	—	—	150
	150	—	—	150
CORPUS (National Association for a Married Priesthood)	—	—	15,000	15,000
Council for Parliament of World Religions (Chicago)	—	—	1,000	1,000
Demysex (sex education program designers, Mexico City)	1,000	—	—	1,000
Dom. Center for Human Rights (Mexico City)	1,000	—	—	1,000
Espace Femmes International (Switzerland)	—	—	3,000	3,000
GodTalk Foundation (Falls Church, Virginia)	—	—	2,000	2,000
Grupo de Información en Reproducción Elegida (Mexico City)	2,000	—	—	2,000
International Association of Buddhist Women	5,000	—	—	5,000
International Network for the Rights of Female Victims of Violence in Pakistan (INRFVVP, Louisville, Kentucky)	—	1,000	—	1,000

Grants and Allocations Given by Catholics for a Free Choice, 1998-2000 (cont.)	1998	1999	2000	Total
International Movement We Are Church	—	5,000	750	5,750
(Versailles, France)	—	5,000	750	5,750
Irish Family Planning Association	1,300	—	—	1,300
(affiliate of IPPF)				
Janet Gallagher	—	—	7,237	7,237
(New York, research)				
Modemujer (Mexico)	—	10,000	—	10,000
National Latina Institute				
for Reproductive Health (DC)	—	—	5,000	5,000
National Organization for Women				
(NOW, Washington, DC)	100	—	—	100
Quixote Center				
(Hyattsville, Maryland)	—	5,000	—	5,000
St. Stephen's Episcopal Church				
(Washington, DC)	50	—	—	50
Sophia Center (Oakland, California)	15,000	5,000	—	20,000
Total grants and allocations	**610,90**	**444,536**	**454,202**	**1,510,641**
Grants to Latin America	490,053	422,036	410,715	1,322,804
Percent of Total Grants to Latin America	80.2%	94.9%	90.4%	87.6%

Table 5

**Annual Program Expenditures,
Catholics for a Free Choice, 1998-2000**

		1998	1999	2000	Totals
IIIa.	**Education and Communications -** Raise awareness of reproductive health issues through publications, public speaking, media and seminars.	360,727	414,522	546,002	**1,321,251 (18.8%)**
IIIb.	**Constituency Building -** Participation in coalitions and training, organizing and collaborating with Catholic and interfaith activists, leaders and organizations.	307,903	255,617	247,104	**810,624 (11.5%)**
IIIc.	**Research -** Research and monitoring related to the Catholic health care system and the initiatives of the Catholic bishops.	167,242	388,132	277,833	**833,207 (11.9%)**
IIId.	**International Program -** Educational activities in several European countries and translation and distribution of foreign language publications.	264,947	158,413	237,270	**660,630 (9.4%)**
IIIe.	**Latin America Program -** Education and communications projects in Latin America including Spanish-language publications, workshops, and policy analysis.	756,769	619,915	685,046	**2,061,730 (29.4%)**
	Religion Counts - To provide a positive, ethically sensitive religious contribution to discourse on issues surrounding population, reproductive health, and development policies.	125,000	208,532	323,125	**656,657 (9.4%)**
	Religion and the United Nations - Participation in United Nations conferences and meetings.	189,373	316,655	171,544	**677,572 (9.6%)**
IIIf.	**Total Annual Program Expenses**	**2,171,961**	**2,361,786**	**2,487,924**	**7,021,671 (100.0%)**

Part 2

Answering CFFC's Arguments

Why It is Important to Learn CFFC's Arguments.

In order to fight an opponent effectively, you must know how he thinks. You must be especially familiar with his arguments and how to refute them. This may require several hours of study, but it is the most powerful weapon you have (after prayer) in support of your mission, which is saving souls and protecting the Catholic Faith. If you do not have knowledge of your opponent and his propaganda, all of your efforts will be in vain: "My people are destroyed for lack of knowledge" [Hosea 4:6]. This is the basic principle of apologetics.

The primary defenses of abortion given by Catholics for a Free Choice are twelve in number. These are divided into theological arguments (the ones you can prove false with logic) and secular arguments (the ones you can prove false with facts).

Like all other pro-abortion arguments, CFFC's are designed primarily to *distract* the listener and divert attention from the subject of abortion. In order to be effective, pro-lifers must be able to render these arguments ineffective by bringing attention back to the basic issue: Abortion.

CFFC's Theological (Faith-Based) Arguments

(1) "The Bible says nothing about abortion."
(2) "You are not guilty of sin if you follow your conscience."
(3) "The fetus is not a person."
(4) "The church's ban on abortion is not infallible."
(5) "Dissent is necessary for the life of the Church."
(6) "We respect the ability of women to make good decisions."

CFFC's Secular (Fact-Based) Arguments

(7)   "Please don't call us 'pro-abortion.' Nobody is *for* abortion. We are 'pro-choice'."

(8)   "The majority of Catholics are pro-choice."

(9)   "If you want to cut the abortion rate, you must support the widespread availability of contraception."

(10)   "The celibate male priesthood has no right to pronounce doctrine in areas outside its expertise."

(11)   "The Church's teachings on abortion have changed many times over the centuries."

(12)   "We respect the right of others to hold opinions different from our own."

In addition to the detailed rebuttals that follow, Human Life International has produced a short summary of responses to CFFC's arguments.

This sixteen-page booklet is entitled "How 'Catholics' for a Free Choice Distorts Catholic Teaching on Abortion." It is suitable for distribution at events and talks organized by CFFC, for putting in your church's literature rack with your pastor's permission, and for reference when you are calling in to radio talk shows.

It is also available in Spanish.

You can order 100 copies for $15.00 from;

Human Life International
4 Family Life
Front Royal, Virginia 22630, USA
Order hotline: 1-800-549-LIFE
Web site: http://www.hli.org

Vida Humana Internacional
45 Southwest 71st Avenue
Miami, Florida 33144
Telephone: (305) 260-0525
FAX: (305) 260-0595
E-mail: vhi@vidahumana.org
Web site: http://www.vidahumana.org

CFFC Argument #1:
"The Bible says nothing about abortion."

What Catholics for a Free Choice Says.

> "There has been no systematic thinking in Jewish-Christian tradition on abortion. There is nothing in the Bible on it."
> — Former CFFC board member and ex-priest Daniel C. Maguire.[113]

Summary of the Response.

(1)   It is true that the Bible does not directly condemn abortion. However, the Bible teaches that there is a child in the womb, and it *does* condemn the killing of the innocent — specifically the practice of child sacrifice.[114] Preborn children are undeniably innocent, because they lack the intent to commit sin or do harm.

(2)   All religious people agree that God opens and shuts the womb and infuses the human body with a soul. This means that He certainly intended to create a human life, and we have no right to interfere with His will regarding its creation.

(3)   This argument is only a diversion, because CFFC heartily approves of many acts *specifically* condemned by the Bible, including fornication, adultery, homosexual acts and divorce.

(4)   The Bible does not *support* the availability of abortion.

(1) The Bible *Indirectly* Condemns Abortion.

CFFC's statement that abortion is not explicitly mentioned in the Bible is technically correct. However, this does not automatically mean that the Bible *approves* of abortion.

The modern horror of suctioning babies from the womb for money would have been wholly foreign and unimaginable to the minds of people in Biblical times, so an explicit condemnation of abortion would not have even occurred to the authors of the various books of the Bible.

There are many sins that the Bible condemns implicitly, or indirectly. For instance, the Commandment "thou shalt not kill" certainly applies to sins such as serial killing, terrorism and the indiscriminate bombing of civilians during warfare, though these are not specifically mentioned in the Bible.

How, then, may we know that the Bible *indirectly* condemns abortion?

We may do so through the following simple logical process.

(a) The Bible condemns the killing of the innocent, i.e., the sinless.[115]

(b) A preborn child is obviously innocent of any crime or actual sin, because he or she cannot possess the *intent* of doing evil. Pro-abortionists sometimes justify abortion by casting the pre born child in the role of an "aggressor." This is illogical, because aggression requires conscious intent.

(c) The Bible teaches that human life, *created and nurtured by God*, is present in the womb of the woman from the very beginning. Psalm 139:13,15 praises God in these words: "For thou didst form my inward parts, thou didst knit me together in my mother's womb. ... my frame was not hidden from thee, when I was being made in secret, intricately wrought in the depths of the earth."

Furthermore, God personally named and honored seven men before they were even born. Only *persons* merit names. These seven are Ishmael (Genesis 16:11); Isaac (Genesis 17:19); Josiah (1 Kings 13:2); Solomon (1 Chronicles 22:9); Jeremiah (Jeremiah 1:5); John the Baptist (Luke 1:13); and Jesus Himself (Matthew 1:21).[116]

God is not inconsistent. He has loved us all with an infinite love for all eternity — long *before* we were even conceived. He has said to us "I have loved thee with an everlasting love" [Jeremiah 31:3]. If He values men He named, He values *all* of his created preborn human beings.

(d) The conclusion is inevitable. If the Bible condemns the killing of the innocent (paragraph a, above), if preborn children are innocent (b, above), and if human life is present from fertilization (c, above), then the Bible also condemns the killing of

58

preborn children.

No other conclusion is possible.

(2) Only God Has the Power to Open and Shut the Womb.

Religious persons on both sides of the abortion issue agree that God gives life, and that God gives the person a soul.

Martin Luther said that "Even if all the world were to combine forces, they could not bring about conception of a single child in any woman's womb nor cause it to be born; that is wholly the work of God alone."[117]

There are more than a dozen Biblical references to God opening and shutting the womb.[118]

Now, if we all agree that God gives life and confers the soul, by what right may we interfere with His will? God does not act randomly or without reason, despite what CFFC says in its literature.[119] He creates every child for a purpose. Psalm 127 specifically refers to children as a "gift of the Lord" and as a "reward." We do not have the right to disrupt or destroy His plans. Abortion is a supremely arrogant act because it imposes our will over God's.

Is this not the definition of *all* sin — stubbornly refusing to do God's will for our lives?

(3) The Biblical Argument is Just Another Diversion by CFFC.

Perhaps we should leave aside what the Bible does or does not say about abortion for a moment, and consider this question: Would Catholics for a Free Choice repudiate abortion if Scripture *specifically* and *directly* prohibited it?

The Bible repeatedly and forcefully condemns other sexual sins such as homosexual activity, divorce, fornication, and adultery,[120] yet CFFC tolerates and even embraces all of these as "basic human rights." In spite of more than fifty Biblical passages denouncing these sins, Frances Kissling casually stated that "I really think God cares very little about the sexual rules, about who is sleeping with whom, other than to wish that we treat each other well and with respect."[121]

CFFC is obviously using the Bible as a diversion in exactly the same manner as it uses its fetal pain, fetal personhood, ensoulment and viability arguments. Even if theologians could somehow decisively prove that the Bible condemned abortion, CFFC would certainly not cease to advocate it, because CFFC does not *care* what the Bible says — *unless it can use the Bible as a mere tool to support its ideology.*

Frances Kissling proves this when she said that "... we all have the obligation to interpret the gospels in light of the times. Anyone who thinks that the gospels were so explicit that they do not call for a strong element of interpretation is really not on this planet."[122]

(4) What *Else* Isn't in the Bible?

In order to be balanced and fair, we must ask the leaders of Catholics for a Free Choice a simple question: If they insist upon talking about the Bible, where does it *justify* abortion?

There is no phrase in the Bible remotely *approaching* the phrases "freedom of choice," "woman's body, woman's choice," "plan your family," "use your conscience," or any of the other popular pro-abortion slogans.

There is, however, the phrase *"choose life*, therefore, that you and your descendants may live" [Deuteronomy 30:19].

Conclusion.

It is true that the Bible does not use the word "abortion" in the way we use it and mean it in the modern day. However, if we examine Scripture *in toto*, we can only conclude that it repeatedly addresses the great value of human life, that human life is created in the image and likeness of God (even the preborn John the Baptist recognized the preborn Jesus as God), and that God loves each of us with an infinite love — a love so great that He even sent His only Son to redeem us.

In light of this, there is no way a person who is honestly seeking the truth can conclude that the Bible supports prenatal killing in any way. Anyone who believes that it does is simply deceiving himself: "There is a way that seems right to a man, but its end is the way of death" [Proverbs 14:12].

CFFC Argument #2:

"You are not guilty of sin if you follow your conscience."

What Catholics for a Free Choice Says.

"Church law affirms both the right and the responsibility of a Catholic to follow his or her conscience, even when it conflicts with church teaching. ... Catholic theology tells individuals to follow their own consciences on moral matters, even when one's conscience is in conflict with church teachings."
— *Conscience* Magazine.[123]

Summary of the Response.

    (1)   CFFC's understanding of "conscience" is fatally flawed. It wrongly believes that conscience is the *source* of morality, instead of the *witness* to the moral law, of which God is the source.

    (2)   Regarding the principle of probabilism: When there is doubt regarding the presence of human life, the benefit of the doubt should always be given to life. This is true not only regarding Church teachings, but in everyday life as well.

    (3)   CFFC consistently misuses the documents of Vatican II to support its concept of the human conscience.

(1) CFFC's Understanding of Conscience is Fatally Flawed.

CFFC's Concept of Conscience. Catholics for a Free Choice so heavily emphasizes the role of conscience in making decisions *for* abortion that even its newsletter ["A Newsjournal of Prochoice Catholic Opinion"] is entitled *Conscience.*

By contrast, a *properly*-formed and informed Catholic conscience is fully aware of the evil and murderous nature of abortion, and is led to vigorously oppose it at all times.

CFFC recognizes that it cannot logically support its pro-abortionism unless it misrepresents the true purpose of the human conscience. In order for a person's conscience to be conditioned to accept abortion and other evils, it must first decisively turn away from God's teachings and proclaim that it can determine for *itself* what is right and wrong, even ignoring all external standards if necessary to reach the desired conclusion.

In other words, CFFC must justify its position by stating that the only legitimate guide for the human conscience is moral relativism. This is the theory that there are no moral principles that exist independently of one's own opinions and feelings, and that there is no morality that is binding on all persons, everywhere and at all times. Of course, if each person's conscience is the *source* of morality, then morality is individualistic and therefore also relativistic and entirely subjective. This leads to "might is right" thinking, where the strong dominate the weak and justice is simply discarded in favor of utilitarianism and convenience. Examples of where this kind of thinking leads abound in modern society: Abortion, racism, sexism, rape, incest, euthanasia, terrorism, infanticide, and trafficking in women and children.

CFFC outlines its concept of 'conscience' in a pamphlet written by ex-nun Marjorie Reiley Maguire and ex-priest Daniel C. Maguire entitled "Abortion: A Guide to Making Ethical Choices."[124]

The section of this pamphlet addressing conscience is shown below, followed by comments. Paragraphs are lettered for clarification.

(a)   **CFFC:** "We are not born with something called conscience. Conscience is something that has to be formed. Conscience is our progressively refined ability to think about situations in which we are involved and evaluate their moral goodness or badness for us."

Comment: This first paragraph is theologically correct. However, this is a common CFFC tactic: Begin by stating the truth, and then smoothly and seamlessly transition into falsehoods.

(b)   **CFFC:** "To make this evaluation we bring to bear on the situation the reasoning process of our mind, the feelings of our heart, the standards of moral behavior we have learned from society, and, where appropriate, religious teachings. ..."

Comment: This statement shows that CFFC has no problem with *deliberately* misinforming a person's conscience. In fact, this is the primary mission of CFFC — to provide an "alternative" view of the Catholic Church's teachings on abortion and other sins. Notice that CFFC relegates "religious teachings" to last place in its list of moral determinants and, even then, only "where appropriate." CFFC claims that the "feelings of our heart" and *society's* morality are the primary yardsticks of what is right and wrong — not Church teaching.

The Church has *never* taught that we should derive our morality from our feelings or emotions, or even from the standards set by the world. After all, if a church follows the world and not Christ, it is humanistic and not godly. Instead, we should develop our morality from studying Scripture and revelation as interpreted by the Church.

The *Catechism* identifies the primary danger of CFFC's brand of moral relativism: "The education of conscience is indispensable for human beings who are subjected to negative influences and tempted by sin to prefer their own judgment and to reject authoritative teachings" [¶1783].

(c)   **CFFC:** "Catholicism also teaches that the conscience of the person is the final guide to be followed when deciding to act. ... "

Comment: This statement is completely false. Some actions — including abortion — can *never* be "right," regardless of what our consciences tell us [see the *Catechism*, ¶1751, 1778, 1780 and 1790]. To illustrate how illogical this statement is, consider the parallel in the secular world. If we "follow our conscience" and break a law, the law still considers our actions a crime, and *will* hold us accountable.

CFFC sees the conscience as a teacher and as the supreme judge of moral truth. By contrast, the Catholic Church teaches that the individual conscience must be schooled to *recognize*, not to *determine*, what is and is not moral activity.

To illustrate, let us imagine for a moment that your pharmacist cannot read the dosage on the prescription for the heart medicine you need in order to stay alive. Would you prefer that he make a personal determination based on his life

63

experience, or check with the proper authority — the issuing physician — to confirm the dosage?

The *Catechism of the Catholic Church* states that "Objective rules of morality express the rational order of good and evil, *attested to* by conscience ... It is by the judgment of conscience that man *perceives* and *recognizes* the prescriptions of the divine law" [¶1751, 1778].

Once again, CFFC quotes Church teachings — but only when they seem to support CFFC's ideology. CFFC simply does not believe that Christ speaks with His authority through the Magisterium of the Catholic Church and the Pope and the bishops in communion with him. Nor does it believe that the Magisterium is the *only* authentic interpreter of the Word of God, whether written in the Bible or oral in sacred tradition [see *Dei Verbum*, ¶10].

(d)   **CFFC:** "You are not guilty of sin if you follow your conscience, even if most people in the Church would consider your action wrong. ..."

Comment: Once again, the Church has repeated many times that *no* abortion is licit, and that individual conscience must yield to Church teachings regarding the sanctity of human life. Sin is defined as rejecting God and His laws [*Catechism*, ¶398]; people or groups are not free to redefine "sin" to suit their own purposes.

(e)   **CFFC:** The Catholic Church, when considered in its rich diversity, teaches that some abortions can be moral and that conscience is the final arbiter of any abortion decision."

Comment: CFFC does not even represent its *own* positions accurately in its literature. CFFC considers *all* abortions moral. In its view, the only qualification for a "moral" abortion is that the woman wants it. CFFC even fought hard against the Partial-Birth Abortion Ban Act, which would have prohibited the killing of near-term preborn children by delivering all but the head and then suctioning the brains out and collapsing the skull. How CFFC can defend such a ghastly procedure in the name of "Catholic justice" is incomprehensible.

CFFC distributes this brochure in bulk to abortion clinics. It is quite obvious that its purpose is to salve the consciences of Catholic women in the abortion clinic's waiting rooms so that its abortion 'sales' may go smoothly.

Unilateral Conscience. Other CFFC documents show that one of the primary features of its concept of "conscience" is that it is unilateral. This invalidates its philosophy regarding the role of conscience, because, in order to be consistent, rights regarding conscience must be extended to *all* people — not just to those who hold the "approved" political ideology.

CFFC claims that "pro-choice" politicians must follow their consciences and vote *for* abortion even when the majority of their constituents are pro-life — but that pro-life politicians must *not* follow their consciences, regardless of the beliefs of their constituents — they *must* vote for abortion as well!

CFFC writer Christine E. Gudorf presents us with a glaring example of this kind of hypocrisy;

> A politician should not acquiesce to the wishes of the majority when they contradict his or her conscience, as Mario Cuomo has attested in thrice vetoing capital punishment laws desired by the majority in New York State. At the same time, when fundamental moral values are in conflict, as they are in the abortion instance, and strong popular support for the conclusion reached by the legislator's conscience is absent, a strong case can be made for Catholic legislators' refusing to impose their conclusions of conscience on others.[125]

CFFC's other writings prove that its definition of "conscience" is nothing more than a tool to hoodwink legislators.

CFFC believes that, when a large majority of people have a politically conservative viewpoint that contradicts the view of a "pro-choice" politician, he must not contradict his own conscience by voting as the people want. However, if a large majority of the people demand a ban on, say, partial-birth abortions, then a pro-life legislator must not "impose his beliefs" on them by voting pro-life. As one CFFC writer claims, "A Catholic who believes abortion is immoral in all or most circumstances can still support its legality."[126]

As Argument #12 shows, CFFC admits that pro-lifers see abortion as murder, but then condemns *all* pro-life activities, from rescue missions to political organizing. Meanwhile, CFFC claims the right to commit any act in *support* of abortion — including setting up abortion mills in countries where abortion is illegal.

In other words, CFFC declares that pro-lifers may not follow their consciences and fight abortion in any way, which is a gross violation of the consciences of those who oppose abortion. This attitude is not only hypocritical, it is blatantly unjust.

In summary, CFFC's concept of the role of conscience is not only in direct conflict with Church teachings, it is inconsistent because it is applied *conditionally*, depending entirely upon one's beliefs regarding abortion. This means that CFFC's concept of the human conscience is invalid.

It is true that Catholics must follow their consciences, but their consciences must be formed by the Word of God, which is authentically interpreted and taught only by the Magisterium of the Catholic Church, to which Christ entrusted His authority to teach in His Name.

Pro-Lifers Must Be Forced to Conform. We can conclude that Catholics for a Free Choices does not really believe its own rhetoric when it so firmly states that "All Catholics have the right to follow their informed consciences in all matters."

As we can see from Argument #12, CFFC stridently condemns every activity by pro-lifers, even those as innocuous as helping pregnant women so they may carry their babies to term.

CFFC's glorification of "conscience" is a mere smoke screen. In practical effect, CFFC believes that only "pro-choice" Catholics have the right to follow their consciences.

In 1990, CFFC decisively proved, in the *Paquette v. Regal Art Press* case, that it has no regard for the consciences of those who disagree with it.

Chuck and Susan Baker are Catholics who run a private printing press named Regal Art in Vermont. In 1990, Linda Paquette, a member of the Vermont chapter of Catholics for a Free Choice (VCFC), asked the Bakers to print membership forms for her organization. The Bakers refused on the grounds that CFFC deliberately distorts Catholic teachings regarding abortion and contraception.

Incredibly, Paquette alleged that the Bakers should be forced to print her material, since VCFC "promotes freedom of conscience" and "tolerance." She also argued that pro-abortionism was part of her "religious creed." She complained to the Vermont Human Rights Commission, which threatened the Bakers with a $10,000 fine and a lawsuit for compensatory and punitive damages on the grounds of "religious discrimination."

Note that the Bakers operate a *private* printing press. They receive no government money, and are not a tax-deductible charity. In other words, they are a private small business — but CFFC attempted to *force* them to print material that violates their religious beliefs and their consciences.

Eventually the lawsuit was dismissed, but only after a long and expensive court fight.[127]

With astounding hypocrisy, Marie Baldwin, head of VCFC, said that "We need reasoned debate, respectful dialogue, acknowledgement that each of us is entitled to opinions emanating from that secret core inside of us where we are alone with God. That core is conscience. It cannot be coerced, or controlled, or made to conform to the conscience of another."[128]

(2) On the Moral Principle of Probabilism.

CFFC's Interpretation of Probabilism. CFFC relies upon the moral principle of `probabilism' to support its notion of an unformed and unrestricted conscience.

Former CFFC Board member and ex-priest Daniel Maguire defines *his* version of this concept;

> The Catholic doctrine of *probabilism* ... blesses diversity of opinion in morally debated areas. ... *Ubi dubium, ibi libertas* — "where there is doubt there is freedom" — is probabilism's cardinal principle. ... The hallowed Catholic tradition of probabilism taught that in respectably debated issues, where good people for good reason disagree, conscience is free.[129]

Maguire continues by defining two ways in which probabilism may be used — with external sources and with internal judgment;

> *Extrinsic probabilism* involves reliance on authority figures, which in the past usually meant finding five or six reputable moral theologians who held the liberal view. ... Thus, if you found five or six theologians, known for their "prudence and learning" who held the liberal dissenting view, you could follow them in good conscience even if the other ten thousand

theologians — including the pope — disagreed.

Intrinsic probabilism is attained by the individual in a do-it-yourself manner; it is accomplished when an individual person perceives the inapplicability of a particular teaching even without help from theologians or other authority figures.[130]

CFFC's Omissions. Maguire is brazenly omitting crucial qualifiers regarding the use of the principle of probabilism.

(a) The fundamental principle of probabilism is *lex dubia non obligat* or "A doubtful law does not bind." This leads to the obvious conclusion that an established law *does* bind, and that the principle of probabilism may never be used when a prohibiting law is certain, as is the Church's pro hibition of abortion.[131]

Maguire's statement that "... probabilism taught that in respectably debated issues, where good people for good reason disagree, conscience is free" is obviously a thinly-disguised endorsement of situational ethics, and is completely false.

Our Sunday Visitor's Catholic Encyclopedia describes the proper role of probabilism: "Probabilism asserted that liberty from a law was to be held in possession until the opposite was held to probably be the case."[132]

Theologians originally proposed the principle of probabilism *only* for those very rare instances where scientific or theological knowledge of a subject was incomplete, or where the Church had not yet clearly out lined its teachings on the subject.

There is no doubt whatsoever about the Church's condemnation of abortion, sterilization and contraception. Probabilism can never apply to a universal moral prohibition. Therefore, the principle of probabilism does not apply in these cases.

Regarding abortion, no prudent person could possibly conclude that Church law is *un*certain. Therefore, as the National Council of Catholic Bishops Committee on Doctrine has stated, "Catholic theology does not allow the application of the theory of probabilism in cases which contradict Church teaching or where the risk of taking life is present."[133]

In summary, when the Church has definitely prohibited an act, all Catholics must abstain from performing it.

CFFC is clearly abusing the principle of probabilism. We must remember that CFFC's primary mission is not to clear up doubt regarding abortion, but to *generate* it. Groups like CFFC can only flourish in a fog of confusion and uncertainty.

(b) Maguire appears to be paraphrasing the 1917 *Catholic Encyclopedia* which states, "The prevailing theory amongst Probabilists holds that if five or six theologians, notable for prudence and learning, independently adhere to an opinion their view is solidly probable, *if it has not been set aside by authoritative decisions or by intrinsic arguments which they have failed to solve*"[134] [emphasis added].

If Maguire is indeed using the *Catholic Encyclopedia*, he omits the portion of the above quote that is italicized. Once again, the Church has declared repeatedly and forcefully that abortion is *never* licit. Therefore, the principle of probabilism is inapplicable to abortion.

(c) The same 1917 *Catholic Encyclopedia* article Maguire appears to use also warns that "All moralists agree that mere flimsy reasons are insufficient to give an opinion solid probability, and also that the support of many theologians who are mere collectors of the opinions of others is unable to give solid probability to the view which they maintain."[135]

A review of CFFC literature shows that the most compelling reasons the organization offers to support the free availability of abortion do not even reach the standard of `flimsy.' The most authoritative declarations by CFFC theologians either profess ignorance or arrive at unsupported and obviously false conclusions, i.e., "We don't know when life begins" and "the fetus is not human."

CFFC would not dare use the principle of probabilism in the secular sphere. No judge would accept probabilism as a defense if civil law was abundantly clear, because "ignorance of the law is no excuse." In civil society, if a person has any doubt whatever regarding the legality of an act, he studies the law further, and acts with prudence until its parameters are clear in his mind. He does not simply remain willfully ignorant and do whatever he pleases, intending to present probabilism as a defense in court.

(d) CFFC applies probabilism inconsistently, and only to its own advantage. A theological principle, in order to be valid, must apply *univer sally* to all situations. CFFC no more sincerely believes in the principle of probabilism than it believes in the primacy of conscience, because it

69

protests vociferously whenever social conservatives or pro-lifers employ either of these in support of their objectives.

CFFC's loud and persistent criticism of Pope Paul VI is the most obvious example of this double standard. Patty Crowley grumbles that "Twenty-five years later I feel betrayed by the church. If, as the majority of the [Papal birth control] commission believed, birth control is not intrinsically evil and if most Catholics practice birth control, how can the official church uphold *Humanae Vitae?*"[136]

Let us suppose for the sake of argument, that, under the guidance of the Holy Spirit, Pope Paul VI employed the principle of probabilism when he adopted the minority report of the Papal Birth Control Commission when writing the 1968 encyclical *Humanae Vitae*. Certainly there were many more than "five or six" theologians who agreed with him on the topic of contraception. Yet we see no defense of probabilism by CFFC in *this* case; instead, we see only complaints — and lots of them.[137]

(e) Finally, Maguire neglects to mention that probabilism was discarded as a theological construct long ago because of its obvious vulnerability to exactly the kind of abuses that CFFC promotes so vigorously.

Our Sunday Visitor's Catholic Encyclopedia describes the ultimate fate of probabilism: "probabilism degenerated into voluntarism and experienced all of the problems involved in that system of moral analysis." Voluntarism is the "moral doctrine which holds that the moral malice of actions is determined by the status of the agent's will or intention."[138] Voluntarism is one of the disconnections between freedom and truth described in *Veritatis Splendor*, Pope John Paul II's encyclical on moral principles.

The Dangers of Misusing Probabilism. To demonstrate how unworkable, illogical and hypocritical CFFC's application of the theory of probabilism really is, consider a person who holds an outrageous viewpoint that not even "five or six theologians" in the whole world will support.

What if this person is an American Nazi who believes in a White homeland in the Northwestern United States, where other races are excluded? What if he is a member of an organized pedophile group like the North American Man-Boy Love Association (NAMBLA)? What if he is someone who believes that murdering abortion clinic workers is "justifiable homicide?"

Not to worry — in such a case, ex-priest Daniel Maguire says that we may just depend upon our own opinions to arrive at a decision with intrinsic, or "do-it-yourself" probabilism, as quoted above.

This misuse of the principle of probabilism leads to CFFC stating

> If you carefully examine your conscience and then decide that an abortion is the most moral act you can do at this time, you're not committing a sin. Therefore, you're not excommunicated. Nor need you tell it in confession since, in your case, abortion is not a sin.

Maguire is backed up by Alberto Munera, S.J., who takes this reasoning to its logical conclusion: "That is to say, an act can be considered morally wrong only in an individual's conscience. And because only God can judge conscience, nobody can declare a specific human behavior "intrinsically wrong"."[139]

In other words, CFFC would rewrite Jesus's words in John 20:23 to read "If you forgive the sins of any, they are forgiven; if you retain the sins of any, they are retained, unless, of course, that person feels comfortable with what they did."

There are great dangers inherent with this interpretation of the principle of probabilism, which is indistinguishable from a straightforward statement of moral relativism.

If this reasoning were true, it could logically be extended to every area of moral theology, just as CFFC has done in the area of sexual ethics. This means that a lax Catholic could violate any Commandment or any of its derivative laws, and still claim to be a "faithful Catholic." This is a classic example of *reductio ad absurdum*. No member of CFFC would dare defend himself or herself in a civil court of law with such a specious argument.

A parallel situation illustrates these pitfalls.

Let us say for a moment that a certain self-professed "pro-lifer" is seriously considering shooting a local abortionist. Perhaps he has read the declaration justifying the use of deadly force against abortionists, which was signed by several self-styled "theologians." Perhaps, as CFFC has noted, he has seen the statement by Father David Trosch that people who work for abortion rights should be "sought out and terminated as vermin are terminated."[140]

Certainly this potential shooter could find several theologians (not necessarily Catholics) who support the use of deadly force to rescue preborn children. However, even if he could find *no* theologians to support this view, he could simply use Maguire's intrinsic probabilism to "perceive the inapplicability of a particular teaching" against murdering abortionists — in his *own* case.

Undoubtedly, abortion clinic bombers have said to themselves (to paraphrase the above CFFC statement);

> I have carefully examined my conscience and decided that bombing an abortion clinic is the most moral act I can do at this time, so I'm not committing a sin. Therefore, I'm not excommunicated. Nor need I tell it in confession since, in *my* case, bombing an abortion clinic is not a sin.

Obviously, CFFC would *never* permit the use of either extrinsic or intrinsic probabilism to justify the murder of an abortionist or the bombing of an abortion clinic. Yet it robustly defends the use of probabilism to rationalize abortion. This is blatant hypocrisy.

In summary, CFFC's application of probabilism is selective, and depends entirely upon its ideology regarding the issue being discussed. However, in order to be valid, a theological principle must apply consistently and universally in all possible situations. It may not be used unilaterally — that is, to support only one viewpoint.

Unilateral Probabilism. CFFC's defense of unilateral (one-way) probabilism is evident in every issue of its journal *Conscience*. It continually tries to marginalize the beliefs of pro-lifers by claiming that "the majority of Catholics are pro-choice" (see Argument #8). In fact, the average issue of *Conscience* contains at least a dozen references to various polls and surveys.

If CFFC truly believes that probabilism is a valid theory, why does it continue to condemn pro-lifers as a "small and vocal minority?" If, as Daniel Maguire claims, we must respect the views of "five or six out of ten thousand," why does CFFC not respect the views of a much *larger* percentage of society — the many millions who consciously describe themselves as pro-life?

CFFC has distorted the principle of probabilism far beyond its permissible boundaries in order to suit its own purposes.

In reality, the principle of probabilism cannot be used to justify *any* type of violence against human beings, whether abortionists or the preborn.

(3) CFFC's Misuse of Vatican II Documents.

Introduction. Catholics for a Free Choice is one of the many dissenting groups that frequently appeal to an ill-defined "Spirit of Vatican II" to support their demands for change in the Church. These groups use nebulous terms such as "renewal," "reinvigoration" and "rejuvenation" to describe their plans, all the time claiming that Vatican II would have blessed their goals.

Significantly, these organizations rarely quote documentation from Vatican II — and, when they do, they invariably misinterpret the documents or misquote them entirely.

The two documents CFFC most often abuses are *Dignitatis Humanae* and *Gaudium et Spes*.

The *Declaration on Religious Freedom*. Dissenters frequently quote the Vatican II document *Dignitatis Humanae* ("Declaration on Religious Freedom") in support of their contention that people should be able to do anything their "consciences" do not object to.

For example, CFFC claims that "According to the Vatican II, "Declaration on Religious Liberty;" *"The Christian faithful have the civil right of freedom from interference in leading their lives according to their conscience"*."[141] Frances Kissling says "In its approach to the [abortion] issue, the organization [CFFC] relied on the Declaration on Religious Freedom, the Second Vatican Council's endorsement of the separation of church and state, pluralism, and the primacy of conscience."[142]

Father John Courtney Murray, S.J., principal author of the *Declaration*, anticipated this type of mendacity.

He stated in a footnote to the Abbott-Gallagher edition of the Council texts that

> The *Declaration* does not base the right to the free exercise of religion on "freedom of conscience." Nowhere does this phrase occur. And the *Declaration* nowhere lends its authority to the theory for which the phrase frequently stands, namely, that I have the right to do what my conscience tells me to do, simply because my conscience tells me to do it. This is a perilous theory. Its particular peril is subjectivism — the notion that, in the end, it is my conscience, and not the objec-

tive truth, which determines what is right and wrong, true or false.[143]

CFFC conveniently neglects to mention paragraph 8 of the *Declaration*, which notes that "... not a few can be found who seem inclined to use the name of freedom as the pretext for refusing to submit to authority and for making light of the duty of obedience."

Pope John Paul II defined the correct relationship between freedom and truth as it *should* be perceived by the conscience, and also described the role of the Magisterium, in his encyclical *Veritatis Splendor* ("The Splendor of Truth"), ¶61-62;

> Consequently "in the practical judgment of conscience," which imposes on the person the obligation to perform a given act, "the link between freedom and truth is made manifest." Precisely for this reason conscience expresses itself in acts of "judgment" which reflect the truth about the good, and not in arbitrary "decisions." The maturity and responsibility of these judgments — and, when all is said and done, of the individual who is their subject — are not measured by the liberation of the conscience from objective truth, in favor of an alleged autonomy in personal decisions, but, on the contrary, by an insistent search for truth and by allowing oneself to be guided by that truth in one's actions.
>
> Christians have a great help for the formation of conscience "in the Church and her Magisterium." As the [Second Vatican] Council affirms: "In forming their consciences the Christian faithful must give careful attention to the sacred and certain teaching of the Church. For the Catholic Church is by the will of Christ the teacher of truth. Her charge is to announce and teach authentically that truth which is Christ, and at the same time with her authority to declare and confirm the principles of the moral order which derive from human nature itself." It follows that the authority of the Church, when she pronounces on moral questions, in no way undermines the freedom of conscience of Christians.

Frances Kissling tries to raise the specter of the entanglement of Church and

State, which is anathema to all dissenters, as she states that "Catholic acceptance of the principle of the separation of church and state is very recent. It was only some thirty years ago, at the Second Vatican Council, that it was definitively accepted in the "Declaration on Religious Liberty"."[144]

In reality, the *Declaration* nowhere even *mentions* the separation of Church and State. Instead, it delineates the duties of the State with relation to the Church, stressing that all believers should be allowed to worship as they please.

Gaudium et Spes. CFFC also misrepresents *Gaudium et Spes* ("On the Church in the Modern World") when it claims that

> While we may consider certain behavior morally wrong, some-body in his or her conscience may see no error or wrongdoing in it and thus commits no moral error in engaging in that behavior (*Gaudium et Spes* 26). That is to say, an act can be considered morally wrong only in an individual's conscience. And because only God can judge conscience, nobody can declare a specific behavior "intrinsically wrong."[145]

One must wonder if CFFC writers actually *read* the documents they quote. *Gaudium et Spes* [¶26] says nothing at all about conscience, but instead address-es the dignity ascribed to every human person. In fact, no passage in the entire document says anything even remotely approaching the above passage, even allowing for wide latitude in different translations.

However, *Gaudium et Spes* [¶16-17] *does* address the role of the human con-science. It says;

> Conscience frequently errs from invincible ignorance without losing its dignity. The same cannot be said for a man who cares but little for truth and goodness, or for a conscience which by degrees grows practically sightless as a result of habitual sin. ... Only in freedom can man direct himself toward goodness. Our contemporaries make much of this freedom and pursue it eagerly; and rightly to be sure. Often however they foster it perversely as a license for doing whatever pleas-es them, even if it is evil. ... Before the judgment seat of God each man must render an account of his own life, whether he

has done good or evil.

Gaudium et Spes also contains a passage regarding practical atheism which may have been written with groups like CFFC in mind: "Undeniably, those who willfully shut out God from their hearts and try to dodge religious questions are not following the dictates of their consciences, and hence are not free of blame ..." [¶19].

CFFC, which appeals to *Gaudium et Spes* frequently, never mentions that it squarely condemns the use of abortion and contraception;

> Children are really the supreme gift of marriage and contribute very substantially to the welfare of their parents. ... in their manner of acting, spouses should be aware that they cannot proceed arbitrarily, but must always be governed according to a conscience dutifully conformed to the divine law itself, and should be submissive toward the Church's teaching office, which authentically interprets that law in the light of the Gospel [¶50].

Gaudium et Spes repeatedly condemns abortion, going so far as to call it an "unspeakable crime" [¶51].

It is really not surprising that CFFC, which relies so heavily on the "Spirit of Vatican II," picks and chooses among its teachings, just as it picks and chooses which Catholic doctrines it deems convenient.

Conclusion.

Catholics for a Free Choice possesses a fatally flawed concept of conscience, treating it as a teacher, not a pupil. Conscience is indeed a decisionmaker, but it must be freely submitted to the law of God, to which it is a witness, not an arbiter.

The primary error of CFFC lies not in affirming the freedom of conscience to decide, but in misinterpreting the *nature* of such freedom. Freedom of conscience must be at the service of moral truth, but can never be its determinant.

CFFC's erroneous notion of freedom results in its many ideological inconsistencies and its schizophrenic antagonism between freedom and moral law. Moral law is the *guide* to authentic freedom so that it can reach its fulfillment in God ("You shall know the Truth, and the Truth shall make you free" [John 8:32]).

Instead, CFFC "... chooses to disobey and do evil, an abuse of freedom that leads to "the slavery of sin"" [Romans 6:17].

In support of its twin goals of confusing the faithful and making Catholic women comfortable with choosing abortion, CFFC stretches the principle of probabilism until it resembles no more than a simple statement of situational ethics.

Finally, CFFC grossly misquotes Vatican II documents in support of its notions of conscience and free choice, and ignores the fact that the documents repeatedly condemn abortion in the most forceful terms.

Catholics for a Free Choice also proves by its own words and actions that it does not believe its own rhetoric regarding the role of conscience in making informed moral decisions, because it reserves the right to act to *pro-choice* individuals alone, while stridently condemning every pro-life activity. It also has no problem with coercing pro-life Catholics into supporting its activities.

In summary, the primary role of 'conscience' for CFFC is to serve as a confusing diversion and a cover for its many abortion-promoting activities.

CFFC Argument #3:

"The fetus is not a person."

What Catholics for a Free Choice Says.

"Yet, in a 1974 document, the "Declaration on Procured Abortion," the Vatican stated that it does not know when a fetus becomes a person — just as each person in this room in all honesty would have to say."
— Frances Kissling.[146]

Summary of the Response.

(1) Kissling states that she "does not know when a fetus becomes a person." She does not seem aware that revoking the person hood of a person or group constitutes the basis of *all* oppression — of women, of minorities, of Jews, etc. It is necessary for all oppressors to deaden their consciences by dehumanizing their victims so that they may kill or exploit them.

(2) CFFC simply states as a fact that preborn human beings are not persons, without supporting its view with any proof or evidence whatever. CFFC cannot prove that preborn children are *not* human or persons. Therefore, since even CFFC admits that it cannot answer this question, we must err on the side of safety, because abortion *might* be taking the life of a person.

(3) Contrary to what CFFC claims, the Catholic Church does indeed consider preborn children to be persons. In fact, the "Declaration on Procured Abortion," which Frances Kissling quotes above, equates abortion to murder.

(4) This argument is another diversion, because CFFC claims the right to revoke the "personhood" of a preborn child even *after* acknowledging it.

(5) CFFC feigns ignorance about the timing of "personhood" and "ensoulment" as justification for allowing abortion throughout pregnancy. Once again, if we do not *know* if a preborn child is a person or has a soul, we must err on the side of safety.

(1)   Revoking Personhood is the Basis of All Oppression.

When it casually dismisses or avoids the question of the personhood of the preborn child, CFFC is emulating the oppressors who have killed and enslaved millions throughout human history.

The Nazis followed this well-worn path. They acknowledged only that they were destroying "human weeds" and "life not worth living," and officially classified their living human victims as "non-persons."

The slavers also took this course. They recognized the obvious life in their slaves (after all, dead slaves can't work), and their obvious humanity (other species weren't intelligent enough to follow orders), but drew the line at their *personhood*. Slaves were, according to the United States Supreme Court's 1857 *Dred Scott v. Sanford* decision, officially "non-persons."

And now, all pro-abortion groups simply dismiss the preborn child as "less than human."

They have no solid evidence to back up their claims.

Nor did the Nazis or slavers.

The pro-abortion "non-personhood" argument has one purpose and one purpose *only* — to confer a false veneer of respectability upon the elimination of human beings whom the pro-abortionists deem "unwanted" or "inconvenient." Such mental mendacity allows otherwise rational people to participate in the killing with clear consciences. The only reason CFFC calls preborn human beings "non-persons" is so that it may continue to promote abortion.

The 1985 edition of *The American Heritage Dictionary* describes CFFC's attitude perfectly: "Non-Person. n. A person whose expunction from the attention and memory of the public is sought, esp. by governmental action and usually for reasons of ideological or political deviation."

Ironically, while it denies preborn children equal rights, CFFC writers often complain about the Vatican, which they allege denies women full "personhood" by refusing to allow women's ordination.

It is the height of hypocrisy for CFFC to complain that women are being oppressed, when it is one of the most outspoken oppressors of the most helpless human beings — preborn children.

(2)   CFFC Cannot Prove that Preborn Children Are *Not* Human.

CFFC says that we cannot know if preborn children are persons, and so we may abort them for any reason we like.

CFFC's thinking is fundamentally flawed. Simple logic tells us that we must give the benefit of the doubt to life in any situation where our actions may endanger life.

For instance, take the case of a construction company that has been given a contract to demolish a derelict building. They don't go ahead and knock the building down if they don't know if there are any people in it. They thoroughly search the building first.

We may not fire a weapon in the direction of a schoolyard we cannot see if we don't know if there are any children playing in it.

And we may not drop heavy objects from the top of a tall building if we don't know if there are any people below.

Yet CFFC claims that we may freely abort preborn children because we *don't know* if a person is present!

The Vatican's 1974 "Declaration on Procured Abortion" [¶13] sets a reasonable and simple standard to follow;

> It is not up to biological sciences to make a definitive judgment on questions which are properly philosophical and moral such as the moment when a human person is constituted or the legitimacy of abortion. From a moral point of view this is certain: even if a doubt existed concerning whether the fruit of conception is already a human person, it is objectively a grave sin to dare to risk murder.

(3) The Catholic Church Considers Preborns to be Persons.

What Kissling Says. In 1999, Francis Kissling casually stated to a study group of the British Parliament that "Even in Catholic theology, the word murder is not used in connection to abortion."[147]

Apparently Kissling has not bothered to read the documents she quotes so often in *support* of CFFC's pro-abortion ideology. Or perhaps, since she believes that preborn children are not persons, she cannot imagine how anyone *else* could consider them persons.

Whatever her motivations, Kissling is dead wrong — the Catholic Church has repeatedly referred to abortion as "murder," plain and simple.

What the Church Teaches. For example, the 1930 encyclical *Casti Connubii* ("On Chastity in Marriage") refers to abortion as the "direct murder of the innocent" [¶64].

The 1974 "Declaration on Procured Abortion" quotes Tertullian, who called abortion "anticipated murder" and Pope Stephen V, who said "That person is a murderer who causes to perish by abortion what has been conceived" [¶6 and 7].

The 1995 *Charter for Health Care Workers* of the Pontifical Council for Pastoral Assistance refers to abortion as "deliberate murder" [footnote 261].

The 1997 "Vademecum for Confessors Concerning Some Aspects of the Morality of Conjugal Life" of the Pontifical Council for the Family states that "The moral gravity of procured abortion is apparent in all its truth if we recognize that we are dealing with murder and, in particular when we consider the specific elements involved. The one eliminated is a human being at the very beginning of life" [¶52].

In addition to Vatican statements, Bishops' councils and individual prelates all over the world have condemned abortion as murder literally hundreds of times.

One of the most eloquent of these statements is the 1991 document entitled "The New Campaign Against Life," by the Bishops of Chiapas, Mexico. The Bishops call abortion "the murder of a helpless and innocent human being" [¶1]. In his 1998 letter "The Inalienable Right to Life and Partial-Birth Abortion," Eusebius J. Beltran, Archbishop of Oklahoma City, says that this "cold-blooded murdering of the unborn" is "beyond my understanding."

Most significantly, abortion is specifically referred to as "murder" in an encyclical widely criticized (and therefore presumably read) by CFFC writers — *Evangelium Vitae*: "The moral gravity of procured abortion is apparent in all its truth if we recognize that we are dealing with murder ..." [¶58].

In addition to recent statements, many of the early Church Fathers specifically taught that abortion was murder — including Tertullian, Hippolytus, and St. John Chrysostom (see Appendix B).[148]

It is one thing to state that one *disagrees* with the Church's teaching that abortion is murder. It is another thing entirely to claim that the Church *does not teach* that abortion is murder.

CFFC writers and speakers often represent themselves as experts and authorities in Catholic theology. For a so-called "expert" or "authority" to simply claim that the Church does not associate the word "murder" with abortion is inexcusable.

But Forgiveness Waits ... Although abortion is a heinous sin, God can forgive it through His Church, because the Church, like Christ, is compassionate.

Murder is the direct killing of an innocent human being with full knowledge and intent, and is a mortal sin. "Mortal sin is sin whose object is grave matter and which is also committed with full knowledge and deliberate consent" [*Catechism*, ¶1857].

There are two primary circumstances that may decrease the subjective guilt of abortion;

(1) **Extreme fear or pressure.** When a young girl or woman is in such terror or under such pressure that rational thinking is impossible, her subjective guilt is diminished to a certain extent. We do not refer here to the young college girl who is pregnant and is uncomfortable with what her parents may think, or whose boyfriend threatens to leave her if she refuses to abort; we are referring to parents or boyfriends who threaten her with physical violence or other extreme consequences. A pregnant mother should defend her preborn child with the same vigor she would defend one of her born children, but sometimes, because of an extreme fear caused by no fault of her own, this just *seems* to be impossible.

(2) **Ignorance.** Unfortunately, the pulpits of our churches are largely silent regarding abortion. When a girl grows up surrounded by people of tepid faith, trendy and inoffensive bishops and pastors, and pro-abortion groups telling her that it is perfectly all right to abort, she may truly believe that she is not committing a sin. One of the primary goals of Catholics for a Free Choice is to keep women ignorant of authentic Catholic teaching regarding the life issues.

Many women who have aborted their preborn children find out too late that the pro-abortionists have lied to them. There are thousands of post-abortive women now working tirelessly against the wholesale killing of the preborn. Many of these women confessed their abortions years or even decades after they occurred, and all of them know that Christ, through His Church, forgives all sins that are sincerely repented of.

The *Catechism of the Catholic Church* says that "There is no one, however wicked and guilty, who may not confidently hope for forgiveness, provided his repentance is honest. Christ who died for all men desires that in his Church the gates of forgiveness should always be open to anyone who turns away from sin" [¶982].

(4) The "Personhood" Argument is Just Another CFFC Diversion.

Echo of the Eugenics Movement. Frances Kissling shows that she thinks like a slave owner when she claims that "The child whom you see as precious and irreplaceable is that way because you have made it so. We each become a person through a process — a process that includes having parents, teachers, schools, friends, and lovers who all contribute to the person we are today."[149]

This shows that Kissling believes that a child has no intrinsic worth — that its value is conferred by others, which is dehumanizing and the basis of all oppression. She would certainly not tolerate any man saying that *women*'s value is conferred by men!

Kissling says that people *become* persons through a "process" involving interactions with many other people. This dangerous belief is a justification for active eugenics and infanticide, and would lead us to judge that babies up to four or six months old are "non-persons," because they have not yet begun actively participating in the "process" of others contributing to their personhood, and because they cannot actively interact with these persons to the degree required by the decisionmakers.

Personhood is Irrelevant to CFFC. When all is said and done, we find that the "personhood" argument for justifying the availability of abortion is just another diversion by CFFC.

Marjorie Reiley Maguire and ex-priest Daniel C. Maguire show that CFFC believes that women should be able to have abortions *even if they believe their preborn children are persons*;

> It is important to understand that while abortion does involve the taking of a human life — because all life that is in and of a human being is human life — in order to call it murder we

83

would have to believe that prenatal life in the early stages of pregnancy is a human person and that there were absolutely *no* reasons that justified the taking of that life ... [However], you may feel you have reasons that justify abortion regardless of your beliefs about personhood.[150]

Frances Kissling takes this view a step further when she insists that even those who believe persons are being killed by abortion have no right to interfere with the availability of abortion: "Even if you are convinced that abortion takes a life of a person you have a responsibility to respect the views of other religions."[151]

This is equivalent to a slaver or a racist saying that "Even if you are convinced that lynching takes the life of a [Black] person, you have a responsibility to respect the views of other religions and not interfere in any way."

(5) Ensoulment = Life?

Who Bestows the Soul? "Ensoulment" is that instant when God confers the soul upon a human body. According to Catholic teaching, God fuses body and soul at the instant of fertilization, when the sperm meets the egg.

This is the only logical time that ensoulment could possibly occur. The process of human development is an unbroken and seamless continuum from fertilization until natural death. All that changes is the location of the person.

CFFC recognizes the folly in denying that preborn children are alive and human, because life and humanity are both scientifically provable traits. Instead, CFFC writers often use the timing of "ensoulment" — a question that science literally will never be able to answer — in order to justify its abortion advocacy.

This is classic 'mystagoguery,' or employing a higher degree of obscurity. It is the polar opposite of trying to clarify an issue, because it is a deliberate attempt to render a question so complicated or murky that it can never be answered. This, of course, assures maximum freedom of action.

Pro-abortionists despise what they call "anti-choice black and white" thinking, because it clearly exposes their crimes and sins, and dispels the cloak of confusion and uncertainty with which they attempt to enshroud all their activities.

CFFC writers employ 'mystagoguery' to assert that personhood does not begin until the child gets its soul — and that it is not God, but the *mother*, who ensouls it. For example, Marjorie Reiley Maguire of CFFC said that "Personhood begins when the bearer of life, the mother, makes a covenant of love with the developing life within her to bring it to birth. It is in the nature of things that woman creates the `soul` just as much as she nourishes the body of developing human life."[152]

This is outright heresy, and in direct contradiction to what the Church has always taught. The *Catechism of the Catholic Church* says that "every spiritual soul is created immediately by God — it is not "produced" by the parents" [¶366]. The 1974 *Declaration on Procured Abortion* states that "Created immediately by God, man's soul is spiritual and therefore immortal" [¶8].

Conclusion: Give Life the Benefit of the Doubt. By saying that we cannot determine when ensoulment takes place, CFFC is admitting that ensoulment *may* take place at fertilization. If we choose to debate the timing of ensoulment, we must go back to the basic concept that we must always give human life the benefit of the doubt.

It is immoral to approve of a particular action just because human life might *not* be taken.

Society forbids behavior that *may* take life, even if the chance of such an occurrence is small. We are not allowed to poison Halloween treats on a supermarket shelf, just because human life *might not* be taken. And we have many local laws and ordinances that forbid smoking in crowded areas, because secondhand smoke *may* be injurious to others.

Once again, the Vatican's 1974 "Declaration on Procured Abortion" tells us the uncertainty is no rationalization for unrestricted freedom of action: "In the course of history, the Fathers of the Church, her Pastors and her Doctors have taught the same doctrine — the various opinions on the infusion of the spiritual soul did not introduce any doubt about the illicitness of abortion" [¶7].

In summary, the question of ensoulment is just another pro-abortion red herring. If scientists and theologians somehow achieved a breakthrough whereby they could prove that a preborn child received its soul at the instant of fertilization, we can be quite certain that ensoulment would suddenly become "irrelevant" in CFFC's view.

CFFC Argument #4:

"The church's ban on abortion is not infallible."

What Catholics for a Free Choice Says.

"... contrary to popular belief, the prohibition of abortion has never been declared an infallible teaching. This fact leaves much more room for discussion on abortion than is usually thought."
— *Conscience* Magazine.[153]

Summary of the Response.

(1)   CFFC completely disregards the fact that Church teachings on a subject such as abortion can be considered infallible through the *ordinary* magisterium.

(2)   CFFC ignores the teachings of the Church even when they *are* declared infallible. This means that, even if the Pope solemnly declared infallible the teaching that abortion is the murder of a human person, CFFC would simply disregard his proclamation. Therefore, CFFC is merely using the "infallibility" argument as another diversion.

(3)   A number of CFFC writers have declared that it is *impossible* to speak infallibly on any topic. Once again, even if the Pope declared the Church's teaching on abortion infallible, CFFC would simply ignore him. Yet CFFC treats women's choices *for* abortion as infallible, since it says we must *always* trust women to make good decisions.

(1)   How Can We Discern if a Teaching Is Infallible?

Ex Cathedra Declarations. There are two primary means by which the Church may declare a teaching infallible.

The most definitive statement of infallibility is the Pope's solemn declaration *ex cathedra* that a matter of faith or morals must be assented to in order for a Catholic to attain salvation.

One example of such a pronouncement is the 1854 Apostolic Constitution of

Pope Pius IX entitled *Ineffabilis Deus* ("The Immaculate Conception"), which proclaimed the perpetual sinlessness and virginity of Our Lady.[154]

Every Catholic must assent by faith to an infallibly proclaimed doctrine. Anyone who disbelieves or dissents from such a teaching cannot be called Catholic.

The Ordinary Magisterium. The second means by which Catholics may know that a Church teaching is infallible is by examining the ordinary Magisterium. This is the usual day-to-day expression of the Church's teaching authority, and does not require a solemn declaration by the Pope or by the assembled Bishops.

The Second Vatican Council's Dogmatic Constitution *Lumen Gentium* addressed the degree of assent that Catholics must give to the teachings of the Pope;

> ... loyal submission of the will and intellect must be given, in a special way, to the authentic teaching authority of the Roman Pontiff, even when he does not speak *ex cathedra* in such wise, indeed, that his supreme teaching authority be acknowledged with respect, and sincere assent be given to decisions made by him ... [¶25].

The Church may also teach infallibly through the authority of the Bishops.

The Canon of St. Vincent of Lorenz declares that any doctrine that has been taught *semper ubique ab omnibus* — always, everywhere, and by everyone — makes it part of the ordinary and universal Magisterial teaching.[155]

Ancient and modern Catholic theologians have always condemned the practice of abortion, as shown in the response to Argument #11. Therefore, the Catholic Church has indeed prohibited abortion *semper ubique ab omnibus*.

Lumen Gentium restates and applies the Canon to the Bishops;

> Although the bishops, taken individually, do not enjoy the privilege of infallibility, they do, however, proclaim infallibly the doctrine of Christ on the following conditions: Namely, when, even though dispersed throughout the world but preserving for all that amongst themselves and with Peter's successor the bond of communion, in their authoritative teaching

concerning matters of faith and morals, they are in agreement that a particular teaching is to be held definitively and absolutely.

This is still more clearly the case when, assembled in an ecumenical council, they are, for the universal Church, teachers of and judges in matters of faith and morals, whose decisions must be adhered to with the loyal and obedient assent of faith [¶25].

This means that Pope Paul VI's 1968 encyclical *Humanae Vitae* did not create some new doctrine or dogma. It once again *announced* and *recognized* the infallible doctrine, already more than nineteen centuries old, that human life is sacred from fertilization to natural birth and thence to natural death.

Because of Her constant and unwavering condemnation of abortion, always, everywhere, and by all of the Bishops, we may state without fear of authoritative contradiction that the Catholic Church's ban on abortion is, indeed, an infallible doctrine.

Why Doesn't the Pope Formally Declare Pro-Life Teachings Infallible? Pro-life theologians have debated the wisdom of having the Church's teachings on abortion and contraception be formally declared infallible, and have decided that this would not be advisable in the larger scheme of things.

Such a pronouncement in the realm of morals (as opposed to fundamental Catholic beliefs) would give the impression that all other moral teachings of the Church were optional. This might lead to a situation where disbelief would run rampant in the areas not specifically addressed *ex cathedra*, and would lead to more and more demands for such declarations in almost every area of Church teaching.

(2) CFFC Simply Disregards Those Teachings that *Have* Been Declared Infallible.

Yes, It's Another Diversion. CFFC's argument that "the ban on abortion is not infallible" is simply another diversion — one of many it throws out to muddy the waters and confuse the issue.

Even if the Pope *did* declare the Church's teachings on birth control and abortion infallible, CFFC would simply deny the liciteness of such a pronouncement.

This is especially true in the area of sexual morality.

Rosemary Radford Ruether says that "An effort to declare the ban on contraception "infallible" would have the immediate effect of focusing Catholic dissent on the doctrine of infallibility itself. ... A storm of dissent, and even ridicule, directed at infallibility itself would ensue from such a declaration."[156]

When Pope John Paul II convened a November 1988 conference under the auspices of the John Paul II Institute for Studies on Marriage and the Family entitled "*Humanae Vitae:* Twenty Years Later," the Pope and Monsignor Carlo Caffarra stated that *Humanae Vitae* must be assented to by the faithful.

CFFC immediately accused the Pope of "abusing the Magisterium." One of its writers displayed a profound ignorance of the nature of Church teaching authority when she said that "In theological terms, they [the dissenters] see this as blurring the distinction between the changeable positions of the ordinary magisterium and the unchangeable truths of the extraordinary magisterium."[157]

Shortly thereafter, 163 dissenting theologians signed a statement entitled "Against Incapacitation — for an Open Catholicism," popularly known as the Cologne Declaration. CFFC published this Declaration in the March/April issue of its newsletter *Conscience*.

They said that "We observe an attempt, theologically highly questionable, to enforce and overstep in an inadmissible way the Pope's competence in the field of doctrinal teaching alongside that of jurisdiction."[158]

The dissenter's statements show that, even if the Holy Father infallibly declared abortion to be prohibited, they would simply ignore him. Therefore, any statement by CFFC that "the Church's teachings against abortion are not infallible" is simply a diversion, since the dissenters would attack any teaching against abortion that *was* solemnly declared infallible.

Our Lady's Perpetual Virginity. In 1854, Pope Pius IX published the Apostolic Constitution *Ineffabilis Deus* ("The Immaculate Conception"), which infallibly proclaimed the perpetual virginity of the Blessed Virgin Mary.

Yet, even though this teaching was declared *ex cathedra* infallibly, CFFC dismisses it. This proves again that, even if the Pope *ex cathedra* declared abortion to be murder infallibly, it would not alter CFFC's ideology one iota.

CFFC Board member Rosemary Radford Ruether has said that "The methods of history, used in an unbiased manner, would almost certainly conclude that Jesus had normal siblings."[159]

CFFC has no problem with simply denying Our Lady's perpetual virginity if it advances the pro-abortion cause. This is because CFFC perceives anti-woman conspiracies behind every Church declaration, and ascribes the most absurd motives to Church leaders who are trying to focus on purely theological matters.

CFFC says that

> Because of her perpetual virginity, Mary has become the standard bearer for conservative and static notions of gender relations, reproductive rights, and, of course, sexuality. ... By celebrating Mary's lack of sexuality, the church denigrates the sexual. ... Mary's sexuality is largely a church construction. Any belief that human beings construct, we can deconstruct and rebuild. This reconstruction is taking place all the time in the lives of women who look to Mary for spiritual strength.[160]

Notice CFFC's warped concept of sexuality. It says that a virgin "lacks sexuality." This implies that CFFC sees sexual acts as the *only* expression of human sexuality, and that a person who refrains from sexual activity is somehow incomplete.

Once again, this kind of nonsense proves that CFFC simply does not believe that the Magisterium of the Church can interpret the word of God. This is a fundamental act of disobedience and is, of course, another heresy. CFFC does not simply deny specific teachings, but rejects the very authority of the Catholic Church to teach in God's name.

(3) CFFC Believes It is *Impossible* to Speak Infallibly.

CFFC: "Infallibility "R" Us." CFFC argues that the teachings of the Church against abortion are not infallible.

This is a mere diversion.

As stated above, even if the Pope *did* declare *ex cathedra* that all Catholics must believe that abortion is murder, CFFC would simply ignore his declaration — because it actually believes that it is *impossible* for anyone to speak infallibly.

Daniel C. Maguire says that "Making infallible statements through the medium of fallible language is a naïve dream."[161]

If we take Maguire at his word, then our language constrains us from speaking of or describing *any* definitive truth. This is merely a clever way of insinuating situational ethics into the discussion on the morality of abortion.

In any case, Maguire cannot really believe that it is impossible to make "infallible" statements. CFFC's strange creed features several articles of faith from which none of its members may dissent under pain of 'excommunication:' That abortion is a "basic human right;" that the Catholic Church has oppressed women for centuries; and that women must be trusted as good decisionmakers.

Any member of CFFC who raises his or her voice in disagreement against these dogmas would be shunned and expelled from the organization.

For CFFC, Consensus = Infallibility. When a person or group departs from the truth and tries to create their own reality, the result is inevitably an erratic and contradictory ethos, as described in *Veritatis Splendor*. Nowhere is CFFC's inconsistency more glaringly evident than in its discussion of infallibility.

First CFFC says that the Pope has not declared the Church's teaching on abortion infallible, so Catholics may ignore it.

Then it says that, even if the Pope *did* declare this teaching infallible, Catholics may *still* ignore it.

Then it claims that it is *impossible* to speak infallibly.

Finally, it asserts that any statement agreed upon by *everyone* is infallible — even though it rejects the Canon of St. Vincent of Lorenz, which says exactly the same thing!

After sorting through all of its wildly inconsistent claims, it seems that CFFC does not consider a teaching infallible unless literally everyone agrees with it. The group refers to a vaguely-defined "voice of the people" [*sensus fidei*] and argues for a kind of religious consensus stating that a teaching can only be infallible if *everyone* agrees on it.

Naturally, since there is no Church teaching that *everyone* can agree on, no teaching at all can be considered infallible. Once again, this is nothing more than pure situational ethics dressed up in fancy theological language.

CFFC relies upon dissenting theologian Richard P. McBrien to describe this concept: "Alternatively, dogma can come through the "ordinary and universal magisterium," that is, what is espoused and taught by all bishops, or theologians, or perhaps believers. ... Traditional criteria of infallibility include reception by the church at large."[162]

McBrien is wrong, of course, and he directly contradicts the definition of the Magisterium provided in the *Catechism of the Catholic Church* [¶85]. The Catholic Church has *never* considered "reception by the church at large" to be a necessary criteria for an infallible teaching. CFFC does not recognize the higher authority of the Church and therefore cannot imagine submitting its will in obedience to Her. Therefore it attempts to forcibly superimpose democratic principles upon the Church, which is *itself* a coercive and non-democratic act.

The Second Vatican Council addressed the role of the people when it emphasized the indissoluble bond between the *sensus fidei* and the guiding role of the Magisterium, saying that "these two realities cannot be separated" [*Lumen Gentium*, ¶12]. If the people choose to separate themselves from the guidance of the Magisterium, the result is division, disunity and a falling into the slavery of sin, all of which are evident in the writings of Catholics for a Free Choice. The *Catechism* tells us that "Where there are sins, there are also divisions, schisms, heresies, and disputes. Where there is virtue, however, there also are harmony and unity, from which arise the one heart and one soul of all believers" [¶817].

CFFC Argument #5:

"Dissent is necessary for the life of the Church."

What Catholics for a Free Choice Says.

"I also believe that dissent is the lifeblood of the church. Without people, without women willing to dissent, to stand up and challenge the church and indeed take a prophetic stance on the issues that affect us, the church will be a dead organism. ... God wills dissent to reach the blindness and hardness of heart of many church leaders. Dissent is a constructive, not a destructive, activity in the religious community ..."
— Frances Kissling and Marjorie Reiley Maguire.[163]

Summary of the Response.

(1) The goal of legitimate discussion on points of moral theology is to clarify and instruct. For CFFC, the objective of dissent is to force the Church to change Her teachings and to bend to CFFC's will through sheer persistence and continual agitation.

(2) The ultimate danger posed by organized pressure to change Church teachings is that She will become just another permissive pseudo-religious social organization. This, of course, is exactly what CFFC wants to achieve.

(3) Professional dissenters do not actually seek the truth. They seek submission of others to their wills. CFFC-style dissent in no way resembles an authentic search for the truth, because its members have already firmly established in their minds their version of the truth, which is completely independent from guidance given by Scripture and the Magisterium.

(1) What is the Objective of Organized Dissent?

The Character of Organized Dissent. There exists today a vast network of organizations dedicated to sustained and comprehensive dissent against Church teachings, particularly in the pivotal area of sexual ethics. Many of these groups are formally affiliated with umbrella organizations such as Catholic Organizations for Renewal (COR) and Call to Action (CTA).

In order to effectively oppose the dissenters, we must understand *why* they seem to be bent on endless agitation and confrontation. We must perceive the Church and the world from *their* point of view.

The question most often asked by bewildered orthodox Catholics is: "Why don't they just *leave?*"

Maryknoll Sister Rose Dominic Trapasso has written a succinct summary of the Church from the feminist dissenter's point of view. This passage is important, because almost all dissenters adopt these ideas, regardless of whether they are male or female. Trapasso says that:

> Feminism arises from the recognition that the oppression of women has been universal, it is global and it is derived from structures. And we know that the kind of change feminists want has to take place at a structural, ideological level. Feminism has helped us see the connections among many kinds of oppression. Whether it is racial, military or economic oppression, there are connections. And they are all linked in the fundamental domination, the original domination, which is that of male over female in a patriarchal system. It is the basis of our order, our hierarchy. So we are talking not just about the liberation of women or about equality with men, but about a much deeper questioning of society and the types of relationships found in the hierarchical ordering of society. ... The Church has not modified its position or criticized injustices against women because it has been and continues to be a patriarchal institution.[164]

Breaking this passage down into segments, we have the following ideas;

(1) Men have always oppressed women.
(2) Men use "structures" to oppress women.
(3) The Catholic Church's all-male hierarchy is the paramount patriarchal "structure," because it promulgates a belief system that interferes with all of women's most basic human rights.

The Objective of Organized Dissent — Revolutionn. Given the above, the only just and logical course of action for a dissenter is to reform and reconstruct oppressing "structures" — with special emphasis on the Roman Catholic Church.

CFFC board member Rosemary Ruether said that "As a feminist, I can come up with only one reason to stay in the Catholic Church: To try to change it."[165]

This is why members of CFFC do not simply leave the Church. They allege that, as long as the "patriarchal, hierarchical" church remains in its current form, it will continue to "oppress" *all* women. Naturally, CFFC does not address the *real* oppression its members suffer — the load of guilt they feel because of their immoral activities.

Christine E. Gudorf tells us that "Religion must participate in the purge of patriarchal restrictions from social and religious practice and ideology. It must do so even when, as is often the case, the purge requires the reworking of central religious myths and doctrines and the reinterpretation of revealed truth."[166]

Ruether shows us that CFFC will never be satisfied, no matter how much 'progress' it makes. She says that "No token accommodations will satisfy us. What is required is the *total reconstruction* of God, Christ, human nature, and society."[167]

HLI's book *Call to Action or Call to Apostasy?* describes how dissenters systematically target the four Marks of the Church — one, holy, catholic and apostolic — in their attempts to restrain Her from saving souls, and how the dissenters in particular desire to dilute and destroy the Sacraments of Holy Orders, the Eucharist and Confession.

Mary Hunt and Frances Kissling speak of what they mean by "feministizing" the Catholic Church: "By feministization we mean the process by which values of inclusivity and mutuality, justice and equality are made manifest in previously patriarchal, that is, hierarchical, gender-, class-, race-stratified organizations."[168]

Frances Kissling described the "two complementary strategies employed by Women-church in its struggle for a transformed church:"

> One is the strategy of confrontation and challenge — you know, directing one's attention to the hierarchy. But the other, in [holding] a meeting like this, is ignoring the hierarchy. The name of the conference, Women-church: Claiming Our Power, is just women taking their power and going with it — not wor-

rying about what the bishops have to say, not worrying about what the Pope thinks — in essence, taking their own vision of church and making it a reality.[169]

What is the future "reality" of which Kissling speaks? CFFC's writers give us many clues.

The reformed "catholic" church would embrace;

* **Abortion.** Some extremist feminists have claimed that "If men could get pregnant, abortion would be a sacrament." For CFFC board member Mary E. Hunt, abortion actually *is* a sacrament. She says "Women's right to choose is what I, as a Catholic, dare to call sacramental. ... Reproductive choice is a sacred trust and women are more than equal to the task."[170]

* **Contraception, Divorce and Premarital Sex.** Sister Marie Augusta Neal says that "The rules that will emerge when women are part of the policy process will not resemble the obsolete regulations presently prescribed for men and women with regard to birth control, abortion, divorce, and sexual relations outside a context of love."[171]

* **Homosexual Acts.** Hunt, a lesbian, says that "Once again churches lag behind science. Long after social and behavioral scientists have proven that homosexuality is healthy, good and natural for a certain percentage of our population, the Roman Catholic Church continues to teach antiquated and harmful theology."[172] Hunt wrote an essay entitled "Lovingly Lesbian: Toward a Feminist Theology of Friendship" in an anthology entitled *Sexuality and the Sacred*. She said that "To be a lesbian is to take relationships with women radically seriously, opening oneself to befriend and be befriended, so that by loving, something new may be born. ... When all women are free to have this experience, then, and only then, can we say that any women are free."[173]

  Hunt has also said that "'Love' and 'lesbian' go together like 'love' and 'justice' and 'hearts' and 'flowers'."[174]

  All of this, of course, is in direct contrast to the Church's teaching that "homosexual acts are intrinsically disordered and can in no case be approved" [*Catechism*, ¶2357].

  During the meeting of the National Conference of Catholic Bishops (NCCB) in November 2000, CFFC joined the groups Soulforce and

Dignity in support of homosexual, bisexual and "transgendered" Catholics protesting "discrimination" in the Catholic Church. Frances Kissling said that "Church leaders have to stop treating members of the gay community as though they were second-class citizens."[175] Naturally, she provided no evidence whatever that the Church has *ever* treated homosexuals as "second-class citizens."

* **Homosexual "Marriage."** CFFC is a member of the Women-Church Convergence, and has published its statement that "Indeed, we know many kinds of families that are equally loving and supportive — to name just a few: women in communities; lesbian and gay couples, with or without children; extended families of several generations of women, mostly, who nurture children. ... This is no time to enshrine the so-called traditional, nuclear family."[176]

Another CFFC writer claims that "Many Catholic theologians have supported the principle that both heterosexual and homosexual domestic partnerships based on justice and commitment, rather than the traditional marital contract, are morally valid."[177]

* **All Reproductive Technologies.** Hunt also describes "... lesbian mothers who have the right, not the privilege, to use reproductive technology to choose to have children by self insemination."[178]

* **Women's Ordination.** Rosemary Radford Ruether claims that "There is an increasing demand from Roman Catholic women that they be recognized as full members of the Church. This must include ordination to all priestly ministries."[179] Mary Hunt says that "We do not want the largess of the bishops for a few women deacons who will solve their priest shortage by their boundless energy and ministerial skill, unless the episcopacy is open to women."[180]

* **No Confession.** Holy Orders is not the only Sacrament CFFC would like to rework. It believes that anything in the Church that allows one person to have any kind of "power" over another must be jettisoned. Adelle-Marie Stan refers to Confession as an "... antiquated rite and an invasion of privacy," and predicts that eventually everyone will be granted general absolution.[181]

A Summary of What CFFC Wants. Mary Hunt summarized CFFC's strategic objectives at an April 24, 1988 speech at St. John the Baptist Catholic Church in Schenectady, New York. An observer reported that

97

Lesbian and gay people in church will become as common as candles because the choice will be welcoming diversity or dying on the vine as the people of God. This "diversity," said Hunt, would mean a "shift in power" from the hierarchy to the people of the church, by means of a priesthood that is open to everyone, whether male or female, married or unmarried, sexually active or celibate, homosexual or heterosexual. This is only the first step, however; Hunt said that the ultimate aim is an end to the priesthood and the hierarchy altogether, so that everyone could worship as "a discipleship of equals." The Church would also "celebrate the goodness" of marriage after divorce, and would welcome homosexual marriage. She concluded by stating that "The reality will come first; the theology will come next."[182]

Notice that Hunt is clearly calling not only for women priests, but *an end to the priesthood entirely*. This, of course, means an end to the Sacraments, the primary means by which we obtain grace.

When we look at all of these demands as a body, we can see that the ultimate objective of Catholics for a Free Choice is the transformation of the Catholic Church into a *sexually permissive pseudo-Christian denomination*. As Frances Kissling says, "Yes, we really are talking about revolution. ... I've spent years looking for a government I could overthrow without going to jail, and I've found it in the Church."[183]

(2) The Deadly Dangers of "Reformation."

The "Mainline" Protestant Churches Are Dying. All we need do is examine the plight of the mainline Protestant churches to see where this wide and easy road leads. Dissent means death to a church, not only spiritually but physically. This is true both within and without the Roman Catholic Church.

The eight largest denominations in the United States that teach a traditional sexual ethic are the Assemblies of God (Pentecostal), Jehovah's Witnesses, Lutheran Church (Missouri Synod), Mormon Church, Roman Catholic, Southern Baptist, the Fundamentalist Churches, and Islam. These denominations have each enjoyed a large increase in membership over the past four decades. In 1960, their combined total membership was 61,977,000. In 1999, it was 94,712,000, for a total increase of 53 percent. This rate of increase was slightly greater than the overall U.S. population increase of 51 percent over this time period.[184]

Meanwhile, the four largest mainline Protestant denominations (United Methodist, Presbyterian Church USA, Episcopal and United Church of Christ) have all adopted permissive stances towards sexual issues. Rather than keep pace with the increase in population, their total combined membership has actually *declined* from 19,900,000 in 1960 to 15,659,000 in 1999 — a drop of 21 percent.[185]

It is easy to discern why this is happening. Why bother being a member of a church that gives you permission to do anything you want to do?

Dissent is Deadly to the Clergy. Dissent within the Catholic Church has also caused an enormous amount of damage, particularly to the clergy.

As described in the book *Call to Action or Call to Apostasy?*, Human Life International researchers compiled more than 40,000 statistics from the 1957 to 2001 issues of *The Official Catholic Directory* and the Vatican's *Statistical Yearbook of the Church* for the purpose of charting historical trends regarding the "priest shortage." These statistics included year-by-year figures for every diocese in the United States, and covered the numbers of diocesan and religious priests, religious sisters, priestly ordinations and numbers of baptized and practicing Catholics.

Then two clusters of fifteen dioceses each were examined over the period 1956 to 2000. One cluster consisted of fifteen dioceses that have had a generally orthodox tradition since 1956, and the other cluster consisted of fifteen dioceses that have had a generally permissive tradition over the same period.

This study led to three primary conclusions regarding the "priest shortage," ordinations and women's religious communities:

(a)   There are currently nearly twice as many diocesan priests per million active Catholics in orthodox dioceses as there are in theologically permissive dioceses (2,138 vs. 926). The number of diocesan priests per million active Catholics in orthodox dioceses is actually increasing, while the number of diocesan priests per million active Catholics in theologically permissive dioceses has been steadily declining for four decades, and probably will continue to do so. In orthodox dioceses, there were 1,830 diocesan priests per million Catholics in 1956, and 17 percent *more* (2,138) in 2000. In permissive dioceses, there were 1,290 diocesan priests per million practicing Catholics in

1956, and 926 in 2000, a 28 percent decrease.

(b)   There are currently more than *three times as many* ordinations of diocesan priests per million active Catholics in orthodox dioceses as there are in theologically permissive dioceses (52 vs. 15). The number of ordinations of diocesan priests per million active Catholics in orthodox dioceses is experiencing a strong upward trend, while the number of ordinations of diocesan priests per million active Catholics in permissive dioceses was at an anemic level fifteen years ago and is continuing to decline. In orthodox dioceses, there were 34 ordinations of diocesan priests per million active Catholics in 1986, and 52 in 2000 — an increase of more than 50 percent. In permissive dioceses, there were 16 ordinations of diocesan priests per million practicing Catholics in 1986, and only 15 in 2000 — a six percent decrease [the *Official Catholic Directories* only began tabulating ordinations by [arch]diocese in 1986].

(c)   The impact of feminism has been particularly devastating to women's religious communities in the United States. In 1956, there were 180,000 nuns in this country, and in 2000 there were only 79,500 — a drop of more than 55 percent in just four decades. Interestingly, there are still twice as many nuns per million active Catholics in orthodox dioceses as there are in permissive ones (6,142 per million vs. 3,158 per million). Although mother houses have a great degree of control over their sisters, the atmosphere of a local orthodox diocese often moderates their influence.[186]

Dissent Leads to Destruction. Catholics for a Free Choice writers insist that dissent is healthy for the Church, and will help it "grow in holiness."

However, as the above statistics prove, CFFC's brand of "dissent" will not help the Catholic Church grow, in holiness or in any other way.

In summary, evidence of the pernicious and devastating impacts of widespread dissent are becoming obvious both within the Roman Catholic Church and outside it. Priestly "vocations crises" are focused primarily in permissive dioceses and archdioceses, while the orthodox bishops that CFFC condemns so vehemently have so many seminarians they don't know what to do with them all.

Churches that adhere to their historical moral teachings are flourishing, while those that have accepted abortion, contraception, homosexual acts, divorce, and other evils are dying out.

(3) CFFC-Style Dissent is Not a Genuine Search for the Truth.

How to Deal With Difficulties. We must recognize that the Catholic Church welcomes and seeks to guide every Christian's earnest search for the truth. Coercion and force can never lead to enlightenment; all who approach Christ must do so of their own free will.

Donum Veritas ("Instruction on the Ecclesial Vocation of the Theologian") tells us that "Freedom of research, which the academic community rightly holds most precious, means an openness to accepting the truth that emerges at the end of an investigation in which no element has intruded that is foreign to the methodology corresponding to the object under study" [¶12].

The document continues by addressing in detail how a theologian (or lay person) may deal with difficulties he or she may encounter with a particular Church teaching, whether it be in doctrine or morals.

It concludes this discussion by affirming that

> When the Magisterium proposes "in a definitive way" truths concerning faith and morals, which, even if not divinely revealed, are nevertheless strictly and intimately connected with Revelation, these must be firmly accepted and held. When the Magisterium, not intending to act "definitively," teaches a doctrine to aid a better understanding of Revelation and make explicit its contents, or to recall how some teaching is in conformity with the truths of faith, or finally to guard against ideas that are incompatible with these truths, the response called for is that of the religious submission of will and intellect. This kind of response cannot be simply exterior or disciplinary but must be understood within the logic of faith and under the impulse of obedience to the faith [¶23].

Where Dissent and Truth-Seeking Diverge. It is at this point that dissent and a legitimate search for the truth part company.

Those who submit themselves to the teaching authority of the Church act in humble obedience. They conform their consciences to the will of Christ as expressed by His Vicar and those bishops in union with him.

By contrast, professional dissenters stubbornly insist that particular Church teachings are false or do not apply to them, no matter how frequently the truth is presented and explained to them. More directly, they state that the Church has no *authority* to teach because it is "patriarchal" and "hierarchical," and *by definition* oppresses all women (see Sister Trapasso's quote above).

One basic problem is that many dissenters do not even understand the *definition* of obedience. Barbara Ferraro and Patricia Hussey, signers of CFFC's 1984 pro-abortion *New York Times* ad, said that "This victory confirms our understanding of obedience as responsible decisionmaking."[187]

Obedience does not mean endless decisionmaking — it means that all debate and decisionmaking has come to an end.

Curiously, Frances Kissling presents a cogent argument for obedience to *civil* law, while inconsistently arguing that people can ignore *church* law;

> Implementation of the [civil] law shouldn't be subject to controversy nor the interference of opinions of any kind, no matter how honorable they might be. By establishing a debate instead of a sentence, what prevails is personal and moral opinion, which in addition to inserting a strong portion of hypocrisy and active imagination, distorts the very character of a process that should be far from publicity and strictly linked to the implementation of the law.[188]

Conclusion. CFFC repeatedly insists that dissent is "healthy" for the Catholic Church. We must understand that when CFFC speaks of "dissent," its objective is *not* to find the truth. Its members have already made up their minds. They have *found* their version of the 'truth' — and it differs radically from the truth presented by the Roman Catholic Church.

Donum Veritas describes the ultimate impact of dissent;

> The Church "is like a sacrament, a sign and instrument, that is, of communion with God and of unity among all men." Consequently, to pursue concord and communion is to enhance the force of her witness and credibility. To succumb to the temptation of dissent, on the other hand, is to allow the "leaven of infidelity to the Holy Spirit" to start to work [§40].

By contrast, Barbara Ferraro and Patricia Hussey coin the oxymoronic term "faithful dissent," and then demand that the Church essentially commit suicide by incorporating the poison of dissent into its very structure;

> We believe that dissent on all controversial issues including reproductive rights is essential for the life of the Church. We believe that the dissent falls within the rights and responsibilities of all Roman Catholics. The official Church has a responsibility to foster a climate in which faithful dissent is incorporated into the ongoing life of the community.[189]

In summary, what we have in the Catholic Church today is a raw struggle for its heart and soul. On one side, we have the Vicar of Christ and the bishops in union with him steadfastly proclaiming truth to an increasingly hostile world. On the other side, there is a vast network of professional dissenters, of whom CFFC is one of the most vocal, who desire to transform the Church and all of its most important teachings until it has been completely assimilated by the values of the world.

CFFC is particularly dangerous because it deceives by calling itself "Catholic," by purporting to speak for a majority of Catholics, and by misinterpreting and misusing authentic Church teachings, thereby presenting itself as a respectable orthodox group to the uninformed.

Each of us has to decide whether or not he or she is going to follow the sure path to the Truth embodied by Jesus Christ — the Church or the world, which is represented by CFFC and other dissenters.

Moreover, we must decide this question as if our eternities depended upon it.

CFFC Argument #6:

"We must respect the ability of women to make good decisions."

What Catholics for a Free Choice Says.

"The Catholic religion makes the fetus into an icon, a figure of religious veneration, which I think is sick, really sick. ... It's not the abortion issue that's at question. The question is: How do we get the Church to acknowledge that women can be trusted to make good decisions? That is what we are trying to do on the abortion issue, to trust women."
— Frances Kissling.[190]

Summary of the Response.

(1)   Just because a human being happens to be female does not mean that she is automatically endowed with the wisdom to make good moral decisions. CFFC does not attribute this kind of wisdom to men. It certainly does not believe men have the good judgment to run the Catholic Church! Therefore, it is being sexist when it makes this statement.

(2)   CFFC's emphasis on respecting women's ability to make good decisions is nothing more than an attempt to lend a thin veneer of legitimacy to the killing of preborn babies. CFFC wants to divert attention away from the concrete and bloody act of abortion and focus it on an abstract question.

(3)   By saying that we must trust women to make moral choices regarding abortion, CFFC is actually saying that *abortion* can be a moral choice. It certainly would not trust a convicted molester to be left alone with little girls, because it rightly considers sexual molestation to be immoral. This contrast shows that CFFC believes there should be no restrictions whatever on women's decisionmaking regarding abortion.

(1)   CFFC Entrusts Only *Women* to Make Moral Decisions.

Catholics for a Free Choice insists that we must trust women to make moral decisions about abortion. It claims that "Abortion can be a moral choice. Women can be trusted to make decisions that support the well-being of their children, families, and society, and that enhance their own integrity and health."[191] CFFC also says that "It is important that the Vatican, which claims love for its believers, should acknowledge the right of women to make choices about their lives."[192]

CFFC seems to believe that the ability to make moral decisions is a sex-dependent trait, reserved only to women. It never speaks of *men's* ability to make good and moral decisions, particularly when addressing the role of men in governing the Catholic Church.

In fact, CFFC is often extremely disrespectful and sexist when speaking of men in general. Frances Kissling contemptuously refers to the Bishops of the Catholic Church as "300 men in dresses," and says that "... in their male rage, and in their fear of losing control, these men behave very badly. ... these men don't deserve good manners. We must get to the point where once we know they don't deserve good manners, we're capable of taking to the streets. ... Nothing will drive them crazier than to be treated without dignity."[193]

We can imagine how CFFC would react if a Bishop referred to women's "female emotionalism," and said that women "don't deserve good manners" and should be treated "without dignity."

CFFC is comprised of professional victims. Nowhere else in the world have women enjoyed so much opportunity as in the United States, yet a former CFFC Board member asserted that "... these rights of women still are consistently, sweepingly, viciously, atrociously violated by men in all cultures I know of, *especially* the one I live in [the USA]."[194]

Catholics for a Free Choice attributes special wisdom and unique decision-making capabilities to women. In fact, CFFC believes that women should evolve their own system of ethics and spirituality separate from men, for the express purpose of attacking men and overthrowing the "patriarchy."

Emily Culpepper says that

> And we know that to be "prochoice," to affirm the value of
> women's lives and *moral agency*, is the most radically prolife,
> genuinely biophilic orientation. Women's moral agency on

our own terms — the development of feminist, womanist ethics — is a direct contradiction to patriarchy. ... To assert our right to choose is to assert that, even more fundamentally than being "she who can bear children," a woman is "she who can create values." ... When women assert our right to reproductive choice, we are asserting our right to make our own world of values, which shatters the standard patriarchal claim to ethical hegemony. ...[195]

Notice that Culpepper would like to entrust women with creating their own value systems. This is the purest statement of ethical relativism, and inevitably leads to moral pandemonium and the grossest violations of justice.

She continues by saying that abortion is not only necessary for women's autonomy, but that it is a direct attack on the hated "patriarchy;"

When we see that the deeper taboo is against women acting as moral agents (that is, shapers of culture), we can more easily see the connections among all the manifestations of reproductive choice that patriarchy would deny us. ... Abortion, and the fact that women may under certain conditions recognize it as a morally defensible choice, *especially* breaches the patriarchal definition of society. ...As we have seen, asserting ourselves as ethical agents breaks such a root paradigm of patriarchy that it is a profound move globally towards women's liberation.[196]

In summary, CFFC perceives abortion as not merely a means for women to gain control over their own bodies, but as a vital tool in its revolutionary work, whose ultimate aim is to overthrow the "patriarchy." This is the primary reason it attributes a moral decisionmaking capacity only to women; to acknowledge any favorable traits in men would undermine its entire ideology, which regards males as universal and omnipresent "oppressors."

Ironically, CFFC's ideology contributes heavily to the irresponsibility of men and their oppression of women. When abortion was illegal, men were much more careful about "sleeping around." Now that it is freely available, many men see abortion as a quick and easy solution to the problem of "unplanned pregnancy." Therefore, men can now shirk responsibility for their own children, and millions of them have presented their wives and girlfriends with an oppressive and coercive decision: "Get rid of the kid or I'm out of here!"

(2) CFFC Wants to Divert Attention from Abortion at All Costs.

CFFC constantly speaks about the necessity of respecting women's ability to make good decisions.

This assertion certainly sounds reasonable on its face. However, we must remember that CFFC looks for the most reasonable sounding language to excuse the grossest possible acts.

Of *course* we should trust women (and men) to make good decisions. The goal of raising children is to train them to make good moral decisions. But CFFC's rhetoric in this area cloaks its real motive: To divert people's attention away from the concrete act of abortion and focus it instead on an abstract concept. CFFC knows that, if it can focus on the "moral agency" of women — or some other nebulous and tangential issue — people will stop thinking about abortion.

Yes, we should trust both men and women to make good decisions. But this trust must have limits. Civil law trusts people too — but only to a point. If society trusted everyone without limit, there would be no need for laws. And if people really *could* be trusted to do the right thing in all situations, there would be no need for a Redeemer.

However, we must face reality. Human beings are fallen creatures. As a result of original sin, no person is completely trustworthy. This is why we have civil law, and why we have canon law.

The purpose of Church and civil law is to instruct human beings as to the boundaries of acceptable behavior.

What CFFC desires is a complete elimination of all civil and Church laws concerning abortion. In other words, its concept of "trust" means absolutely no limits whatever on abortion, because it sees abortion as a "basic human right."[197]

(3) The Real Issue Here is the Morality of *Abortion*, Not the Morality of Women.

CFFC Never Met an Abortion it Didn't Like. CFFC's "moral agency of women" argument is another classic diversion, intended to distract people from thinking about abortion.

In its October 1984 full-page ad in the *New York Times*, CFFC claimed that "A large number of Catholic theologians hold that even direct abortion, though tragic, can sometimes be a moral choice."

CFFC is grossly understating its extremism in this ad. It claims that abortion can "sometimes" be a moral choice, when in reality, it believes that abortion is *always* a moral choice.

One writer in *Conscience* said that "We need to adamantly state that the only criteria for the [abortion] service should be a woman's word."[198]

CFFC has never met an abortion it didn't like. It would not even condemn a decision by a woman to abort her husband's baby so she could look good in the swimsuit she just bought, a situation that has actually been litigated;[199] and it would not criticize a third-trimester abortion done on the healthy and viable baby of a healthy mother just because she changed her mind about raising a child.

This extremism is rooted in CFFC's core belief that a preborn child, no matter how fully developed, can *never* be as valuable as the life of a woman. CFFC speaks endlessly about the "value" of the fetus, and speaks of it as being "precious," but this is simply more distracting rhetoric designed to make CFFC appear humane and benevolent, when it is not.

Frances Kissling says that

> I feel that the value of the fetus, until the third trimester, never outweighs the value of women's well-being or the social importance of acknowledging women's capacity to weigh all the values in making the decision whether or not to continue a pregnancy. I believe that as the fetus comes closer to fulfilling its potential to become a person, more serious reasons are required to morally justify terminating its life. I do not believe that my beliefs in this realm are more factually compelling than others, and thus I am unwilling to see any one of our beliefs enacted into law.[200]

Notice the spongy and flexible terminology Kissling uses in her efforts to sound compassionate and caring. She says that the fetus comes *closer* to being a person, yet never quite goes so far to say that it cannot be killed, even in the third trimester. She concludes by implying that, even if she *did* think the third-trimester preborn baby should be protected, her belief should not be enacted into law.

To show how absurd her reasoning is, consider a parallel case of animal cruelty. Certainly CFFC would not accept a statement by a person who defends sadists who tear puppies or kittens limb from limb, and who evades the question by saying that "animals should be protected, but I am not willing to see my belief enacted into law."

In summary, Kissling believes that preborn children deserve no protection whatever. In contrast to its claims, when real-life situations present themselves, CFFC believes that preborn children are absolutely worthless. In its view, the woman's right to make a decision *always* outweighs the preborn child's right to live, even in the case of a perfectly healthy woman aborting a perfectly healthy child in the third trimester simply because she changed her mind about being a mother.

To show how extreme CFFC's ideology really is, two of its writers went so far as to say that "Any interference in the abortion decision is an attempt to come between a woman and God. This is in our understanding a direct contradiction of the Gospel ..."[201]

Ultimately, There is No `Right' to Make an Immoral Decision. Throughout all of Her history, the Catholic Church has taught that abortion is an *intrinsically evil* act, an act that can *never* be justified under any circumstances, and regardless of what the motives for the act are.

CFFC argues that women should be allowed to make decisions that are irredeemably evil, when in reality there is no such right under either civil or Church law.

To illustrate this principle, civil law does not allow men to rape women, even in extraordinary circumstances (because there is no such thing as a "hard case" to justify rape). The law does not permit women to kill their *born* children, even if they feel that they are at the end of their rope (because there are no mitigating circumstances that can excuse such an act, except perhaps for insanity). Any law that permitted rape or infanticide would be widely recognized as evil and unjust.

By contrast, however, civil law *does* permit women to kill their *preborn* children for any reason they like. This does not mean that abortion is moral; it means that the law *itself* is immoral.

CFFC Argument #7:

"Please don't call us `pro-abortion.' Nobody is for abortion. We are `pro-choice.'"

What Catholics for a Free Choice Says.

"I don't consider myself in any way, shape or form pro-abortion. I think it depends on the circumstances. I think there are women who have been raped — they are few and far between — who would be better off carrying the pregnancy to term. I also think there are many, many reasons for which abortion is justified. ..."
— Frances Kissling.[202]

Summary of the Response.

(1)   Although CFFC prefers the term "pro-choice," its actions show that it is truly *pro-abortion*.

(2)   Liberals have no trouble labeling conservative groups as being "for" something if they fight for its availability. This standard should be applied to CFFC as well.

(1) Why Use the Term "Pro-Choice" in the First Place?

The very term `pro-choice' shows that the pro-abortionists don't really believe their own rhetoric. They know that the word "ABORTION" conjures up vivid pictures of a bloody, cowardly act of outright slaughter, and so they slyly dodge the much more accurate term "pro-abortion."

CFFC has a self-image that it carefully cultivates for public consumption: That of a beneficent, neutral and even prophetic observer passively monitoring abortion from the political sidelines, free of any ideology or self-interest.

However, CFFC's actions by no means accurately reflect its preferred media image;

*   CFFC only supports *one* choice: Abortion. Its writers have repeatedly condemned adoption and do everything they can to direct the woman's so-called "free choice" towards abortion.[203] They write brochures for abortion clinic waiting rooms that are grossly biased towards abortion, and whose sole purpose is to ease the consciences of Catholic women who are about to abort. Not a single word in these brochures even *hints* at any other choice.

* CFFC demands that pro-lifers, along with everyone else, pay for abortions for poor women, both in the United States and overseas. It has even tried to use force of law to coerce Catholic pro-lifers into printing its anti-Catholic and pro-abortion literature.[204]

* CFFC opposes institutional conscience clauses for Catholic hospitals, claiming that they *must* perform sterilizations and distribute abortifacient methods of birth control.[205]

* CFFC vigorously opposes all informed consent laws that would give women more information on the abortion decision.

* CFFC has never condemned the forced family planning programs in China and a number of other countries. In fact, it darkly hints that such coercion should not be "ruled out." One CFFC writer said that " ... human population growth and consumption rates do not seem to be slowing quickly and uniformly enough to rule out future need for coerced contraception and sterilization."[206]

* CFFC provides no help whatever to women who want to carry their babies to term — it *only* supports women who want to abort.

* CFFC has even distributed "liturgies" to celebrate women having abortions — but has no "liturgy" for women who decide to keep their babies.[207]

In summary, when you only support *one* choice, and condemn and oppose all other choices, you are certainly not "pro-choice." It seems that CFFC is less "pro-choice" than any of the *pro-life* groups it denounces so frequently.

One writer in *Conscience* showed how extreme CFFC's pro-abortion position really is. Incredibly, abortion for any reason (or for no reason at all) through all nine months of pregnancy, right up until the instant of birth, is *not enough* for CFFC. It wants the "right" to abortion *expanded;*

> We need to advocate for the expansion of the right to abortion, the removal of all restrictions to access to abortion — eliminating parental or judicial permissions for underage girls and

cutoff points based on fetal viability, rescinding the Hyde
Amendment and other laws limiting federal funding of the
service both here and abroad. We need to adamantly state that
the only criteria for the service should be a woman's word. ...
And we need to be willing to declare that, yea, abortion causes the death of the fetus ..."[208]

Even Frances Kissling occasionally lets slip that her group is a little more *for*
abortion than perhaps it wants known. She said that "We firmly believe that
women are moral agents and as a matter of law should be allowed to make the
decision whether or not to have an abortion with minimal state intervention. If
this is how one defines "abortion on demand," then one would conclude we are
for abortion on demand."[209]

The most certain way to refute the `pro-choice' slogan in a discussion is to
ask the pro-abortionist what they or their group *personally* does to help mothers
carry their babies to term. After all, that's what the term "pro-choice" implies:
Support for all of the choices a mother might make (even though some of those
choices are evil). If the pro-abortionist is an activist whose efforts are entirely
directed towards making sure abortion remains `safe and legal,' then their actions
are not consistent with their words.

This is certainly the case with Catholics for a Free Choice.

(2) CFFC and the National Rifle Association.

The term "pro-choice" is a public relations ploy, mere semantic quibbling.
When a person or organization works for unlimited access to something, and
fights tooth and nail against even the most trivial restrictions upon it, they are
certainly "for" it.

To illustrate this point, let us draw a parallel with NRA activism and gun ownership.

Let us say that, in 1965, there was a total ban on the private ownership of all
guns in the United States. Let us imagine for a moment that a group organizes
for the purpose of having all anti-gun laws thrown out, so that anyone could own
a gun for any reason. Further, after gun ownership was legalized, this group
fights to have the states pay for guns for poor people so that everyone has access
to guns. It also fights against even the most trivial restrictions on gun ownership,
so that children of 10 or 11 can own guns (paid for by the state) without their par-

ents even knowing about it. This group also ignores the thousands of people who are killed by guns each year and refers to people who wants to limit gun ownership in any way as "fanatics" and "lunatics" who want to "control other people's lives." Finally, this group insists that certain people *have* to own guns (such as the Chinese), and that the American people have to pick up part of the tab for forcing the Chinese people to own guns.

Any sane person would call such an organization "pro-gun."

The behavior of the National Rifle Association (NRA) in no way approaches the extreme described above. Yet its opponents call the NRA "pro-gun," and the NRA is honest enough to refer to *itself* as "pro-gun."[210]

Therefore, it is logical to refer to Catholics for a Free Choice, which is much more extreme in its advocacy than the NRA, "pro-abortion."

Conclusion. The term "pro-choice" shows that CFFC is not principled enough to describe itself accurately.

"Pro-choice" *should* mean support for *all* of the choices a mother might make. CFFC's efforts are entirely directed towards making sure abortion remains "safe and legal," which means that its actions are not consistent with its self-description. CFFC criticizes pro-lifers, falsely claiming that they are concerned with children only until they are born, and that they ignore the women — yet CFFC offers mothers who choose to keep their babies no help whatsoever.

Certainly, CFFC frequently bemoans the "oppression" of women in its literature, but talk is cheap. Because its concrete efforts are directed almost exclusively towards preserving the abortion "right," we can accurately refer to CFFC as "pro-abortion."

CFFC Argument #8:

"The majority of Catholics are pro-choice."

What Catholics for a Free Choice Says.

> **CFFC IS THE VOICE OF THE**
> **77% OF AMERICAN CATHOLICS WHO**
> **BELIEVE IN ABORTION RIGHTS.***

— Undated CFFC flyer.

Summary of the Response.

    (1)   CFFC chronically misrepresents the results of various public opinion polls in order to buttress its allegations. In reality, most Catholics and most Americans would ban more than 99 percent of all abortions if given the opportunity to vote on it.[211]

    (2)   CFFC states that many Catholic theologians support the wide availability of abortion. In reality, CFFC's *own polls* show that a theoretical maximum of only six percent of Catholic theologians support unlimited access to abortion, the current situation in the United States.

    (3)   CFFC does not *really* believe that public opinion polls should guide public morality, because it only mentions poll results when they appear to support its position. CFFC simply disregards poll results when they do not agree with its ideology.

(1) How CFFC Uses Opinion Polls to Deceive People.

CFFC Omits Crucial Information. The typical issue of CFFC's journal *Conscience* is sprinkled with more than a dozen references to polls and surveys showing that most American Catholics disagree with or ignore the Church's teachings on sexual ethics. The group is so fixated on polls that *Conscience* sometimes features several full pages plastered with the results of public opinion polls.[212]

But CFFC often deliberately omits crucial information when it reports on the results of these polls.

For example, anyone who sees CFFC's flyer quoted above would simply assume that 77% of all American Catholics believe in abortion law as it now stands, i.e., abortion on demand for any reason (or for no reason at all) through all nine months of pregnancy.

What CFFC neglects to mention is that the 1980 Gallup Poll referred to by the asterisk in "CFFC IS THE VOICE OF THE 77% OF AMERICAN CATHOLICS WHO BELIEVE IN ABORTION RIGHTS*" breaks down as follows;

* 23% of all American Catholics believe that abortion is wrong, even to save the life of the mother, and
* 77% of all American Catholics are distributed among *all* other attitudes, i.e., a single exception for the life of the mother; another exception for rape and incest; yet another for fetal anomalies (eugenics); or all the way to no restrictions whatever.

In other words, if a Catholic believes that abortion should be strictly banned except to save the life of the mother, then CFFC counts him among the "77% of American Catholics who believe in abortion rights!"

Technically, this would mean that CFFC would count even a pro-lifer who would only permit abortions to save the life of the mother as `pro-choice!'

This Gallup Poll is flawed in that it includes many Catholics who do not even practice their faith — so-called "cafeteria Catholics," or, as CFFC sometimes calls them, "Good Enough Catholics."

What Does "Pro-Choice" Mean? Dissenting and liberal groups prefer to use words whose meanings are infinitely flexible and elastic, so they can change them at will to suit their morality. Nowhere is this more evident than in their use of the term "pro-choice."

Catholics for a Free Choice studiously avoids any hard definition of the term "pro-choice," but occasionally one of its writers gives us a hint as to what this expression means.

Ex-priest Daniel Maguire says that

Saint Antoninus, the revered fifteenth-century Dominican bishop of Florence, presented common Catholic teaching when he defended early abortions to save a woman's life — a broad exception in the medical context of his day. Today's Catholic hierarchy might well begin their deliberations with a prayer to St. Antoninus, this pro-choice bishop, canonized a saint in 1523. He is a saintly representative of a pro-choice Catholic view."[213]

CFFC's and Maguire's manipulation of Saint Antoninus' teachings convey the false idea that even people who think that it is legitimate to perform a surgical intervention to save a mother's life, and which unfortunately results in the *indirect* and *unintended* taking of the life of the preborn child, are "pro-choice." We shall explain in more detail the case of "indirect abortion" later. At this point it is sufficient to show how CFFC distorts the historical teachings of prominent Church theologians to support its own agenda.

If a national referendum were held on abortion in the United States today, the people would ban more than 99 percent of all abortions, since the most popular exceptions supported by the general public (to save the life or *physical* health of the mother, rape, incest and eugenics) constitute less than *one percent* of all abortions.[214] Once again, we must stress that a surgical procedure done to save the life of the mother, and which indirectly results in the death of the preborn child, is not classified as an abortion.

The "Double Effect." The very rare cases of pregnancy that pose a real and immediate threat to the mother's life — including uterine cancer and ectopic pregnancies — are a source of great confusion, especially among Catholics.

It is absolutely true that the Catholic Church bans direct abortion to save the life of the mother. However (and this is an *extremely* important point) the mother's life *may be saved* by a surgical procedure that does not *directly* attack the preborn baby's life.

The most common dysfunctions that may set a mother's life against that of her preborn child's are the ectopic pregnancy, carcinoma of the uterine cervix, and cancer of the ovary. Occasionally, cancer of the vulva or vagina may indicate surgical intervention.

In such cases, under the principle of the "double effect," attending physicians must do everything in their power to save *both the mother and the child*. If the physicians decide that, in the case of an ectopic pregnancy, the mother's life can only be saved by the removal of the Fallopian tube (and with it, the preborn baby), or by removal of some other tissue essential for the preborn baby's life, the baby will of course die. But this kind of surgery would not be categorized as an abortion. This is all the difference between deliberate murder (abortion) and unintentional natural death.

The principle of the twofold, or double effect, states that it is morally allowable to perform an action that will produce both good and bad effects as long as the following conditions are *all* met. The example shown is for the treatment of an ectopic pregnancy, where the preborn child is developing in the Fallopian tube. If the child continues to grow there, the tube will eventually rupture and will probably cause the death of both the mother and the child.[215]

(1)   The object of the action to be performed must be good in itself or at least morally neutral. In this case, the object of the surgery is to remove a pathological organ which presents a threat to the life of the woman. By contrast, the object of surgical or chemical abortion is simply to kill the preborn child ["object" is the end toward which an action tends, and does not connote the intention(s) of the operator, as does the word "objective"].

(2)   The good effect must not come about as a result of the evil effect, but must come directly from the action itself. In this case, the good effect (saving the mother's life) is not caused by the bad effect (the death of the preborn child). By contrast, in the case of direct abortion (surgical or chemical abortion), the death of the child is wrongly considered to be the "good" effect.

(3)   The evil effect must not be desired in itself but only permitted. In the case of the removal of an ectopic pregnancy, the surgeon does not intend or want to kill the baby; his death is an unintended and unwanted side effect of the surgery. By contrast, the *intent* of abortion is to kill the preborn child.

(4)   There must be a sufficiently grave reason for permitting the evil effect to occur. In this case, the reason is to save the life of the mother, a good that is greater than or equal to the evil effect of the baby's death. Pro-abortion groups often stretch this principle to absurd lengths, going so far as to justify *all*

(5)   abortions under the principle of the double effect because, as they allege, *all* abortions threaten the life of the mother.[216] Sometimes a fifth condition is added, implicit in (4), above, namely, that there is no other alternative available to solve the problem at hand. If there are alternatives other than the intervention that offer better possibilities to save both mother and preborn child, these of course *must* be used.

     In fact, this last condition is the one that most clearly distinguishes the "indirect abortion" case (the case under the double effect principle) from the "therapeutic" abortion case. "Therapeutic" abortion is *direct* abortion, and therefore is always gravely evil. It is the abortion committed with the (supposed) intention of saving the mother's life, but where one or more of the above conditions are not met. Basically, the doctor in this case *does* have alternatives to save both mother and preborn child, but chooses abortion as the most expedient way to solve the problem at hand. The phrase "therapeutic abortion" is in fact an oxymoron, since no direct abortion is therapeutic, i.e. it does not "cure" anyone of an illness, but instead kills an innocent human being.

     It is perhaps a sign of the times that abortionists see pregnancy *itself* as a disease, and abortion as the "cure" for this dreaded malady. At an Association of Planned Parenthood Physicians conference, Willard Cates compared the miracle of pregnancy to a *venereal disease* when he said that "Unwanted pregnancy is transmitted sexually, is socially and emotionally pathologic ... and has many other characteristics of the conventional venereal diseases. The incubation time, defined as the period between exposure (mid-cycle coitus) and the development of initial symptoms (usually missed menses), averages approximately two weeks."[217] Barbara Roberts said that "It's obvious, therefore, that unwanted pregnancy is the most common venereal disease ... This disease is associated with immense suffering. Seeking to be cured of this disease, women from time have risked pain, mutilation, and death in numbers that really stagger the imagination."[218] And late-term abortionist Warren Hern has said that "[Pregnancy] is an episodic, moderately extended, chronic condition ... defined as an illness ... treated by evacuation of the uterine contents. ... The relationship between the gravid female and the feto-pla cental unit can be understood best as one of host and parasite. Pregnancy should be seen as a biocultural event in the context of *other* human illnesses."[219]

The promotion of "therapeutic" abortion by pro-abortionists in countries where abortion is illegal is a strategy they use to not only legalize abortion in these cases, but also to eventually legalize abortion on demand. Exceptions to direct abortion are not only evil in themselves, they also and *always* lead to abortion on demand.

As medical science advances, surgeons might be able to save the preborn child despite even these serious medical problems. If we ever arrive at the point where the lives of both mother and child can be saved in all cases, the principle of the double effect would not apply.[220]

The principle of the "double effect" also applies to sexual sterilization. If a non-pregnant woman must have a hysterectomy to remove a dangerously cancerous uterus, this will result in her sterilization, but is not a sinful act (provided the above conditions are met). However, if the purpose of the operation is not to heal or safeguard health, but to directly sterilize, then that act is intrinsically evil and is always a mortal sin.[221]

(2) Do Catholic Theologians *Really* Support Abortion?

CFFC's (in)famous 1984 *New York Times* advertisement stated that Catholic theologians take a variety of positions regarding abortion. Naturally, CFFC never revealed just *how many* Catholic theologians described themselves as "pro-choice" — and for good reason.

CFFC had surveyed 2,000 Catholic scholars and theologians. The results of its *own poll* are shown below;[222]

Total surveys mailed:	2,000 (100%)
Responses:	498 (25%)
Of these responses:	
Abortion is unacceptable:	364/498 (73%)
Abortion as it legally stands now is acceptable:	
	30/498 (6%)
Other answers or 'not sure:'	104/498 (21%)

Once again, CFFC's *own polls* show it to be in a tiny minority: In this case, only six percent! And we can bet the farm that this number would be far lower if CFFC had not polled its own sympathetic "house theologians."

(3) Morality is Not Determined by Public Opinion Polls.

CFFC's Inconsistent Use of the Polls. Principled people on all sides of any moral issue seldom listen to the results of public opinion polls. However, Catholics for a Free Choice constantly quotes polls showing that the majority of Catholics use birth control or support abortion.

Why does it do this?

CFFC's primary goal is to influence uninformed Catholics who believe that sexual morality and Church dogma can be determined by popular vote. After all, most American Catholics have never heard abortion, sterilization or contraception condemned from the pulpit. Many have been psychologically conditioned to buy into the "live and let live" philosophy of the Culture of Death. They may believe such acts are immoral or wrong, but they think that they must not "impose their morality" on others by speaking out. CFFC and other pro-abortion groups encourage this silence and misinterpret it as support.

CFFC's use of public opinion polls highlights another of the logical inconsistencies in its actions — it only quotes polls when the polls agree with its ideology.

Certainly CFFC would have approved of the activities of Margaret Sanger (the founder of Planned Parenthood) when the public opinion polls were heavily against her. CFFC itself has agitated in favor of partial-birth abortion when the polls ran a consistent 80% or more against it. The group also pushes for tax funding of abortion even when the people strongly oppose it. In other words, CFFC only mentions poll results if they can be manipulated into supporting its position. If the polls do *not* support CFFC's beliefs, it simply disregards them or distorts them *until* they support abortion.

This proves that CFFC only uses polls as a tool if they support its position on abortion. Therefore, it does not *really* believe that morality can be guided by vote.

CFFC also talks all the time about how a "consensus" should determine morality. However, the group doesn't really believe this either, since, if "consensus" was *against* CFFC, then it can be simply be disregarded.

CFFC writer Mary Segers illustrates this inconsistency;

... Catholic politicians can remind their bishops that in a liberal democracy, not even consensus is controlling, because prudent policy making always looks to the consequences of laws enacted. ... Thus even if a popular consensus develops in favor of restrictive abortion law, a public officeholder is still obliged to judge whether the proposed policy will make sound law.[223]

Conclusion: Where Would We Be Today If ...?

If Jesus and His Apostles had assessed their comparative numerical strength, they would have found that they comprised about 0.0004 percent of the population of their region. If they had taken a public opinion poll, they would have certainly found that they were very unpopular indeed. In fact, Our Lord and eleven of his thirteen Apostles were murdered for the Faith.

If they had given up because the "polls were against them," certainly many people would have breathed a sigh of relief.

But what would the world look like today?

Fortunately, there have been millions of people through the ages who have echoed the words of the Apostle Peter: "Lord, to whom shall we go? You have the words of eternal life; and we have believed, and have come to know, that you are the Holy One of God" [John 6:68-69].

Donum Veritas outlines the Church's teachings on "morality by vote;"

> Polling public opinion to determine the proper thing to think or do, opposing the Magisterium by exerting the pressure of public opinion, making the excuse of a "consensus" among theologians, maintaining that the theologian is the prophetical spokesman of a "base" or autonomous community which would be the source of all truth, all this indicates a grave loss of the sense of truth and of the sense of the Church [¶39].

Once again, we must point out that Jesus Christ entrusted the authentic interpretation of His teachings *only* to the Magisterium, the teaching authority of the Roman Catholic Church. *Only* the Pope and those bishops in communion with him may authoritatively interpret the teachings of Our Lord. In the absence of such unbroken authority throughout the past twenty centuries, the Church would have been reduced from a uniform belief to a diverse and unruly riot of creeds, thereby fatally injuring Her oneness, holiness, catholicity and apostolic mission.

But we must remember that this is exactly what the dissenters want to achieve.

CFFC Argument #9:

"If you want to cut the abortion rate, you must support the widespread availability of contraception."

What Catholics for a Free Choice Says.

> **"NOBODY WANTS TO HAVE AN ABORTION.**
> Picture a world ... where safe birth control is available to everyone who needs it. In this world, abortion isn't legal. It's unheard of. Isn't that the best choice of all?"
> — Full-page CFFC ad.[224]

Summary of the Response.

    (1)   If contraception is so great, why do women still have nearly a million and a half abortions in the United States every year?

    (2)   CFFC's assertion that abortion is a "difficult" and "tragic" choice for all women is a mere public relations smokescreen, and does not reflect the reality: That abortion is a trivial event to many women, equivalent to "removing a wart or straightening a nose," as one pro-abortion writer put it.[225]

    (3)   CFFC neglects to mention that many *men* support abortion, since its legalization was not a victory for women's rights, but for *men's* rights.

Introduction.

In its publications, CFFC portrays abortion as "tragic" and states that "nobody *wants* to have an abortion." It goes on to claim that, if pro-lifers would simply join CFFC to make sure that contraception is available to everyone, abortion would be "unheard of."

Incredibly, CFFC often blames the Bishops of the Catholic Church for the high abortion rate that CFFC itself helps promote!

Frances Kissling says that "The bishops' lack of recognition of birth control as a central and critical tool for achieving a reduction in abortion dooms their [anti-abortion] campaign to failure. They must give up their unrelenting opposition to birth control and come into the mainstream if they truly want to reduce the incidence of abortion."[226] And Rosemary Ruether claims, "It is not too much to say that the Roman Catholic Church, by promoting female subordination and dependency and opposing contraception, is one of the major factors in the high abortion rate globally."[227]

The purpose of CFFC's propaganda, of course, is to make itself appear to abhor the very act that it spends all of its time promoting and spreading.

In fact, because the widespread use of contraception leads to *more*, not *less*, abortions, we might say that CFFC is covering all its bases to make sure that as many abortions are performed as possible.

(1) How Does More Contraception Lead to More Abortion?

Overview. Since contraception is designed to *prevent* pregnancy, it seems contradictory at first glance to say that it leads to *more* "unwanted" pregnancies, and therefore more abortions.

To clarify this matter, we turn to the Alan Guttmacher Institute (AGI), which is the research arm of the Planned Parenthood Federation of America (PPFA).

The AGI's figures show that there are two ways that contraception can lead to more abortion: (a) by being used, and (b) by *not* being used, as described below.

(a) Contraception Fails — Frequently. Western countries are *saturated* with contraceptives. Anyone can get them virtually anywhere, and without restriction.

Yet the abortion rate in all of these nations is high and is holding steady. In some countries such as the United States, the absolute number of abortions is slowly declining, but only in direct proportion to the number of women of childbearing age. If what CFFC alleges is true — that widespread contraceptive distribution leads to less abortions — we should have almost no abortions in the United States today. Abortion should, as CFFC says, be practically "unheard of."

The primary reason that abortion rates are so high in countries where contraceptives are common is that people have been propagandized into believing that "family planning" methods are reliable. In the United States, 57.5% of all abortions are performed on women who were using contraception at the time they became pregnant.[228]

The most commonly used methods of birth control in the United States are the oral contraceptive and the condom.[229]

The user effectiveness rate ("real world" conditions) for the oral contraceptive is 97.0% (89.0% for teenaged girls). The user effectiveness rate for the condom is 86.0%.[230]

This means that, if a girl begins using the oral contraceptive pill on her 15th birthday, the probability of her unintentionally becoming pregnant by the time she is 20 is 44 percent. If her `partner(s)' all use condoms, this probability increases to 53 percent.[231]

Experienced researchers have compared reducing the teen pregnancy rate by making contraceptives freely available to chasing the pot of gold at the end of the rainbow — the more the methods are used, the further the goal of eliminating "unwanted pregnancies" recedes into the distance.

The *Report of the House Select Committee on Children, Youth and Families* concluded that reducing the teen pregnancy rate in this manner is statistically impossible; "The contraceptive failure rate for teens who always use contraceptives is about 10% [annually]. Therefore, hypothetically, if sexual activity among teens reached 100% and the constant use of contraceptives 100%, we would still have a pregnancy rate of about 10%."[232]

Abortion statistician Christopher Tietze stated baldly that women who use contraception are inevitably going to have several "failures" during their reproductive lives:

> The safest regimen of [birth] control for the unmarried and for married child-spacers is the use of traditional methods [of contraception] backed up by abortion; but if this regimen is commenced early in the child-bearing years, it is likely to involve several abortions in the course of her reproductive career for each woman who chooses it.[233]

This is one reason why there are so many abortions in the United States: Half of the *two million* annual contraceptive failures end in abortion.[234]

(b) Many Aborting Women Have Stopped Using Contraception. More interesting are the 42.5% of women who were not using contraception when they became pregnant.[235] This means that they are using *abortion* as birth control.

No matter how perfect a contraceptive scientists develop, it will not affect the pregnancy rate of such women, because they know that they will always have abortion as a backup.

Maria Romero's attitude may be typical: "Sometimes I'm kind of lazy about using my cervical cap ... I think it's wonderful to share the [at-home "do-it-your-self" abortion] experience with my friends."[236]

Pro-abortion author Kristin Luker wrote in her book *Taking Chances: Abortion and the Decision Not to Contracept,*

> To obtain information on these points the author analyzed medical records and conducted lengthy interviews of a large sample of women who were clients of a California abortion clinic. She found that eight out of ten women obtaining abortions had previously used contraception, but then — for reasons that appeared sufficient to them — elected to take chances.[237]

(2) Many Women Think Abortion is a Trivial Event.

Every pro-abortion group, including CFFC, states as fact that "nobody *wants* to have an abortion," or that, for all or most women, abortion is a "tragic" and "difficult" choice.

This is simply not true. The only purpose of such propaganda is to drape a thin mantle of humanity over a brutal and bloody act.

Pro-abortion feminists themselves admit that plenty of women treat abortion as a trivial or even a *desirable* event.

Leslie Savan writes that

> Many women of my generation are replacing having children with having abortions, not only in a literal sense but also as a major rite of passage ... `Wanted unwanted pregnancies' become attractive in the first place because of interacting and not-always conscious motives, among them:
> — A desire to know if we're fertile ...
> — To test the commitment of the man ...
> — Abortion as a rite of passage ... the fact that

more women are aborting makes it more permissible, even intriguing ...

— Torn between `femininity' and feminism, getting pregnant `proves' we are feminine while getting an abortion `proves' we are feminist."[238]

Marilyn Buckham, the director of a large New York abortion mill, said that "`Women don't do this [abortion] lightly.' I'm sick and tired of hearing this. 98 percent of the women *do* do it lightly in here, but I never say that. *And they do it lightly.* They think of abortion like brushing their dime teeth, and that's OK with me."[239]

As long as abortion is easily available as a backup to failed contraception (or no contraception), women will obtain them in vast numbers for reasons that sound incredibly trivial to the majority of Americans.

The Alan Guttmacher Institute performed a major 1988 study designed to find out why women obtain abortions. The primary reasons women gave included;[240]

"I can't afford a baby right now"	21%
"I'm not ready for the responsibility"	21%
"A baby would change my life"	16%
"I have problems with my relationship"	12%
"I'm not mature enough to have a baby"	11%
"I have all the children I want"	8%
"I don't want others to know I was pregnant or having premarital sex"	1%

For such trifling excuses, nearly 4,000 preborn children have their lives snuffed out in the United States *every day.*

Only ten percent of the respondents cited their health, rape or incest, eugenics or pressure from others as reasons to abort. A review of studies in foreign nations revealed that even smaller numbers of women gave serious reasons to abort.[241] Of course, no reason at all justifies the killing of a preborn human being. The point here is that most of the time the reasons women invoke for aborting are trivial.

Since AGI's study contradicted the pro-abortion claim that all abortions are

126

"agonizing decisions made for perfectly good reasons," many pro-abortionists, as Frances Kissling said, "... gave it grief for having done this study because the reasons women gave for having abortions weren't serious enough."[242]

Kissling's admission decisively proves that pro-abortionists do not *care* what the truth is; all that really concerns them is their public relations image — and, of course, the vast amounts of money they make in their grisly business.

(3) The Legalization of Abortion Was a Victory for Unscrupulous Men.

CFFC and other pro-abortionists constantly refer to abortion as a "woman's basic human right." They also relentlessly complain about how men have oppressed women throughout the ages.

Pro-abortionists are so intent on preserving and defending the abortion "super-right" that they are stone blind to the fact that abortion is a tool tailor-made for the millions of men who sexually exploit and abuse women.

Illicit "rights" generated by mortal judges always violate the cardinal virtue of justice on a massive scale. Abortion is a preeminent example of this principle.

Has the easy availability of abortion advanced women's rights? Ask the 14-year old girl who was forced to have an abortion because her parents would have thrown her out of the house if she didn't. Ask the millions of young women whose boyfriends have said to them "Get rid of the kid or I'm leaving you." Ask the frightened teenagers whose boyfriends beat them or even tried to kill them because they refused to have abortions [visit HLI's Web site at http://www.hli.org to find documentation on thousands of extreme incidents of pro-abortion violence, from mass murder and torture to rape and arson. Notice how many women have been beaten and even *killed* by men because they refused to abort their preborn children].

Many men use abortion as a straightforward weapon against women, forcing them to become little more than sterile sex objects. *Roe v. Wade* was a great advance for *men's* rights, because now all they have to do is give their girlfriends a couple of hundred dollars (half the cost of the abortion) and abandon them to let them face the consequences by themselves.

CFFC never mentions the most pitiful cases of all: When older men impregnate young girls and then force them to have abortions to cover up their incest and other sexual abuse. The Johns Hopkins School of Public Health has found that more than 70 percent of all babies born to teenaged girls are fathered by men over age 20, and who are often *much* older. The percentage of older fathers is even greater for babies born to girls 14 years old and younger. Three-fourths of pregnant girls 14 years old and younger report having been coerced into sex by older men.[243] By promoting abortion, Catholics for a Free Choice and other pro-abortion organizations *directly* help many predatory incestuous situations to continue, because it is so easy to destroy the "evidence."

Finally, rich men use abortion as a powerful weapon against women on a national and global scale as well.

In the United States, the abortion rate for minority women is 250 percent greater than the abortion rate for White women.[244]

Most tragically, the legal abortion death rate for minority women is also more than three times higher than that of White women.[245]

Yet CFFC says nothing.

All over the world, abortion and contraception are used as mighty weapons to suppress the fertility of poor women, often by brute force. We all know about the forced abortion and "family planning" program in China, but what about those in Peru, Vietnam, Cambodia, India and a score of other nations? More than three decades ago, feminist writer Lynn Phillips had already identified the strong link between abortion and the oppression of women;

> [Birth control] is an international strategy in application throughout the world; in Vietnam population control of uncontrollables takes the form of outright genocide, but in Latin America, India, here, and in American colonies, birth control is the favored method ... If there is any truth to the idea of a genocide campaign against black and other minority women, our sisterly concern for [illegal] abortion victims begins to look like a blind.[246]

Such genocidal programs are funded by the rich nations of the West and billionaires like Bill Gates, Ted Turner and Warren Hubbard. Their billions also support Asian sex-selection abortion campaigns that have exterminated tens of millions of preborn baby *women*, entirely because they are female — the ultimate in sex discrimination and abuse.

And *still* CFFC says nothing.

What will it take before CFFC *finally* gets sick of the injustices committed against poor women, and stands up and says "Enough!"

Perhaps never, because CFFC derives a large percentage of its income from foundations that specifically earmark their grant money for the suppression of the population in Latin America (see Appendix D). And CFFC would certainly not want to bite the hand that feeds it — even if that hand is helping perpetrate injustice against women on a huge scale.

Summary and Conclusion. It may appear at first impression that the widespread use of contraception would lead to a decrease in abortions. This is precisely what CFFC depends upon — first impressions and false perceptions.

Even the most superficial research reveals that the real reason for the high abortion rate in the United States is a casual attitude towards sex. The AGI study cited above found that more than four in five women obtaining abortions were unmarried. This means that more than 80% of aborting women use abortion as a convenient coverup for premarital sex.[247]

Pro-abortion writer Carolyn Hax expanded on the *real* reason why CFFC and other pro-abortion groups fight so hard to keep abortion legal when she said that;

> The abortion right is being left undefended by its true champions — the women who owe not their lives, but their *lifestyles* to the convenience of legal abortion. ... Abortion has validated a lifestyle that allowed room for irresponsibility. ... Among its perks are extended travel, higher education, unbroken career paths, choosing a different father, limiting family size, and going out and getting drunk after work ...[248]

CFFC Argument #10:

"The celibate male priesthood has no right to pronounce doctrine in areas outside its expertise."

"Would you trust a chef who never eats food? Or a car mechanic who never drives a car? Or a swimming coach who's never been in the water? It's an old liberal complaint, of course — sexual morality being dictated by a celibate, male clergy. But old complaint or not, that sure is a loony place to look for wisdom and guidance on sexuality. ... I don't have an interest in any way in anything the Vatican is likely to say. ...
— CFFC writer Christopher Durang.[249]

"After *Roe v. Wade* in 1973, I attempted to understand how women considering an abortion felt. It was clear to me that men shouldn't speak or advise on this subject. They have no direct life experiences to draw on, I reasoned ..."
— CFFC writer Marie Baldwin.[250]

Summary of the Response.

(1)   CFFC is being grossly hypocritical yet again with this argument. It wants to prohibit men from speaking out *against* abortion, but allows male writers to speak *for* abortion in its journal *Conscience*.

(2)   CFFC alleges that only a person who can experience some thing may speak about it. But CFFC doesn't follow its own rules; women writing and speaking for CFFC constantly criticize the priesthood, even though they will *never* have the experience of being priests.

(3)   Truth has nothing to do with the sex of the person speaking it. To assert otherwise is sexist.

(4)   Attempting to deprive a group of people of their voice because of their opinions is a key element in any program of systematic oppression. CFFC has become an oppressor by attempting to silence men — and, of course, *women* who speak out against abortion.

Background.

CFFC repeatedly asserts that, since the Catholic hierarchy is composed of a male, celibate clergy, it has no standing to speak about sexual morality.

This is simply a repetition of the general feminist complaint that men can't get pregnant, so they have no right to speak out against abortion. One of their favorite slogans is "If men could get pregnant, abortion would be a sacrament."

CFFC's assertion that celibate men may not speak about sexual morality is just another red herring designed to intimidate men into giving up their free speech rights in the area of abortion.

Sex (and Sexual Practice) are Irrelevant to Truth.

The truth (or lack thereof) in an argument has nothing whatsoever to do with the speaker's gender, age, race, religion, sexual preference, or any other personal variable. If a statement or argument is true, then it is *true* — it matters not who is saying it! Anyone who says that bishops or priests have no right to speak on sexual morality — or that men in general have no right to oppose abortion — is, *by definition*, a sexist.

CFFC's rank hypocrisy really stands out when it attempts to ban men from speaking about abortion. As proven by its own writings, the only *real* question is whether or not a person agrees with CFFC on the issues.

Celibacy and gender are mere distractions.

* When a celibate male Catholic bishop agrees with Catholics for a Free Choice on any subject, its writers laud him as being "thoughtful," "carrying out the Catholic tradition of social justice," and "rejoicing in the work of the Holy Spirit."[251] When a celibate male Catholic bishop *disagrees* with Catholics for a Free Choice on any subject, it calls him every filthy name in the book (see Argument #12 for many examples).
* There are plenty of lay Catholic men speaking out *for* abortion — like Teddy Kennedy, Mario Cuomo, Daniel Maguire, Joseph O'Rourke, Kevin Gordon, Andrew Merton, and countless others. None of them will ever get pregnant. None of them will ever face the possibility of abortion. Why does CFFC approve of *them* speaking out on the abortion issue? Why doesn't CFFC tell *them* to mind their own business?
* Nobody agitates for abortion availability more aggressively than

CFFC's president, Frances Kissling, who brags about being sterilized decades ago.[252] If Kissling is never going to face the "agonizing choice" of abortion, and will never experience pregnancy, what gives *her* the right to speak about it?

* We might also ask CFFC to be more consistent when it celebrates *Roe v. Wade*. After all, this decision was handed down by *seven old men* on the United States Supreme Court. Did CFFC reject *Roe*, saying that these men had no right to speak about something they would never experience? Of course not!

It is grossly hypocritical for CFFC to approve of men and sterile women speaking *for* abortion while attempting to intimidate men into not speaking *against* it.

If CFFC would like to be consistent in applying its sexist "no men" standard, then it should say that only those persons of either sex who are fertile and not using any kind of birth control should be able to speak out on abortion.

However, it is generally futile to expect pro-abortionists to be consistent — or honest.

No Rights for the "Unaffected?"

Rosemary Ruether echoes CFFC's opinion that the bishops are "not qualified to speak on the subject of women."[253] This, she says, is simply because they are not women themselves.

If she desires to be consistent, she should mirror this statement by acknowledging that pro-abortion women are "not qualified to speak on the subject of men," and should halt their ceaseless criticism of the Catholic bishops, who of course are all men.

In general, CFFC and other pro-abortion groups seem to believe that only people who may potentially be faced with a certain experience may speak of it. This may sound reasonable until we see how inconsistently they implement this principle.

If we applied this axiom to other issues, only soldiers and those in current or potential war zones could talk about war and only women could speak out against rape and female genital mutilation. Only South African Blacks would have been allowed to speak out against apartheid, because only *they* were adversely affected by it. Only homosexuals could speak out about anti-sodomy laws, because only *they* are directly affected by it. Only Jews would be allowed to speak out about the original Holocaust, American Nazis, and anti-Semitism, because only *they* were and are directly affected by it. Only the poor could defend the rights of the poor. Only drug addicts could talk about drugs. Only cancer patients could speak about cancer. Only people on death row, and their immediate relatives, could speak about capital punishment, because only *they* are directly affected by the death penalty.

Mike Royko's trenchant observation about partial-birth abortion best exposes CFFC's hypocrisy: "True, a man doesn't know what it is like to bear a child. On the other hand, I don't know of any woman who knows what it feels like to have a hole poked in the base of her skull and her brains sucked out, although some talk as if they may have experienced it."[254]

Conclusion.

"Oppression" is defined as any attempt to strip a group of people of their voice. This means that any pro-abortionist who tries to divest men of their right to speak out against abortion is trying to oppress men.

This is significant, in light of the fact that gender feminists constantly grumble that *they* are "oppressed by men." Their assertion is hypocritical, since radical feminists seem to see nothing wrong with oppressing those who disagree with them on the abortion issue.

CFFC's ideal male is a chestless, spineless, gutless creature who will grovel at their feet and conform his thinking to the "approved" regimen, which considers women superior to men in every aspect of their beings — physical, mental, emotional and spiritual. Pro-life men must realize that CFFC is *terrified* of men (and women) who confront it, and strip away its thin shroud of respectability, and expose it for what it really is. The "no men" argument is a mere subterfuge, and even contradicts the so-called "pro-choice" ideology.

Finally, the laws of the United States guarantee that any person can speak out publicly for or against *anything* — despite the wishes of those who would dearly love to stamp out all viewpoints they do not agree with.

The United States Constitution gives men the right to speak out against abortion. Anyone who uses the "men prohibited" slogan should be asked if he or she has heard of the First Amendment to the United States Constitution.

133

CFFC Argument #11:

"The Church's teachings on abortion have changed many times over the centuries."

What Catholics for a Free Choice Says.

"Most people think that the church's current position is the result of 2000 years of unchanged teaching. This is a false perception. The opinion of all church scholars and theologians has never been unanimous on abortion. ... Currently, a majority in the church hierarchy believes that to procure an abortion is a serious sin and grounds for excommunication. This view, however, has only been a part of official church discipline since the *Apostolicae sedis* [sic] of Pius IX in 1869. ..."
— CFFC writer Jane Hurst.[255]

Summary of the Response.

(1)   In contrast to what CFFC alleges, the Catholic Church has *always* taught that abortion is a grave sin. This argument is just another distraction, since CFFC ignores other Church teachings that have never changed through the centuries, including those on divorce, fornication, adultery and homo sexual activity, which have been in place since the very beginning of Church history.

(2)   Various Middle Age-era theories about `formed' and `unformed' fetuses and `delayed ensoulment' or `delayed animation' have nothing to do with the fact that even the theologians who held these theories condemned abortion in the strongest possible terms.

(3)   Let us assume for the moment that the Catholic Church did not ever condemn abortion until *yesterday*. Whatever the history of the Catholic Church's teachings on abortion, the fact remains that the Church condemns abortion unequivocally *today*. Nobody can claim that they are free from a civil law because the law did not exist more than a century ago; yet this is just what CFFC is trying to say we can do with *Church* law.

What CFFC is Trying To Accomplish With This Argument.

The deadliest sin to pro-abortionists is hypocrisy. So they feel compelled to "prove" that pro-lifers are inconsistent hypocrites, just like themselves. They are especially desperate to undermine confidence in Catholic teachings on abortion. They say that, if the Catholic Church has not taught a doctrine since its very inception, then the teaching or doctrine is changeable, and the Church is being "inconsistent" by insisting that its "current position" is the correct one.

Since CFFC knows full well that the Church *has* taught that abortion is gravely sinful from the beginning, it tries to distract attention from the core issues by focusing on various tangential issues, counting on the fact that most Catholics are not intimately familiar with this aspect of Church history.

But CFFC is being inconsistent once again.

CFFC says that Catholics can generally ignore a teaching that has not been held from the very beginning of Church history, with the implication that, if it *had* been taught from the beginning, they would be obliged to obey it. Yet CFFC simply ignores teachings proclaimed by Jesus Christ Himself, including His admonishments against fornication, divorce, homosexual activity and adultery.[256]

This shows that CFFC's emphasis on the "changeability" of the Church's teaching on abortion is just another diversion.

(1) Original Church Teachings Against Abortion.

From the very beginning of Her history, the Church has *always* taught that abortion is gravely sinful.

The *Catechism of the Catholic Church* teaches that

> Since the first century the Church has affirmed the moral evil of every procured abortion. This teaching has not changed and remains unchangeable. Direct abortion, that is to say, abortion willed either as an end or a means, is gravely contrary to the moral law [¶2271].

The earliest known teaching against abortion was the *Didache* of about 100

AD, which commands "Thou shalt not kill the fruit of the womb by an abortion."

Many of the Early Church Fathers condemned abortion. In about 177 AD, Athenagoras wrote that "Those women who use drugs to bring about an abortion commit murder and will have to give an account to God for their abortion." Tertullian, Hippolytus, St. John Chrysostom and St. Augustine all condemned abortion in the strongest possible terms.

The Church's earliest Councils also legislated against abortion. The Council of Elvira, in 305 AD, held that a woman who aborted a child was not to be given communion even at the end of her life.[257]

The Council of Ancyra (314 AD) repeated this teaching, and stated that "Women who prostitute themselves, and who kill the children thus begotten, or who try to destroy them in their womb, are by ancient law excommunicated to the end of their lives. We, however, have lessened their punishment and condemn them to the various appointed degrees of penance for ten years."[258]

Scores of other Early Church Fathers and Councils condemned abortion, and many prescribed excommunication for women who obtained abortions. Appendix B quotes and summarizes many of these pronouncements.

In conclusion, this very brief review of early Church history decisively proves that CFFC's statement alleging that abortion has only been an excommunicable offense since 1869 is completely false. It has, in fact, been a teaching of the Church from the very beginning of Her history.

(2) On `Formed' and `Unformed' Fetuses.

At various times in Church history, certain theologians have expressed opinions that differed from the teachings of the Church. However, such opinions are not binding on Catholics, who have a moral obligation towards the Magisterium of the Catholic Church, which is comprised of the Pope and the bishops in communion with him. Much as CFFC would like to believe otherwise, the opinions of theologians have no binding effect on Catholic consciences.

CFFC's problem is not that it honestly misunderstands the issues; its primary difficulty is that it rejects legitimate Church authority. As Frances Kissling has said, "We are all mavericks. We are people who don't take authority seriously."[259]

CFFC has written about the "inconsistency" of the Catholic Church regarding its ancient belief that there were two classes of preborn children: The "formed" and the "unformed." This concept was sometimes expressed as "delayed animation" or "delayed ensoulment," which was based on the obsolete biology of the Greek philosopher Aristotle, who claimed that God infused the soul in the human body some time after conception.[260]

Despite theological debate over ensoulment, the Catholic Church and all of Her theologians have continued to teach that abortion is always a grave moral evil, though the canonical penalties for aborting a "formed" fetus were for a time greater than those for aborting an "unformed" fetus.

The *Declaration on Procured Abortion* tells us that

> It is true that in the Middle Ages, when the opinion was gen-
> erally held that the spiritual soul was not present until after the
> first few weeks, a distinction was made in the evaluation of the
> sin and the gravity of penal sanctions. Excellent authors
> allowed for this first period more lenient case solutions which
> they rejected for following periods. But it was never denied at
> that time that procured abortion, even during the first days,
> was objectively grave fault. This condemnation was in fact
> unanimous [¶7].

(3) More Recent Teachings of the Church.

As we have seen, the Catholic Church has *always* taught that abortion is murder. However, some confusion exists because the penalties for the murder of a preborn child have been changed several times in the history of the Church.

In 1588, Pope Sixtus V tried to discourage abortion by reserving absolution to the Holy See alone. Because of the numbers of abortions taking place, it soon became evident that such an arrangement was impractical, and so in 1591, just three years later, Pope Gregory XIV returned absolution for abortion to the local ordinary (the local bishop).[261]

Paolo Zacchia, Physician-General of the Vatican, published a book in 1620 entitled *Quaestiones Medico-Legales* in which he argued that ensoulment takes place at conception and that development is a continuum.[262] This was a decisive rejection of the "delayed animation" theory.

In 1679, Pope Innocent XI condemned the writings and teachings of two the-ologians, Thomas Sanchez and Joannis Marcus, who believed that abortion was lawful if the fetus was not yet animated or ensouled and the purpose of the abor-tion was to prevent shame to the woman.[263] This act showed decisively that the

Church did not tolerate abortion, and was willing to prosecute those who spread error regarding prenatal child-killing.

The French Jesuit Theophile Raynaud (1582-1663) believed that indirect abortion of a viable baby to save the mother's life was allowable. This was notable because he was the *first* theologian to hold this view and his teachings were unique in the Church until about 1850. This is an early statement of the principle of the "double effect," as described above.

In 1869, Pope Pius IX took the action that pro-abortionists deliberately misrepresent in order to buttress their views. The Pope officially removed the distinction between the animated and unanimated fetus from the Code of Canon Law.[264] This action dealt not with theology, but with discipline, and merely made the punishment for abortion at *any* stage uniform. The Pope removed the distinction in order to clarify the Church's stance that life and ensoulment both begin at fertilization.

Summary and Conclusion.

With its "historical inconsistency" argument, Catholics for a Free Choice is attempting to show two things: (1) that Church teachings on abortion have changed in the past, so they can be changed again, and (2) Catholics need not obey a teaching that is allegedly "changeable."

However, both of these allegations are invalid because the Catholic Church has *always* taught that abortion is gravely sinful.

Evangelium Vitae confirmed this teaching in an authoritative and solemn declaration:

> Therefore, by the authority which Christ conferred upon Peter and his Successors, in communion with the Bishops — who on various occasions have condemned abortion and who in the aforementioned consultation, albeit dispersed throughout the world, have shown unanimous agreement concerning this doctrine — I declare that direct abortion, that is, abortion willed as an end or as a means, always constitutes a grave moral disorder, since it is the deliberate killing of an innocent human being. This doctrine is based upon the natural law and upon the written Word of God, is transmitted by the Church's Tradition and taught by the ordinary and universal Magisterium.

No circumstance, no purpose, no law whatsoever can ever make licit an act which is intrinsically illicit, since it is contrary to the Law of God which is written in every human heart, knowable by reason itself, and proclaimed by the Church [¶62].

It is true that poorly catechized Catholics may be confused about the Church's teachings on abortion, especially when groups like CFFC *exist* to cultivate such confusion.

However, in light of the constant teaching of the Church against abortion, we must wonder how anyone who has studied the relevant history in any depth — as CFFC constantly boasts it has — can possibly hold that the Church ever has or ever will accept abortion.

CFFC Argument #12:

"We respect the right of others to hold opinions different from our own."

What Catholics for a Free Choice Says.

"We are convinced that only open, honest, and respectful dialogue will bring the Catholic community to some resolution of this problem. ... We hope that the discussion can be carried forward in a manner that is respectful of the consciences and persons of all its participants."
— *Conscience* Magazine.[265]

Summary of the Response.

(1)   CFFC acknowledges that those who believe abortion is murder must morally protest it.

(2)   Yet CFFC stridently condemns *all* pro-life activities. This is schizophrenic, hypocritical and inconsistent.

(3)   CFFC proves, by its constant stereotyping and labeling of Church leaders and pro-lifers, that it does not respect the sincerely held beliefs of anyone who disagrees with it.

(1) CFFC Acknowledges that Pro-Lifers Should Take Action ...

Catholics for a Free Choice frequently claims that it respects the opinions of those people it calls "anti-choicers."

However, both the organization's actions and rhetoric prove that its vaunted tolerance is just another public relations facade.

If a person *really* believes that preborn children are human beings, then he logically believes that abortion is the deliberate murder of these human beings. Anyone of good will who believes that a human being is in danger of being murdered is going to be driven by his conscience to *do* something about it. In fact, rescuing those in danger of death is the *duty* of all Christians — indeed, of all men and women who care about humanity.[266]

Garry Wills acknowledges this point in CFFC's *Conscience* magazine:

"Abortion is like genocide to those who think human persons are being killed —
not a thing one can witness *without* moral protest."[267] Perhaps Wills is referring
to the injunction in Proverbs 24:11-12; "Rescue those who are being taken away
to death; hold back those who are stumbling to the slaughter. If you say,
"Behold, we did not know this," does not he who weighs the heart perceive it?
Does not he who keeps watch over your soul know it, and will he not requite man
according to his work?"

In light of these sincerely held moral beliefs, even those who call themselves
"pro-choice" should respect the motives of activist pro-lifers, even if they do not
agree with them.

(2) ... But CFFC Condemns *All* Pro-Life Activities.

CFFC concedes that men and women who think abortion is murder must take
action to stop it. Yet CFFC betrays the hypocrisy in its thinking by condemning
literally *every* form of peaceful pro-life activity, thereby showing that it cares little about the consciences of pro-lifers.

CFFC would like to prohibit all pro-life street activity. It says that pro-lifers
must not peacefully block clinic doors to save preborn children, because this is
"committing direct violence against women."[268] We may not picket, because this
is "Cromwellian fanaticism."[269] We can't sidewalk counsel, because the women
"have already made their minds up, and any interference will just cause them
pain and distress."[270] We must not quietly pray in front of the clinics, because, as
Frances Kissling says, even *this* "offends and hurts women."[271]

CFFC would also like to ban all behind-the-scenes activities by pro-lifers.
It says that we should not be allowed to offer alternatives to women through
Crisis pregnancy centers (CPCs), which CFFC calls "fraudulent and deceptive
clinics." These CPCs, of course, may never give women factual biological information on fetal development, because this constitutes a "propaganda tool for the
anti-abortion position."[272]

Adoption is off limits, because, as CFFC writers say, it is "misogynist" and
"devastating."[273] Pro-lifers must not try to enact any kind of restrictions on
abortion, even if they are massively supported by public opinion, because such
activity is "a violation of the wall of separation between Church and State." We
can't lobby Congress, because this is "partisanship."[274] We can't organize,
because such activity is a "conspiracy." We must not educate the public, because
we are pushing "anti-choice propaganda." We cannot try to convince others to

141

embrace our position through one-on-one dialogue, because that is "shoving our philosophy down other people's throats," and, believe it or not, "spiritual battering!"[275]

Pro-life priests may *never* mention abortion in their homilies or have a Sanctity of Life Sunday, because this may cause "frustration" and "anger" among so-called "pro-choice Catholics."[276] Bishops cannot even exert any control over their own property by banning pro-abortionists, because this is "controlling public practices."[277] CFFC would even deny pro-lifers the right to express their belief that preborn children are human beings, because this encourages "terrorism."[278] In fact, CFFC alleges that the Catholic Church cannot even *refuse* to donate money to groups it believes to be promoting abortion because, as Frances Kissling says, this is "intimidation," "strong arm tactics," and a "dirty little war" against "every good thing."[279]

Finally, CFFC condemns even pro-life attempts to help women through the aftermath of abortion with programs such as Project Rachel, which Kissling has labeled "offensive" and "dumb."[280] Incredibly, CFFC even denounces pro-lifers who offer money and other aid to pregnant women to help them through their pregnancies and beyond, because, as CFFC says, this is "questionable," "manipulative," "unethical," and "dangerous."[281]

CFFC not only refuses to offer real help to women in crisis pregnancies, it would deny them help from any *other* source as well. No wonder former CFFC Board member Marjorie Reiley Maguire now refers to CFFC as "anti-woman!"[282]

In conclusion, CFFC's claim that it respects the consciences of pro-lifers is laughable, since it condemns every type of pro-life activism without exception. Simultaneously, when referring to aborting women, CFFC hypocritically asserts that "Freedom cannot be refused whole classes of persons on the grounds that some of them might, or even probably would, use that freedom to commit grievous sin."[283]

CFFC constantly asserts that "pro-choice Catholics" must be allowed to "follow their consciences" in all areas, even to the point of disregarding all church and civil laws. Meanwhile, it works tirelessly to force pro-lifers to abandon *their* consciences, because it strenuously denounces every known pro-life activity.

This is not "respect" in any way, shape or form. It is, instead, the most blatant hypocrisy and injustice.

As an aside, Thomas J. Gumbleton, Auxiliary Bishop of Detroit, wrote a letter to *Conscience* magazine praising the United States bishops who supported the peace movement in Latin America, saying that "Strong public statements and actions, including civil disobedience, arrest, and jail mark this involvement."[284] Once again, we see a dazzling display of liberal hypocrisy: If you're on *their* side of an issue, you can do anything you want. If you *disagree* with them, you had just better shut up and do nothing.

(3) CFFC Certainly Does *Not* Respect the Consciences or Persons of Pro-Lifers.

CFFC's Bigotry. CFFC board member Rosemary Radford Ruether defines "bigotry" as "... a stereotyping of an entire other religious or racial group as essentially evil and demonic by nature."[285]

By its own definition, Catholics for a Free Choice is a group of committed bigots, because its literature is saturated with stereotypes and sweeping generalizations about pro-lifers.

CFFC writers are adept at playing the victim, because it garners sympathy and is an effective fundraising ploy.

One CFFC writer sniffled that "We must hold our hands out in friendship even when our faces are slapped. We have to listen and seek to understand even when our ears are assailed with venomous words."[286] Significantly, CFFC also says that "Epithets, on the other hand, lack specific semantic connections, existing only to arouse emotions by circumventing intellectual comprehension."[287]

Yet it is not their "antichoice" opponents, but CFFC, which frequently uses "venomous words." And it is obviously CFFC which constantly attempts to "arouse emotions by circumventing intellectual comprehension."

Even as they plead for tolerance and nonjudgmentalism, Frances Kissling and other CFFC leaders refer to the Pope and the bishops as "absolutist," "angry," "anti-woman," "arrogant," "blind," "bullies," "callous," "coercive," "confused," "cruel," "dangerous," "dogmatic," "dumb," "embarrassing," "fanatical," "hardhearted," "harsh," "hypocritical," "illogical," "imperialistic," "irresponsible," "liars," "loony," "Luddites," "manipulative," "mean," "misogynist," "nasty," "narrow-minded," "obsessive," "obstructive," "pathological," "pernicious," "pig-headed," "prattlers," "ranting," "reactionaries," "rigid," "ruthless," "sanctimonious," "self-righteous," "simplistic," "slippery," "terrible," "totalitarian," "tyrannical," "unethical," "unhinged," "unjust," "unkind," "vehement," "virulent," and "vituperative," and even "betrayers of Christ" and "the seed of Satan," among many other labels.[288] CFFC writers even go so far as to accuse the

Church hierarchy of using "force, threats and violence" to obtain its objectives — but of course never gives examples of such abuse.[289]

Naturally, if a bishop *agrees* with CFFC on any issue, it says that he is "rejoicing in the work of the Holy Spirit," but when he opposes CFFC, it calls him every filthy name it can think of.[290]

You cannot shout insults in a person's face while claiming that you respect him. CFFC's allegation that it respects the beliefs and actions of its opponents is simply more pro-abortion public relations propaganda designed to make it look reasonable and inclusive.

Frances Kissling has boasted that "God put me on earth to give the pope a hard time."[291] She has also said that

> "We are still treating the leadership [of the Church] with an enormous amount of respect. They don't deserve our respect. ... I would like to see women reach the point they understand that every bishop in this country should be so embarrassed that he is afraid to show his face in public. ... But these men [the bishops] don't deserve good manners. We must get to the point where once we know they don't deserve good manners, we're capable of taking to the streets. ... Nothing will drive them crazier than to be treated without dignity."[292]

Once again, we might ask how "giving people a hard time," "treating them without dignity," and "driving them crazy" constitutes showing them respect as human beings.

Many of CFFC's other actions show that they do not respect the Catholic Church they claim to love so much. CFFC's first public action was to ridicule the Church by crowning one of its three founders, Patricia McQuillan, "Pope Joan I" on the steps of St. Patrick's Cathedral in New York City.[293] Since that time, CFFC has continued its tradition of aggressively mocking and attacking the Church and Her Pope. For example, during the 1987 Papal visit to the United States, CFFC ran a full-page advertisement in the *San Francisco Chronicle* entitled "Where Motherhood Kills: The Women's Message for the Papal Visit," condemning the Pope for opposing abortion and birth control. Kevin Gordon, a member of CFFC's national Board of Directors, publicly burned Vatican documents he did not agree with. And, just to rub salt in the wounds they inflicted, CFFC boasted that it "decided in May to play the lead role in organizing and assisting local [abortion] clinics facing threats from antichoice people during the Pope's visit."[294]

Incredibly, after engaging in all of this activism and agitation during the Pope's visit, CFFC accused the *Pope* of causing "dissention and debate ... oppression and pain!"[295]

CFFC's Absurd Stereotyping. One of the most common tactics used by pro-abortion groups is calling their opponent's motivations into question. They know full well that it is hard to whip up hatred against a group of people who sincerely follow Christ's example of loving the sinner while hating the sin. Therefore, they must construct a stereotypical caricature of pro-lifers that is much easier to despise and ridicule.

CFFC writers consistently make ridiculous generalizations about pro-lifers, without making the slightest attempt to understand their motivations.

One must tremble when contemplating the level of fevered paranoia from which such preposterous fantasies arise. CFFC is a conspiracy theorist's dream come true.

For example, according to CFFC, the purpose of the right-to-life movement "... has been to deny women opportunity, to deny women choice, to deny women a moral existence. They are only interested in women in a negative sense."[296] Frances Kissling says that "... hatred of women and fear of sexuality are the roots of Vatican positions on birth control and abortion. ... This lack of respect for women and the palpable aversion to sexuality are timeless. ... This ethic is characterized by historic and present day hostility, even hatred of women, the body, and sexuality."[297] Janet Parker alleges that "... the core of the Religious Right's agenda is to reestablish a white, heterosexual-patriarchal, Christian theocracy. ... The social order that the Religious Right wants to enforce and maintain is a racist, patriarchal system in which white, Christian males dominate and rule nation and family."[298] CFFC board member Rosemary Radford Ruether claims that "... the motivation of the antiabortion movement is primarily about patriarchal control over women and youth and not about concern for life in the broader sense. ... Most of the antiabortion camp has little concern for life after birth."[299]

CFFC often claims to respect pro-lifers. However, it is not respectful to present your own paranoid fabrications about your opponents as established fact, without even the most superficial attempt to understand their true motivations.

As could be expected, CFFC repeatedly pillories and labels the "antichoicers"

145

they claim to "respect" so much. Some of the printable epithets they use to describe pro-lifers in general include "criminal," "deceptive," "fanatical," "fascist," "hypocritical," "irrational," "murderous," "racist," "sexist," "strident," "stupid," "vicious" and "vindictive."[300] In the eyes of CFFC, in fact, there is no such thing as a "good" pro-lifer — unless he or she supports hedonistic sex education and the widespread distribution of contraceptives.

Remember that CFFC claims that "anti-choice rhetoric leads to violence." Perhaps CFFC should listen to itself and turn down its *own* level of hatred and malice a few notches.

Conclusion.

While Catholics for a Free Choice demands that people respect the consciences of people who disagree with Church teachings on abortion and contraception, it engages in a deliberate propaganda campaign that is carefully designed to demonize and stereotype pro-life Catholics.

First CFFC clearly acknowledges that pro-lifers must *do* something to fight an act they consider evil. But then it condemns all of the possible courses of action pro-lifers can take, ridicules them relentlessly, and stereotypes them ruthlessly.

This blatant double standard leads us to conclude that, in CFFC's view, the only consciences worthy of respect are those of so-called "pro-choice Catholics." In fact, CFFC believes that the conscience of a pro-lifer must *always* yield to the conscience of a pro-abortionist in every possible circumstance. To CFFC, the conscience of a pro-lifer has exactly the same value as the life of a preborn child — i.e., exactly none.

This attitude is summed up in a brazenly witless statement by Malcolm Potts, who said that "The most uplifting vision of religious liberty I can envisage for the twenty-fifth anniversary of *Roe v. Wade* [the United States Supreme Court decision that legalized abortion] would be a person who sincerely believes abortion is murder driving a woman with a different belief to an abortion clinic."[301] We must wonder if CFFC would agree that another "uplifting vision of religious liberty would be a person who sincerely believes abortion is acceptable driving a man with a different belief (and a homemade bomb) to an abortion clinic at 3 AM."

Of *course* not. After all, with CFFC, religious liberty goes just one way.

Appendix A

Statements of Catholic Bishops Condemning Catholics for a Free Choice

National Council of Catholic Bishops
Committee on Doctrine
"Abortion and "Free Choice:" The Catholic Church
Teaches Direct Abortion is Never a Moral Good."
November 1984

Among the various contributions to this year's debate on abortion and public policy was a statement issued by a group which calls itself a "Catholic Committee on Pluralism and Abortion," and publicized by "Catholics for a Free Choice."

This statement says it is mistaken to believe that the Catholic Church teaches that deliberately chosen abortion is morally wrong in all instances, and it suggests that abortion can sometimes be a legitimate moral choice.

As the Committee on Doctrine of the National Conference of Catholic Bishops, responding to the general concern of our brother bishops, we want to affirm that such an opinion, however sincerely motivated, contradicts the clear and constant teaching of the Church that deliberately chosen abortion is objectively immoral. It is not a legitimate moral choice [1].

The assertions contained in the statement of the Committee on Pluralism and Abortion which imply that Church teaching about abortion has not always been clear and constant are not correct, and are not substantiated by scholarly research. For example, the statement appeals to philosophical discussions about "ensoulment," and to canonical discussions about when the person who commits the sin of abortion also incurs the penalty of excommunication, as if these dis-

147

cussions provided a basis for legitimate diversity of opinion. But such philosophical and canonical discussions have always presumed the Church's constant teaching about the immorality of abortion. The Committee also appeals to principles of moral theology, such as probabilism, religious liberty, and the centrality of informed conscience, as justifying its opinion. But Catholic theology does not allow the application of the theory of probabilism in cases which contradict Church teaching or where the risk of taking life is present. Furthermore, legitimate freedom of conscience requires the responsible formation of conscience in accord with the truth of the Gospel message as handed on in the constant teaching of the Church.

The members of the Committee on Pluralism and Abortion present a personal opinion which directly contradicts the clear and constant teaching of the Church about abortion, a teaching which they as Catholics are obliged to accept. At the same time, the Committee on Doctrine reaffirms its confidence in the many theologians who explore and present the implications of moral teaching in fidelity to the Catholic tradition.

[1] This teaching was cogently reaffirmed by the Second Vatican Council, which referred to abortion as an "abominable crime" (Pastoral Constitution on the Church in the Modern World, no. 51); it has been authoritatively explained in the *Declaration on Procured Abortion* of the Congregation for the Doctrine of the Faith (1974), and has frequently been restated by the Bishops of the United States in various Pastoral Letters (e.g., *Human Life in Our Day* in 1968, no. 84; *To Live in Christ Jesus* in 1976, nos. 637-65; *The Challenge of Peace* in 1983, nos. 286-289), and numerous other statements.

"Statement Regarding Catholics for a Free Choice"
Administrative Committee
National Conference of Catholic Bishops
November 4, 1993

During Pope John Paul II's recent visit to this country, programs about dissent in the Catholic Church often included a spokesperson for a group calling itself "Catholics for a Free Choice" (CFFC). Both before and since World Youth Day, because of CFFC's presuming to speak for American Catholics, and because of the attention the media have paid to the group, many people, including Catholics, may be led to believe that it is an authentic Catholic organization. It is not. It has no affiliation, formal or otherwise, with the Catholic Church.

In fact, Catholics for a Free Choice is associated with the pro-abortion lobby in Washington, D.C. It attracts public attention by its denunciations of basic principles of Catholic morality and teaching — denunciations given enhanced visibility by media outlets that portray CFFC as a reputable voice of Catholic dissent.

CFFC can in no way speak for the Catholic Church and its 59 million members in the United States. Most of CFFC's funding is from secular foundations supporting legal abortion in this country and abroad. It shares an address and funding sources with the National Abortion Federation, a trade association which seeks to advance the financial and professional interests of abortionists.

Therefore it is important to educate the public, especially Catholics, about CFFC's insistence on claiming a Catholic label. This group has rejected unity with the Church on important issues of longstanding and unchanging Church teaching. In fact, there is no room for dissent by a Catholic from the Church's moral teaching that direct abortion is a grave wrong.

Our Catholic position embraces the truth regarding the sacredness of every human life, before as well as after birth. CFFC endorses the violent destruction of innocent unborn human beings and regularly issues legal briefs and other publications endorsing legalized abortion for all nine months of pregnancy and for any reason. Most Americans do not support its extreme agenda.

Because of its opposition to the human rights of some of the most defenseless members of the human race, and because its purposes and activities deliberately contradict essential teachings of the Catholic faith, we state once again that Catholics for a Free Choice merits no recognition or support as a Catholic organization.

"Status of `Catholics for a Free Choice'"
Bishop Joseph A. Fiorenza of Galveston-Houston,
President of the National Conference of Catholic Bishops,
United States Catholic Conference
May 10, 2000

For a number of years, a group calling itself Catholics for a Free Choice (CFFC) has been publicly supporting abortion while claiming it speaks as an authentic Catholic voice. That claim is false. In fact, the group's activity is directed to rejection and distortion of Catholic teaching about the respect and protection due to defenseless preborn human life.

On a number of occasions the National Conference of Catholic Bishops (NCCB) has stated publicly that CFFC is not a Catholic organization, does not speak for the Catholic Church, and in fact promotes positions contrary to the teaching of the Church as articulated by the Holy See and the NCCB.

CFFC is, practically speaking, an arm of the abortion lobby in the United States and throughout the world. It is an advocacy group dedicated to supporting abortion. It is funded by a number of powerful and wealthy private foundations, mostly American, to promote abortion as a method of population control. This position is contrary to existing United Nations policy and the laws and policies of most nations of the world.

In its latest campaign, CFFC has undertaken a concentrated public relations effort to end the official presence and silence the moral voice of the Holy See at the United Nations as a Permanent Observer. The public relations effort has ridiculed the Holy See in language reminiscent of other episodes of anti-Catholic bigotry that the Catholic Church has endured in the past.

As the Catholic Bishops of the United States have stated for many years, the use of the name Catholic as a platform for supporting the taking of innocent human life and ridiculing the Church is offensive not only to Catholics, but to all who expect honesty and forthrightness in public discourse. We state once again with the strongest emphasis: "Because of its opposition to the human rights of some of the most defenseless members of the human race, and because its purposes and activities deliberately contradict essential teachings of the Catholic faith, ... Catholics for a Free Choice merits no recognition or support as a Catholic organization" (Administrative Committee, National Conference of Catholic Bishops, 1993).

Excerpts from
The Bishops of Chiapas, Mexico
"The New Campaign Against Life"
July 1, 1991

On the occasion of the so-called "National Forum on Voluntary Motherhood and the Decriminalization of Abortion" held in the city of Tuxla Gutierrez, Chiapas, we, the Bishops of Chiapas, proclaim the following:

1. Moral laws and objective truth are not determined by the amount of pressure exerted on the Legislative Authorities. Therefore, even though many people might unite to urge that the congress of the State of Chiapas proceed with its Decriminalization of Abortion bill, and were our congressmen to allow themselves to be swayed by publicity, acceding to such demands, indeed abortion would still be a crime, simply because it is the murder of a helpless and innocent human being.

7. To this Forum was invited a group of foreigners that calls itself "Catholic Women for Choice," [Catholics for a Free Choice], that is, women who say they support legalized abortion. If this be true, we have to affirm with utmost clarity that such a position nullified their claims to be Catholics. They have excommunicated themselves; they have placed themselves outside the Church. A truly Catholic woman is one who accepts the Church's doctrines. If she does not accept them, she is free to change her religion or to lose it; but she has no right to use the word "Catholic"; because she is not a Catholic. Such manipulation of this word is deplorable, for only confusion results. Could it be a ploy by the organizers of the Forum to make people believe that within the Church there is no unanimity on this point? The Devil works that way.

Samuel Ruiz Garcia, Bishop of San Cristobal de Las Casas
Felipe Aguirre Franco, Bishop of Tuxla
Felipe Arizmendi Esquivel, Bishop of Tapachula

Appendix B

Early Teachings of the Catholic Church Against Abortion

"You shall not kill an unborn child or murder a newborn infant."

— *The Didache* ("The Lord's Instruction to the Gentiles through the Twelve Apostles"). II, 2, translated by J.A. Kleist, S.J., *Ancient Christian Writers*, Volume 6. Westminster, 1948, page 16.

"You shall love your neighbor more than your own life. You shall not slay the child by abortion."

— Barnabas (c. 70-138), *Epistle*, Volume II, page 19.

"For us [Christians], murder is once and for all forbidden; so even the child in the womb, while yet the mother's blood is still being drawn on to form the human being, it is not lawful for us to destroy. To forbid birth is only quicker murder. It makes no difference whether one takes away the life once born or destroys it as it comes to birth. He is a man, who is to be a man; the fruit is always present in the seed."

— Tertullian, 197, *Apologeticus*, page 9.

"Those women who use drugs to bring about an abortion commit murder and will have to give an account to God for their abortion."

— Athenagoras of Athens, letter to Marcus Aurelius in 177, *Legatio pro Christianis* ("Supplication for the Christians"), page 35.

"It is among you that I see newly-begotten sons at times exposed to wild beasts and birds, or dispatched by the violent death of strangulation; and there are women who, by the use of medicinal potions, destroy the unborn life in their wombs, and murder the child before they bring it forth. These practices undoubtedly are derived from a custom established by your gods; Saturn, though he did

152

not expose his sons, certainly devoured them."

— Minucius Felix, theologian (c. 200-225), *Octavius*, p. 30.

"... if we would not kill off the human race born and developing according to God's plan, then our whole lives would be lived according to nature. Women who make use of some sort of deadly abortion drug kill not only the embryo but, together with it, all human kindness."

— Clement of Alexandria, priest and the "Father of Theologians" (c. 150-220), *Christ the Educator*, Volume II, page 10. Also see *Octavius*, c.30, nn. 2-3.

"Sometimes this lustful cruelty or cruel lust goes so far as to seek to procure a baneful sterility, and if this fails the fetus conceived in the womb is in one way or another smothered or evacuated, in the desire to destroy the offspring before it has life, or if it already lives in the womb, to kill it before it is born. If both man and woman are party to such practices they are not spouses at all; and if from the first they have carried on thus they have come together not for honest wedlock, but for impure gratification; if both are not party to these deeds, I make bold to say that either the one makes herself a mistress of the husband, or the other simply the paramour of his wife."

— St. Augustine, Bishop of Hippo (354-430), *De Nuptius et Concupiscus* ("On Marriage and Concupiscence"), 1.17.

"Some virgins [unmarried women], when they learn they are with child through sin, practice abortion by the use of drugs. Frequently they die themselves and are brought before the ruler of the lower world guilty of three crimes; suicide, adultery against Christ, and murder of an unborn child."

— St. Jerome, Bible Scholar and translator (c. 340-420), *Letter to Eustochium*, 22.13.

"The hairsplitting difference between formed and unformed makes no difference to us. Whoever deliberately commits abortion is subject to the penalty for homicide."

— St. Basil the Great, priest (c. 329-379), *First Canonical Letter*, from the work *Three Canonical Letters*. Loeb Classical Library, Volume III, pages 20 to 23.

"Accordingly, among surgeon's tools, there is a certain instrument, which is formed with a nicely-adjusted flexible frame for opening the uterus first of all, and keeping it open; it is further furnished with an annular blade, by means of which the limbs within the womb are dissected with anxious but unfaltering care; its last appendage being a blunted or covered hood, wherewith the entire foetus is extracted by a violent delivery. There is also a copper needle or spike, by which the actual death is managed in this furtive robbery of life: they give it, from its infanticide function, the name of enbruosphaktes, the slayer of the infant, which was of course alive ... life begins with conception, because we contend that the soul also begins from conception; life taking its commencement at the same moment and place that the soul does."

> — Tertullian, theologian (150-225), *Treatise on the Soul*, pages 25 and 27.

"Those who give drugs for procuring abortion, and those who receive poisons to kill the foetus, are subjected to the penalty for murder."

> — Trullian (Quinisext) Council (692), *Canons*, 91.

Summary of the Most Significant Early
Catholic Church Teachings Against Abortion

The *Apocalypse* of Peter.

Hippolytus, Bishop of Pontius and theologian (died 236), *Refutation of All Heresies*, 9.7.

Origen, theologian of Alexandria (185-254), *Against Heresies*, page 9.

Cyprian, Bishop of Carthage (c. 200-258), *Letters*, page 48.

Council of Elvira in Granada, Spain (305), *Canons*, 63 and 68.

Council of Ancyra in Galatia, Asia Minor (314), *Canon*, 21.

Ephraem the Syrian, theologian (306-373), *De Timore Dei*, page 10.

St. Basil the Great, priest (c. 329-379), *Letters*, 188.2, 8.

St. Ambrose, Bishop of Milan (c. 339-397), *Hexameron*, 5.18.58.

Apostolic Constitutions (late Fourth Century)

St. Augustine, Bishop of Hippo (354-430), *Enchiridion*, page 86.

St. John Chrysostom, Bishop of Constantinople (c. 347-407), *Homily 24* ("On

The Book of Romans")
Council of Chalcedon (451)
Caesarius, Bishop of Arles (470-543), *Sermons*, 1.12.
Council of Lerida (524).
Second Council of Braga (527), *Canons*, 77.
Consillium Quinisextum (692).

Appendix C

How to Defeat Catholics for a Free Choice at the Local Level

"Therefore, having this ministry by the mercy of God, we do not lose heart. We have renounced disgraceful, underhanded ways; we refuse to practice cunning or to tamper with God's word, but by the open statement of the truth we would commend ourselves to every man's conscience in the sight of God. And even if our gospel is veiled, it is veiled only to those who are perishing. In their case the god of this world has blinded the minds of the unbelievers, to keep them from seeing the light of the gospel of the glory of Christ, who is the likeness of God ... We are afflicted in every way, but not crushed; perplexed, but not driven to despair; persecuted, but not forsaken; struck down, but not destroyed; always carrying in the body the death of Jesus, so that the life of Jesus may also be manifested in our bodies."
— 2 Corinthians 4:1-4,8-10.

Getting Started.

> "Therefore it is important to educate the public, especially Catholics, about CFFC's insistence on claiming a Catholic label."
> — National Conference of Catholic Bishops. "Statement Regarding Catholics for a Free Choice," November 4, 1993.

Every faithful Catholic is deeply concerned about what is happening in the Church today, not only in Canada and the United States, but all over the world. The Catholic Church is literally under siege by those who would undermine or even destroy its most basic dogma and teachings.

This has been the situation since the founding of the Church at the original Pentecost, and it will be this way until Our Lord returns again.

Unfortunately, concern alone will not safeguard the Faith. Decisive *action* by

156

a large number of priests and lay people is also required if the Church is to persevere.

The late Father John Hardon, S.J. said at the 1996 Call to Holiness conference that "The Church cannot be destroyed, but let's be clear: The Church in any particular country *can* be wiped out. We have some 1,900 extinct dioceses in the world today. Barring a miracle of grace, one diocese after another in the United States will disappear."

There are many things an individual Catholic can do to defend the One True Faith, and these actions fall into two general categories. You can either confront the dissenters directly, or, if for some reason you cannot do this, you can support those who are battling on the front lines.

This Appendix includes suggestions for fulfilling your role as a member of the Church Militant. These proposals are only a starting point; anything you can do to blunt or lessen the baleful influence of the Modernist dissenters is precious in the eyes of God and Holy Mother Church.

How CFFC Operates.

The Situation. All dissenting organizations, including Catholics for a Free Choice, operate primarily by stealth. They use a tactic called "infiltration and subversion," which means that they present themselves as Catholic scholars who preach and teach about social justice, freedom, inclusiveness and toleration. Meanwhile, they actively conceal their true beliefs and goals.

CFFC's primary mission is to undermine the teachings of the Catholic Church. To this end, it attempts to influence the organizations and individuals that have the greatest amount of influence on the largest number of people. CFFC therefore focuses on Catholic and secular universities, other learning institutions, religious orders, politicians, the media, and the United Nations. Occasionally it will attempt to exert influence at the diocesan or parish level, especially if the bishop or pastor has been effective at opposing its agenda.

Once established, CFFC does its real work, which is the *subversion*, or undermining, of authentic Catholic teaching regarding sexual ethics.

How does an ordinary group of Catholics fight such expert and experienced deception and treachery?

Faithful Catholics often feel helpless and anxious as they see what dissenters are doing to Holy Mother Church, and the almost universal indifference towards the systematic subversion of Church teachings. They know that, if they attempt to take action against the dissenters, they may be stonewalled, stereotyped and ridiculed. This leads to a kind of paralysis among orthodox Catholics and a resulting unwillingness to take action against heresy. They think "What's the use? If I raise my head and protest, I'll simply be labeled a fanatic."

Experienced dissent fighters have heard this plaintive story from bewildered Catholics many times, and know that it springs from a feeling of helplessness and anxiety.

What is the answer to this problem?

How can average Catholics effectively defend their Faith? How can they ensure that their efforts bear fruit?

The Solution. A feeling of helplessness is caused by a lack of power, and a lack of power is caused by disorganization. Anxiety is caused by uncertainty, and uncertainty is caused by lack of knowledge.

Knowledge dispels anxiety and gives us confidence.

Organization eliminates helplessness and gives us power.

The purpose of this short Appendix is to give concerned Catholics basic information on the theory of dissent and dissenters in general, and some practical information on how to organize against CFFC in particular. It supplements the book, which defines and explains Church teaching in certain critical areas, so that readers can discern between truth and the subtle and polished falsehoods presented by dissenting groups.

Before we can defeat Catholics for a Free Choice and its agenda, we must look upon ourselves as members of the Church Militant who have enlisted as Soldiers of Christ (*miles Jesu*). Next, we need to study CFFC in order to learn exactly what kind of people we are dealing with and what their beliefs are. Then we must examine their tactics and their arguments and learn how to defeat them. Finally, we must take concerted and organized action against them, while realizing that it is Satan, not the dissenters themselves, who is the real enemy.

How to Defeat Them? With the "POPE."

"Training, at once many-sided and complete, is indispensable if the apostolate is to attain full efficacy. ... Not a few types of apostolate require, besides the education common to all Christians, a specific and individual training, by reason of the diversity of persons and circumstances."

—   Vatican II, *Apostolicam Actuositatem* ("Decree On the

Apostolate of the Laity"), November 16, 1965. ¶28, "The Need for Training."

Over the years, experienced dissent fighters have developed a very effective method for fighting Catholics for a Free Choice and the hundreds of other dissenting groups that lead so many souls astray.

This general procedure is summarized by the acronym "**POPE**" — **P**ray, **O**rganize, **P**lan and **E**xpose. The following paragraphs describe these steps in detail.

The First Step: *Pray.*

General Intentions. If you feel called to fight Catholics for a Free Choice and other dissenters, you must first of all *pray.*

Every true Catholic must *pray for Holy Mother Church* and Her faithful priests and religious. The battle between the Culture of Life and the Culture of Death is like an iceberg; the part of the struggle that is visible to us is only a small portion of the conflict. The vast majority takes place in the invisible supernatural sphere. Prayer for the general intentions of the Church and the Holy Father is essential to the success of our temporal efforts, and prayer for specific intentions regarding the defense of the Faith is also most efficacious.

In particular, we should remember that the most powerful enemy of Satan and his minions is the Mother of God, Mary Most Holy. Our prayers to Mary, particularly on behalf of Pope John Paul II, who has such devotion to her, will not go unanswered.

Keep in mind that the holy sacrifice of the Mass is the most powerful prayer of all. If you can, try to attend at least one weekday Mass a week, and offer intentions for the conversion of specific dissenters.

Specific Intentions. Eventually you must determine your specific role in fighting dissent. Ask God for guidance, and ask Him to make your course of action perfectly clear. Listen to what He has to say with a willing heart and an open mind. If He has a mission for you, He will make it clear to you. But you have to faithfully listen in order to hear.

You must recognize that you will be facing an implacable opponent that represents a direct and immediate threat to the Catholic Faith. This opponent, knowingly or unknowingly inspired and directed by Satan, naturally uses all of his tools, including lies, deception, and the most vicious of personal attacks.

If you become effective at fighting dissent — and you must *set out* to become effective — the dissenters will relentlessly attack you, both directly and indirectly. You must assess your own personal situation, and that of your family, and insure that both can hold up under the additional stress you will inevitably have to endure.

Keep in mind that this is no abstract or hypothetical war. *Every* Catholic is called to defend the Faith. Throughout the ages, the Catholic Church has been in continuous danger because She has been under constant attack by the Devil, who roams throughout the world seeking the ruin of souls [1 Peter 5:8-9]. As terrible as attacks from the outside can be, they pale in comparison to attacks from *within* by people who represent themselves as Catholics while actively undermining the Faith.

We must stress that many souls are at stake. Those who believe the dissenters are being deceived by Satan; those who hold fast to the Truth will be saved. When you fight error and heresy, you are contributing *directly* to the salvation of souls and following in the footsteps of a long line of Saints who have done exactly the same thing.

Remember that fighting for the Faith requires sacrifice. It can be a difficult and even dangerous task at times. You *will* be reviled and mocked; you *will* feel alone and abandoned; and you *will* feel like giving up and quitting the field of battle at times.

But if you endure, Our Lord will reward you richly with something that all human beings long for: Perfect peace and joy, the likes of which you can find no place else on earth! You will be able to confidently proclaim with Saint Paul: "I am filled with comfort. With all our affliction, I am overjoyed" [2 Corinthians 7:4].

No reward could possibly be greater.

Pray for the Dissenters. While we recognize that Satan might be influencing the dissenters, we must also remember that most of them might be sincere individuals who have been deceived by others, so that it is quite possible that they are not conscious of the fact that there is a diabolical influence at work upon them. Very few dissenters are deliberately malicious. Instead, they sincerely believe they are working for the liberation of people they believe are oppressed.

Some dissenters have suffered much in their lives, causing them to misdirect their rage against the Church. They may have suffered harsh treatment at the hands of members of the Church leadership or family members. Some may even have been victims of bigotry or domestic violence. Many women have had their husbands abandon them. Others have been wounded by the abortion industry, which is geared to protect the (usually male) abortionists, not the women, as proven by its fanatical resistance to regulation by any official body whatsoever. It also completely denies the existence of post-abortion syndrome or any suffering after abortion, thus abandoning women to their fate.

When people have been hurt, they tend to band together and take action against a common `enemy.' In this case, their foe is the Catholic Church, which they perceive as sexist and repressive. They do not see that their pain and suffering has been inflicted by the world and their own bad decisions. All they see is the Church, and they believe the Church is condemning them along with their actions.

While you diligently work against their plans, pray for the dissenters with equal fervor. Of all the people on earth, those who have heard the Truth and have rejected it need prayers most of all. Pray for conversion and healing in the hearts of the dissenters. Pray that they will find peace in Jesus Christ. Pray that they will return to the Sacraments and once again become faithful sons and daughters of the Catholic Church. Pray that *you* will never lose *your* Faith.

The Second Step: *Organize.*

One Voice is Powerless. Seasoned campaigner Edmund Burke once said that "When bad men combine, the good must associate [with each other]; else they will fall one by one, an unpitied sacrifice in a contemptible struggle."

Never has this been so true as in the struggle for the heart of the Roman Catholic Church in America. A single person who raises his or her voice in opposition to heresy, schism and apostasy will quickly be crushed under a tidal wave of ridicule, condemnation and vituperation; but a *dozen* well-organized true Catholics or, better yet, a *hundred* with truth on their side will be an obstacle that even a permissive diocesan hierarchy will be unable to ignore or overcome.

If you have organized dissent in your parish or diocese, you have a problem that is endangering souls. You absolutely must *organize* as quickly as you possibly can.

A bishop, parish priest, director of religious education (DRE) or Catholic school principal will probably not listen to one or two people complaining about dissent or false teachings; but if a dozen or two dozen determined Catholics begin to raise their voices as one and promise to take concrete action, they *will* listen.

You cannot do anything by yourself; so immediately start to ask your orthodox Catholic friends (you know who they are) to get involved. Make up a list of names and a telephone or computer e-mail tree.

Many Voices Acting Together Are Powerful. Don't worry about sheer numbers; the Lord will raise up exactly enough missionaries to do His work effectively. If you have only three friends who feel as strongly you do, surely they will know others. See if you can get a dozen together. Fifty, of course, would be even better.

It is also essential to have a good spiritual director who will guide your steps and give you the "inside information" on the diocese you will need to operate effectively. You know who he is: The faithful priest who has spoken up fearlessly for truth many times and who is an object of ridicule and contempt to quite a number of the laity and his brother priests.

He is the one you need.

Getting Started. Regular meetings are essential, especially in the beginning of any group's existence. Remember three tactical principles as you get started;

*   **Anonymity.** Don't give the opposition an easy target to attack. The minute the dissenters learn the name of your group, they will undertake a systematic campaign of slander and ridicule at the local level which is designed to undermine your effectiveness and your credibility.

This is standard operating procedure (SOP) for social liberal and dissenting groups, and it is a very effective tactic. It does not matter that they know nothing about your group beyond your name; suddenly local clergy and Church lay leaders will hear that you are "fanatics," "anti-woman," "extremist" and "divisive."

You can take measures to blunt or completely avoid this kind of crippling attack.

We must use prudence and discretion when engaged in fighting dissent, because in some situations and some places it is impossible to know who to trust completely. Dissent busters must be very selective when disclosing information, especially in the early stages of the existence of a group or of the development of a plan. Remember that dissenters are expert at infiltration and propaganda; never do or say anything they can legitimately use against you.

* **Security.** Keep your plans confidential for as long as you possibly can. Operate strictly under a "need to know" principle — only inform the minimum number of people required to plan your activities effectively. This will allow you to avoid attacks by the dissenters and will give you the element of surprise, which is a decisive advantage. Your objective is to achieve a stunning victory on your first try. This will boost the *esprit de corps* of your people and demoralize the dissenters.

* **Information.** You should begin gathering information on the dissenters as soon as you possibly can. In a group of a dozen or more people, there are generally one or two who enjoy doing research and investigation.

    The information you should look for includes;

* the dissenter's viewpoints and attitudes, the way they think, and their psychology. When dissent busters understand their opposition, they can accurately project what they will do in the future and how they will react to their initiatives.

* The dissenter's level of morale and their opinions on what directions the Catholic Church is taking.

* Concrete and specific information about dissenting organizations, to include how many people they have, what resources they have, where their money comes from, and who backs them. This is especially important if you are facing a local affiliate of a national group like CFFC.

* The dissenter's long-range plans (strategies) and short-term plans (tactics).

When you are gathering and processing your information, remember the four "X"s:

(1) *Explore:* Take some time right "up front" to research the most likely sources of relevant information so that you will use your time in the most efficient manner. These include the dissenter's Web sites and newsletters.

If they have a local chapter, have one of your people join it and gather information. This is absolutely the best way to keep an eye on the dissenters. But be careful that you remain in the background and do not contribute economically to them or make statements contrary to Faith or morals. Your job is strictly to *observe*, not to contribute to the ruin of souls.

(2) *Examine:* Carefully scrutinize the information you gather and rank it according to relevancy and usefulness. Should you take the time to process and use it right away, or should you file it for future use?

(3) *Explain:* Compile the information you have gathered from various sources into a single readily understandable and handy document that is clear and pertinent to the situation. *Be very careful to document everything you publicly write or say about the dissenters, or you may expose yourself and your organization to costly and distracting litigation.*

(4) *Exchange:* Give your processed information to whatever groups or individuals will find it most useful, both at the local and national levels.

You do not have to learn all of this information by researching it yourself. There are several nationally-based dissent-fighting groups that can give you information and expertise. These include;

HUMAN LIFE INTERNATIONAL™
4 FAMILY LIFE, FRONT ROYAL, VA 22630
TELEPHONE: (540) 635-7884
WEB SITE: HTTP://WWW.HLI.ORG/

HLI has hundreds of extreme quotes by leaders of Catholics for a Free Choice on its Web site, under the "Anti-Life Quote Archive."

———————

Vida Humana Internacional (*VHI*)
45 Southwest 71st Avenue
Miami, Florida 33144
Telephone: (305) 260-0525, FAX (305) 260-0595
Web site: http://www.vidahumana.org/

VHI is the Hispanic Division of Human Life International, and possesses an unparalleled collection of materials in Spanish for defending life, Faith and family. VHI has information on Catholics for a Free Choice on its Web site.

_____

Catholics United for the Faith (CUF)
827 North Fourth Street, Steubenville, Ohio 43952
Telephone: (614) 283-2484 or 1-800-693-2484
Web site: http://www.cuf.org/

_____

Roman Catholic Faithful, Inc. (RCF)
President: Steven Brady
Post Office Box 109, Petersburg, Illinois 62675
Telephone: (217) 632-5920, FAX: (217) 632-7054
Web site: http://www.rcf.org

_____

Adoremus Society for the Renewal of the Sacred Liturgy
Post Office Box 3286, St. Louis, Missouri 63130
Telephone: (314) 863-8385, FAX: (314) 863-5858
Web site: http://adoremus.org
Newsletter: *Adoremus Bulletin.*

_____

Keep the Faith
810 Belmont Avenue, Post Office Box 8261
North Haledon, New Jersey 07508
Telephone: (201) 423-5395

_____

St. Joseph Foundation
11107 Wurzbach, No. 601B, San Antonio, Texas 78230-2570
Telephone: (210) 697-0717
Web site: http://www.st-joseph-foundation.org
Newsletter: *Christifidelis*

The St. Joseph Foundation provides assistance to orthodox Catholics whose rights have been violated by dissenting groups or their pastors or bishops.

_____

Please keep these organizations in your prayers, because they are on the front lines of defending the Faith.

Beginning Your Field Work. After you have gathered a group of committed people and have organized them properly, your *real* work begins. Every member of your group must educate themselves regarding the field of battle and the dissenters.

You must learn the following things;

(A)   Background on the dissenting groups that are causing trouble in your diocese or parish. How do they operate? Who funds them? What are their standard operating procedure (SOPs)?

(B)   You must also educate yourself regarding the standard propaganda that the dissenting groups use. There is nothing more effective, powerful and inspiring than having a faithful Catholic stand up and debunk the lies of the dissenters on the spot, in front of a crowd of people. However, you cannot do this until you know *exactly* what the dissenters are going to say, and until you study the many weak points in their arguments.

Fortunately, dissenters tend to be notoriously unoriginal and inflexible thinkers. They repeat the same falsehoods and distortions over and over again, and become confused and flustered when confronted with a knowledgeable opponent.

Part 2 of this book answers in detail the twelve arguments Catholics for a Free Choice uses most frequently to deceive the faithful. It will probably take you several hours to learn this material, but it will be time well spent. Not only will this knowledge permit you to defend the Faith against Her enemies, but it will strengthen *your* resolve and embolden you to do more for the Church as well.

It will be easier for you to learn this material with others in your group. Get together a couple of times and practice rebutting CFFC's arguments with each other. Practice builds confidence and boldness.

If you would like to write about CFFC, or do more in-depth research on it, visit HLI's "Anti-Life Quote Archive" at http://www.hli.org. It contains several hundred quotes by CFFC by category, to include pro-abortion quotes, anti-religious quotes, and bigoted quotes.

The Third Step: *Plan.*

Take Advantage of the Experience of Others. When you have a number of people willing to help you, meet with them as soon as possible and decide exactly what your mission is, and how you intend to accomplish it.

Whatever course of action you take, it is often very helpful to have an experienced dissent-buster speak to your group in order to train it in strategy and tactics. If you do not have outside expertise, you are much more likely to fail in your mission, because the struggle between truth and dissent at the diocesan or parish level is fraught with pitfalls and concealed obstacles. You may even be able to bring in several speakers and hold a mini-conference open to the public, which would be a great recruiting tool. After the conference, you could have the speakers instruct the leaders of your group during a confidential session in the art of thwarting dissent.

It is also absolutely necessary that you have an orthodox priest as your spiritual advisor. When you finish your preparation phase and step out to fight the dissenters, you will encounter spiritual obstacles you never dreamed existed. A good priest can help you get through these difficult times and can help you prepare yourself for the abuse and ridicule you are likely to suffer. He can help you avoid the bitter and complaining nature that some orthodox Catholics fall prey to, and can instead help you become an optimistic and effective fighter for the Faith. Additionally, the priest can give you insight as to diocesan and parish politics when you need such information.

The Mission Planning Statement. You can maximize your chances of success by writing a mission planning statement and sticking with it. This statement is a summary of the following six elements.

(1)   **The Mission.** What *exactly* do you want to accomplish? How will you know if you were successful in your mission? The dissenters work by stealth and infiltration, so your primary objective is to raise their profile by exposing them and showing to the world what they really believe. The primary rule is: **Do not bite off more than you can chew!** Begin small and work your way up from there, giving your people experience and confidence in their dissent-busting activities.

(2)   **The Focus.** Who are you trying to influence? Select your focus and tailor your plans accordingly. Are you trying to influence your bishop to take action against a conference featuring dissenting speakers, or are you trying to focus your efforts on a DRE [director of religious education] who refuses to remove a scandalous sex education program from your Catholic school?

(3) **The Opposition.** Who are the persons and organizations that will directly or indirectly try to stop you from accomplishing your mission, and what are the strategies and tactics they commonly employ? If you know this information, you can better prepare yourselves to blunt the reaction of the dissenters to your initiatives.

(4) **Resources.** What qualities, persons, and equipment will you need to accomplish your mission? If you are missing some thing vital, can you obtain it? Make certain you have budgets for tangible resources that you follow closely during the execution of your mission.

(5) **The Environment.** What are the physical and psychological conditions under which you must work to accomplish your mission? Are your people ready to operate in this environment?

(6) **Tactics.** What concrete methods will you employ to accomplish your mission or prevent the dissenters from accomplishing *their* objectives?

***Really* Learn Your Faith!** Do you know how to confidently and accurately answer a dissenter who claims that "we can use birth control now, because the Vatican said that we can use our consciences in the *Declaration on Religious Freedom*?"

Can you clearly explain the Church's "double effect" principle as it applies to abortion for the mother's life and to sterilization?

Can you convincingly demonstrate *why* the Church cannot ordain women to the ministerial priesthood?

If you can do all three of these, congratulations — you are among the select group of only about *one percent* of Catholic lay people who can do so.

These are the issues you *will* encounter when you fight dissent on any level. You will not just hear them from professional dissenters and agitators; you will also hear them from friends, family members, fellow parishioners, and even uninformed priests.

Learning how to defend the Faith is a difficult process, but is mandatory if you are to be effective. The best way to do this is to study the *Catechism of the Catholic Church* in detail, with the same level of attention as you would give a college course. It is best to study by yourself and then meet on a weekly basis for a couple of hours with the other members of your dissent-busting group to strategize and discuss difficult concepts and how to explain them clearly.

This process may take a year or more, but it will transform you into a much more effective soldier for Christ.

Learn the Battlefield! You cannot be effective unless you know the topography of the battlefield. Educate yourself about the Church's situation. You can do this by reading good books on the history of dissent, learning about its origins, history and current forms. Then you can become familiar with the current situation in the Church by subscribing to one or more of the journals which are dedicated to fighting dissent and promoting the truth. The idea behind all this reading is to familiarize yourself with both the theory behind dissent and current news and trends in the Church.

The best place to go for accurate information on Church teachings is, of course, the Church. Documents that explain Catholic doctrine regarding the life issues include;

• "Declaration on Procured Abortion." Sacred Congregation for the Doctrine of the Faith, November 18, 1974. This is the most succinct and authoritative expression of the Catholic Church's position on abortion, and is written to be easily understandable. Paragraphs 6 and 7 include an especially useful summary of Church history on abortion. The Declaration is available as a compact 4" X 6" 27 page booklet from the Daughters of St. Paul, 50 St. Paul's Avenue, Jamaica Plain, Massachusetts, 02130. The complete text of the Declaration is also available on the World Wide Web at: http://www.priestsforlife.org/magisterium/quaestiodeabortu.htm.

• *Donum Veritas* ["Instruction on the Ecclesial Vocation of the Theologian"]. Sacred Congregation for the Doctrine of the Faith, May 24, 1990. This excellent and concise document explores the proper role of the theologian in the Catholic Church, pointing out that his function is not to lead, but to explore and advise. The document also shows how a person with a genuine difficulty with a Church teaching may resolve it. The complete text of this document is available on the World Wide Web at: http://www.ewtn.com/library/CURIA/CDFTHEO.HTM.

• *Humanae Vitae* ("Human Life: On the Regulation of Birth"). Pope Paul VI's historic Encyclical Letter dated July 25, 1968. This letter may be obtained in booklet form from the Daughters of St. Paul, 50 St. Paul Avenue, Boston, Massachusetts 02130, telephone: (617) 522-8911. The complete text of *Humanae Vitae* is also available on the World Wide Web at : http://www.priestsforlife.org/magisterium/humanaevitae.htm.

• *Pascendi Dominici Gregis* ("On the Doctrine of the Modernists"). Pope St. Pius X's encyclical of September 8, 1907. Though nearly a century old, this timeless encyclical reads as if it were written yesterday. Pope St. Pius X explores the roots and methods of Modernism, delves into the sources of human error, and explains how to combat heresy and dissent at every level. The complete text of *Pascendi* is available on the World Wide Web at http://listserv.american.edu/catholic/church/papal/pius.x/pascendi.html.

• Most Reverend Rene H. Gracida, D.D., Bishop of Corpus Christi. Pastoral Letter on Abortion and Excommunication, "Choose Life, Not Death!" September 8, 1990. See especially Appendix A, "An Historical Review of Law Relating to Abortion." The complete text of this Pastoral Letter is available on the World Wide Web at http://www.priestsforlife.org/magisterium/gracida.htm.

• Theological Observations by Archbishop Tarcisio Bertone, S.D.B., Archbishop Emeritus of Vercelli and Secretary of the Congregation for the Doctrine of the Faith. "Magisterial Documents and Public Dissent." July 1998. The complete text of this document is available on the World Wide Web at: http://www.ewtn.com/library/CURIA/MDPD.HTM.

• Sacred Congregation for the Doctrine of the Faith. "Concluding Formula of the *Professio Fidei.*" June 29, 1998. This document clearly explains the various grades of Church teachings and the degree of assent every Catholic is obligated to show them. This commentary was issued coincident with the promulgation of Pope John Paul II's *Ad Tuendam Fidem*, which modified the Oriental and Latin Codes of canon law. The complete text of this document is available on the World Wide Web at http://www.ewtn.com/library/CURIA/CDFADTU.HTM.

• Sacred Congregation for the Doctrine of the Faith. "Regulations for

Doctrinal Examination" (New Vatican Norms on Theological Dissent), June 29, 1997. The complete text of this document is available on the World Wide Web at :

http://www.vatican.va/roman_curia/congregations/cfaith/documents/rc_con_cfaith_doc_19970629_ratio-agendi_en.htm.

There are literally hundreds of magazines and journals devoted to fighting abortion, euthanasia, the homosexual rights movement, pornography, population control and other evils. When fighting dissent, you should instead subscribe to orthodox journals and magazines that specialize in this area or at least address it on a regular basis. These include;

The Catholic Answer
Our Sunday Visitor, Inc., 200 Noll Plaza, Huntington, Indiana 46750
Telephone: (210) 356-8400
Issued bimonthly; $18 annually.

Catholic World Report
Post Office Box 591300
San Francisco, California 94159-1300
Telephone: 1-800-651-1531
11 issues per year; $39.95 annually.
In-depth reporting on specific attacks on the Faith around the world.

Crisis: Politics, Culture & the Church
Post Office Box 10559, Riverton, New Jersey 08076-0559
Telephone: 1-800-852-9962, e-mail: crisis@catholic.net
11 issues per year; $29.95 annually.
 A mixture of short articles and current news and trends in the Church.

Envoy: Catholic Apologetics & Evangelization
Subscription Department, New Hope, Kentucky 40052-9989
Telephone: 1-800-553-6869, web site: http://www.envoymagazine.com
11 issues per year; $28.99 annually.

Fellowship of Catholic Scholars Quarterly
Box 495, Notre Dame, Indiana 46556

First Things: A Monthly Journal of Religion and Public Life
Post Office Box 3000, Department FT, Denville, New Jersey 07834
Telephone: 1-800-783-4903
10 issues per year; $29 annually.

Several long articles and book reviews in each issue, along with Father Neuhaus' observations on religion and public life. Past issues are available on *First Thing's* Web site at http://www.firstthings.com.

HLI Reports Magazine
Human Life International, 4 Family Life, Front Royal, Virginia 22630
Telephone: (540) 635-7884, FAX (540) 636-7363, web site: http://www.hli.org/
Issued monthly; $37 annually.

Homiletic and Pastoral Review
Ignatius Press, 2515 McAllister Street, San Francisco, California 94118
Telephone: 1-800-651-1531
11 issues per year; $24 annually.
Past issues are available on *HPR*'s Web site at :
http://www.catholic.net/RCC/Periodicals/Homiletic/index2.html.

Human Life Review
Editorial Office, 215 Lexington Avenue, 4th Floor, New York City, New York 10016
Issued quarterly; $20 annually.

A fine scholarly journal, with several long articles each issue by leading orthodox Catholic scholars.

Inside the Vatican
St. Martin de Porres Lay Dominican Community, New Hope, Kentucky 40052-9989
Telephone: 1-800-789-9494, FAX (502) 325-3091
Issued monthly; $49.95 annually.

National Catholic Register
Post Office Box 5158, Hamden, Connecticut 06518-5158
Telephone: 1-800-421-3230,   FAX: (203)   288-5157,   e-mail:

cmedia@pipeline.com

Issued weekly; $49.95 annually.

Not to be confused with the dissenting *National Catholic Reporter*, this newspaper keeps up on current trends in the church and often features articles on dissent and dissenters.

New Oxford Review

1069 Kains Avenue, Berkeley, California 94706

Telephone: (510) 526-5374, FAX (510) 526-3492

Issued 10 times per year; $19 annually.

Sursum Corda!

Foundation for Catholic Reform

Subscription Department, 1331 Red Cedar Circle, Fort Collins, Colorado 80524

Telephone: (970) 483-8781

Issued quarterly; $26.95 annually

Family-oriented magazine with short articles and current news in the Church.

This Rock

Post Office Box 17490, San Diego, California 92177

Telephone: 1-888-291-8000, FAX (619) 541-1154

Web site: http://catholic.com/rock/thisrock.htm

Issued monthly; $29.95 annually

Voices, Voices, Voices

Women for Faith and Family, Post Office Box 8326, St. Louis, Missouri 63132

Telephone: (314) 863-8385, FAX: (314) 863-5858, e-mail: 72223.3601@compuserve.com

---

The Wanderer

201 Ohio Street, St. Paul, Minnesota 55107

Telephone: (612) 224-5733.

Weekly; $40.00 annually.

This weekly newspaper is the best available source for specific and very timely information on dissent in the American Catholic Church. *The Wanderer* is not afraid to name names!

Orthodox books that examine the subject of dissent in detail include the following. You may be able to find these in your local public or diocesan libraries, but don't count on it. Your dissent-busting organization may wish to purchase these books and pass them around among its members. In order to keep up with the latest offerings, make sure that you subscribe to catalogs from orthodox book publishing companies such as;

- **Keep the Faith**, 810 Belmont Avenue, Post Office Box 8261, North Haledon, New Jersey 07508, telephone: (201) 423-5395.
- **Ignatius Press**, Post Office Box 1339, Fort Collins, Colorado 80522, telephone: 1-800-651-1531.
- **Neumann Press**, Route 2, Box 30, Long Prairie, Minnesota 56347, telephone: (320) 732-6358.
- **Our Blessed Lady of Victory Mission**, Rural Route 2, Box 25, Brookings, South Dakota 57006-9307, telephone: (605) 693-3983.
- **Our Lady's Book Service**, Servants of Jesus and Mary, Post Office Box 93, Constable, New York 12926, telephone: 1-800-263-8160.
- **Roman Catholic Books**, Post Office Box 2286, Fort Collins, Colorado 80522-2286.
- **Sophia Institute Press**, Box 5284, Manchester, New Hampshire 03108, telephone: 1-800-888-9344.
- **Tan Books and Publishers**, Post Office Box 424, Rockford, Illinois 61105, telephone: 1-800-437-5876.

Some of the most detailed books written by orthodox authors on the dissent movement include;

- Donald DeMarco, Ph.D. *In My Mother's Womb: The Church's Defense of Natural Life*. An eloquent defense of the Catholic Church's defense of human life. An examination of abortion's terminology and perspectives, the preborn, contraception and bio-engineering. DeMarco also covers the Church's perspective on new technologies, including *in-vitro* fertilization, surrogate motherhood, fetal experimentation, and genetic engineering. See especially Chapter 1, "Abortion and Church Teaching," pages 7 to 25.
- Father John Ford, Germain Grisez, Joseph Boyle, John Finnis, and William E. May. *The Teaching of Humanae Vitae: A Defense*. Five of the

most respected theologians in the world explain why *Humanae Vitae* is the inevitable product of Catholic moral principles. The writers show that the Encyclical is valid and universally applicable to all Christians, and that it also fulfills the requirements of infallibility under Vatican II's *Lumen Gentium*.

• Human Life International. *Call to Action or Call to Apostasy?: How Dissenters Plan to Remake the Catholic Church in Their Own Image.* A detailed description of exactly how Call to Action (CTA) and other dissenting organizations plan to undermine Church teachings and authority by attacking Her four marks: One, holy, catholic and apostolic. Order from Human Life International, 4 Family Life, Front Royal, VA 22630, telephone: 1-(800) 549-LIFE.

• Monsignor George A. Kelly. *Keeping the Church Catholic with John Paul II*. Order from Ignatius Press. Interesting background and history of the Church mechanism for decisionmaking, and detailed information on dissent and the battle for the soul of the Church, particularly with regards to contraception and obedience to the Pope.

• Father Vincent P. Miceli. *Women Priests and Other Fantasies*. Order from Keep the Faith, address given above. The author examines the pandemonium that results in the Christian Church (particularly the Catholic Church) when the senses of the sacred and supernatural are lost. The instant that Holy Scripture is judged by secular standards, the message of Christianity is hopelessly compromised and lost.

• William Oddie. *What Will Happen to God?: Feminism and the Reconstruction of Christian Belief.* Order from Ignatius Press. The Neofeminists are striving to eliminate from all church documents and prayers what they consider to be "sexist" language. Oddie exposes the fallacies of this goal, and shows what will happen if we allow radical feminism to continue to dictate to the Church. The elimination of so-called "sexist" language is only the beginning!

• Donna Steichen. *Ungodly Rage: The Hidden Face of Catholic Feminism*. San Francisco: Ignatius Press. 1992, 420 pages. A very detailed and absorbing account of how the Roman Catholic Church in the United States has been infiltrated and subverted by radical feminists and dissenters for the express purpose of blunting its effectiveness in its reaction to evils such as divorce, abortion, and euthanasia. This book has much detailed information on many dissenters and dissenting organizations, with an emphasis on feminist and "New Age" groups.

175

- Hans Urs von Balthasar, Joseph Cardinal Ratzinger, Walter Kasper, *et.al. The Church and Women: A Compendium*. Order from Ignatius Press. A collection of articles by leading Church scholars on the role of women in the Catholic Church today and contemporary issues regarding feminism, including the ordination of women and the role and importance of the family. The role of women is developed in a context faithful to Scripture, tradition, and the Magisterium of the Church.

- Dietrich von Hildebrand. *The Devastated Vineyard*. Order from Sophia Press. The author describes in harrowing detail the destruction of the Roman Catholic Church in America and in Europe, and the methods of infiltration and subversion now being used to confuse and paralyze all orthodox Christian churches in our country today. Order from Keep the Faith, 810 Belmont Avenue, Post Office Box 8261, North Haledon, New Jersey 07508, telephone: (201) 423-5395.

The Final Step: Expose Them.

Introduction. Take confidence in the fact that the one thing the dissenters cannot *stand* is opposition. Lies only flourish when a shroud of darkness and secrecy surround them; they will wither up and die when you shine the powerful light of truth on them.

Remember that dissenters work by the principle of *infiltration and subversion*, which requires secrecy. Remove the secrecy and they cannot function.

The Gospel of John tells us

> And this is the judgment, that the light has come into the world, and men loved darkness rather than light, because their deeds were evil. For every one who does evil hates the light, and does not come to the light, lest his deeds should be exposed. But he who does what is true comes to the light, that it may be clearly seen that his deeds have been wrought in God [John 3:19-21].

Dissenters speak endlessly about tolerance and inclusiveness, but you will soon learn that they ardently desire to stamp out any viewpoint but their own. They know that they can only hoodwink people if alternative voices cannot be heard.

Take Two Simultaneous Courses of Action. When countering dissenters, you should initiate two concurrent courses of action: (1) attempt to influence the responsible decisionmakers before the event in question, and (2) plan to be at the event to influence the public and the dissenters themselves.

The first course of action involves identifying the decisionmaker(s) who are responsible for inviting the dissenters into their diocese, parish, school, university, order, or other Catholic organization. Contact these people by letter and provide them with solid evidence that the specific dissenting groups and/or individuals depart radically from approved Church teaching on various issues. Ask for a meeting so that you can discuss what positive alternatives can be taken at this point.

It is human nature for people *not* to admit their mistakes, reverse their decisions or modify their plans, so expect indifference or active resistance. Most commonly, the decisionmaker(s) will simply not respond to your requests for a meeting, and will try to "run out the clock," doing nothing so that the event featuring the dissenters goes on exactly as planned.

If the decisionmaker stonewalls you, do not simply give up. Continue to try to contact him or her, and keep a record of your attempts. If it becomes obvious that the decisionmaker is not interested in talking to you, do not waste any time. Approach the authority at the next higher level, which is usually your local ordinary, or bishop, and repeat the process.

If your bishop refuses to listen to you, continue up the "chain of command." Contact the Apostolic Nuncio. By this time, the event in question may have already occurred, but don't give up. It is vital that the Nuncio and the Vatican be informed of what is happening, so that they have the information and documentation they need in order to take action later.

The second course of action involves being at the event in question and attempting to influence the public and the dissenters themselves. As Americans and Catholics, you have certain rights. Do not be afraid to exercise them, regardless of how loudly the dissenters complain or condemn you.

Your objectives are to present authentic Catholic teaching on the issues and to derail the dissenter's plans to present themselves as the "mainstream," which is one of their primary deceptive tactics. At the dissenter's event, you can use certain tactics to get your message across;

*   Picket the building where the event is taking place, whether it is a church, school building, or other public arena. Check beforehand to

make sure that you know where you may and may not picket. Even if you are standing on public property, the dissenters will use every trick in the book to get you to move as far away as possible. Don't budge! Know exactly what your limits are.

* Leaflet the building where the event is taking place. Use documentation you obtain from the dissenting groups themselves, or from a dissent-busting group, to draw up a leaflet that features extreme quotes from their leaders and extracts from their manifestos showing how anti-Catholic their beliefs really are. Human Life International's Web site at http://www/hli.org features an "Anti-Life Quote Archive" that lists hundreds of quotes by leaders of Catholics for a Free Choice and other dissenting groups. You can also pass out copies of HLI's sixteen-page pamphlet entitled "How 'Catholics' for a Free Choice Distorts Catholic Teaching on Abortion," described above.

* Stand up during the question and answer period (if there is one), ask pointed questions and quote authentic Catholic teachings. Do not let them waffle or dodge your questions. Keep after them! If they refuse to answer or try to evade your questions, they will look deceitful and misleading.

* Once again, document everything. When confronted, many dissenters become outraged and will slander and libel you and your organization. This is fertile ground for legal action against the dissenter and his or her organization. There is no better way to divert the attention of dissenting groups and use up their resources than through litigation. Pro-lifers have suffered at the hands of lawsuit-happy pro-abortionists for years, so let's turn the tables!

The objective of this second course of action is not pure confrontation, but to demonstrate that the dissenters are distorting authentic Catholic teaching. Once again, your objective is to save souls and preach the truth in charity and love.

If, as a side effect, lots of publicity is generated by the conflict, the dissenters will probably not be invited back. All the better!

Summary. The general idea is to operate in *two* ways simultaneously; within the "system," documenting and watching and gathering information; and, since this might take months or even years, *outside* the "system" with leafletting, preaching and publicity.

The wellspring of hope is entrusting the outcome of your efforts to God. You should never feel depressed or despairing when fighting for the Faith and for souls, which is truly the most important work on earth.

Taking action will remove your feeling of helplessness and will heighten your fervor once again. Your watchwords should be vigilance, endurance and courage. No dissenter can beat this combination.

Concluding Notes.

Maintain the Right Attitude. As a dissent-buster, there are several things you must be.

You must be immune to discouragement. The dissenters exist because they cause concern among Catholics by constantly exaggerating the problems in the Church. Remember that their primary objective is the deconstruction and recon-struction of the Church to fit their own false ideology, and that things are nowhere near as bad as they say. Also keep in mind that there is an ongoing revival in the Catholic Church today, and *you* can be a vital part of it. Above all, remember 1 Corinthians 15:58: "Therefore, my beloved brethren, be steadfast, immovable, always abounding in the work of the Lord, knowing that in the Lord your labor is not in vain."

You must be eternally watchful. Examine the catechetics and sex education programs in your Catholic schools, keeping in mind that any program, no matter how orthodox, can be changed on the spot by Modernist teachers with an agen-da. The only way to ensure that your children are raised chaste and faithful is to teach them yourself at home — something that half a million families are doing in the United States today.

Don't be lulled into complacency by the fact that most dissenters are over 50 years of age, and that they are obviously not doing a good job of recruiting from the young. Keep in mind that these are the people who are still infected with the iconoclastic mood of the 1960s and therefore continue in their activism. Modernism and indifferentism are not high ideals that young people want to fight for, and so they are not replenishing the ranks of dissenting groups. Instead many youth simply live lazy, spiritless lives, which is just as dangerous to their Faith as outright dissent.

You should also keep an eye on the literature rack in your church. Dissenting groups often manage to establish a "beachhead" there, because the pastor does-n't have time to read everything that goes in the rack. Read the literature yourself, and if it contains dissent, show your pastor the problems in doctrine or dogma and ask him to remove the material. If he refuses, ask him in the name of "diversity" to include authentic Catholic literature. If he denies *this* request, you will know that you have a close-minded pastor, and you may have to take measures such as leafletting the church.

Finally, **you must be prepared to go for the long haul.** Many chanceries are infested with dissenters who have held their positions for many years and may seem to be almost unassailable because of their many connections and because their bishop may be afraid to take them on. You should accumulate information on these people and let them know that you are carefully watching them. This alone will usually make them less brazen in their dissent. Above all, remember that if you watch enough, document enough, agitate enough and pray enough, the toughest and most entrenched dissenter will eventually give up.

If you have a particular complaint that receives a negative response or no response from your pastor or bishop, you may want to take the matter up with higher authority. There is a specific procedure you must follow if you want to be certain that your protest will be properly attended to at higher levels. You can get this procedure, entitled "Effective Lay Witness Protocol," from Catholics United for the Faith, 827 North Fourth Street, Steubenville, Ohio 43952, telephone: (614) 283-2484 or 1-800-693-2484.

Think Papally, Act Locally. A soldier would never be sent into an armed conflict without intense and appropriate training.

Your work is infinitely more important than that of even the highest ranking general. You will be ready to step onto the battlefield only after you have established a firm foundation of prayer, organized with other orthodox Catholics, and learned your Faith and the tactics of the dissenters. It may take you a year or more of preparation before you are ready to act; but do not become discouraged. The better prepared you are, the more effective you will be as a soldier in the eternal struggle between the Culture of Life and the Culture of Death. Your spiritual advisor and seasoned dissent-busters will be able to help you determine when you are ready to engage in battle against the Modernists.

Appendix

Foundation Funding of Catholics for a Free Choice

Abbreviations

CDD: *Católicas por el Derecho a Decidir* [Catholics for the Right to Decide, or Catholics for a Free Choice in Latin America]

FGI: *Foundation Grants Index*, published by The Foundation Center, 79 Fifth Avenue, New York, New York 10003-3076, telephone (212) 620-4230.

FGIQ: *Foundation Grants Index Quarterly*, published by The Foundation Center.

TFR: *Taft Foundation Reporter*, Taft Group, 12300 Twinbrook Parkway, Rockville, MD 20852; telephone: (301) 816-0210.

NOTE: Foundations often support multiple projects for a particular group in one year. Therefore, this list may show more than one grant for each foundation in a specific calendar year.

Mary Reynolds Babcock Foundation
102 Reynolds Village
Winston-Salem, North Carolina 27106-5123
Telephone: (910) 748-9222
Web address: http://www.mrbf.org/
Assets: $117,939,218 (December 31, 1999)

* **1992:** $20,000 "for "New Approaches Project: Reaching Out to the Uncommitted Middle"" [*FGI*, 1995, page 214].

* **1983:** $20,000 to CFFC Public Information Program "for 2nd year of funding to distribute press kits and participate in media interviews, provide technical assistance to other Catholic organizations wishing to discuss abortion, and conduct a direct-mail campaign to acquaint Catholic activists with pro-choice position and need for addressing the issue" [*FGI*, 1985, page 442].

* **1981:** $20,000 to CFFC Media Program "for campaign to educate public on Catholic position favorable to responsible family planning, contraception, and abortion" [*FGI*, 1983, page 343].

Total donations to Catholics for a Free Choice by the Mary Reynolds Babcock Foundation: $60,000.

Brush Foundation
3135 Euclid Avenue, Suite 102
Cleveland, Ohio 44115
Telephone: (216) 881-5121
Note: The mission statement of the Brush Foundation is "To ensure that family planning is acceptable, available, accessible, affordable, effective and safe."

* **1999:** $37,500 [IRS form 990-PF, "Return of Private Foundation," Brush Foundation, 1998].
* **1998:** $22,500 [IRS form 990-PF, "Return of Private Foundation," Brush Foundation, 1998].
* **1991:** $20,000 [Brush Foundation *Quadrennial Report*, 1989-1992].
* **1986:** $5,000 [CFFC's 1986 Federal income tax return].
* **1983:** $30,000 [CFFC's 1983 Federal income tax return].
* **1981:** $21,103 [CFFC's 1981 Federal income tax return].
* **1980:** $28,750 [*The Brush Foundation: 1928-1980*, page 21].

Total donations to Catholics for a Free Choice by the Brush Foundation: $164,853.

Buffett Foundation
209 Kiewit Plaza
Omaha, Nebraska 68131
Assets: $57,195,568 (June 30, 2000)

* **2000:** $125,000 "for general support" [Foundation Center DIALOG search by Mr. Bruce Gumm requested by Human Life International dated September 10, 2001].
* **1999:** $125,000 "for general support" [*FGI*, 2001, page 297; *TFR*, 2002, page 132].
* **1998:** $125,000 "for general support" [*FGI*, 2000, page 285].
* **1996:** $100,000 "for general support" [*FGI*, 1998, page 227].
* **1995:** $100,000 [*TFR*, 1998, page 149].
* **1994:** $100,000 "for general support" [*FGI*, 1996, page 217].

Total donations to Catholics for a Free Choice by the Buffett Foundation: $675,000.

Cabot Family Charitable Trust
70 Federal Street
Boston, Massachusetts 02110
Telephone: (617) 451-1744
FAX: (617) 451-1733
E-mail: RCSCABOT@aol.com
Assets: $19,476,984 (December 31, 1999)

*   **1992:** $5,030 "for general support" [1992 *Annual Report* of the Cabot Family Charitable Trust].

*   **1983:** $2,500 "for general support" [1983 *Annual Report* of the Cabot Family Charitable Trust].

Total donations to Catholics for a Free Choice by the Cabot Family Charitable Trust: $7,530.

Robert Sterling Clark Foundation
135 East 64th Street
New York, New York 10021
Telephone: (212) 288-8900
Web address: http://fdncenter.org/grantmaker/rsclark/
Assets: $141,216,231 (October 31, 2000)
Note: In 2000 alone, the Robert Sterling Clark Foundation, through its "Protecting Reproductive Rights and Ensuring Access to Comprehensive Reproductive Health Information Services" program, gave $1,756,000 to the most fanatical pro-abortion groups in the United States — The Abortion Access Project, the Alan Guttmacher Institute (the research arm of the Planned Parenthood Federation of America), the American Civil Liberties Union's Reproductive Freedom Project, the Feminist Majority Foundation, the Ms. Foundation for Women, the NARAL Foundation, the National Abortion Federation, the National Family Planning and Reproductive Health Association (NFPRHA), the National Women's Law Center, the Planned Parenthood Federation of America, the Pro-Choice Public Education Project (PEP), the Pro-Choice Resource Center, the Religious Coalition for Reproductive Choice Educational Fund, the Sexuality Information and Educational Council of the United States (SIECUS), the Women's Law and Public Policy Fellowship Program, and the Women's Law Project [Robert Sterling Clark Foundation's *Annual Report 2000* at http://fdncenter.org/grantmaker/rsclark/repro.pdf].

*   **1999:** $15,000 (2 years) "for continued support of CFFC's research on the Catholic Right, mergers of Catholic and non-Catholic hospitals, and a new initiative challenging the Vatican's obstruction of the United Nation's delivery of reproductive health care internationally" [Robert Sterling Clark Foundation *Annual Report*, 1999].

*   **1998:** $75,000 "to support research on Catholic Right and mergers of Catholic and non-Catholic hospitals, and to establish coalition of progressive Catholic groups to challenge Catholic Right" [*FGI*, 2000, page 288].

*   **1997:** $65,000 "for research and monitoring of the Catholic Right and establish coalition of progressive, pro-choice Catholic groups" [*FGI*, 1999, page 251].

*   **1996:** $60,000 "for continued support for research on the Catholic Religious Right and its education and mobilization of Catholic community" [*FGI*, 1998, page 230].

*   **1994:** $50,000 "for study of Catholic health care system in U.S. and reprinting of report on conservative Catholic organizations and allied non-Catholic organizations" [*FGI*, 1996, page 838].

* **1994:** $60,000 "to expand its publication program, focusing on the activities of religious anti-abortion organizations" [*The Chronicle of Philanthropy*, June 14, 1994; *FGIQ*, September 1994, page 60].

* **1993:** $60,000 "for expansion of publication program, focusing on activities of religious anti-choice organizations" [FGI, 1995, page 204].

* **1991:** $47,000 "for research, production and dissemination of a series of fact sheets/booklets on role of Catholic Church in shaping public policy on family planning services and availability of contraception" [*FGI*, 1993, page 737].

* **1985:** $25,000 "for program to educate American Catholics about wide diversity of opinion that exists within Church on issue of reproductive freedom, and to provide Catholic citizens with rational alternative to Church doctrine" [*FGI*, 1986, page 329].

Total donations to Catholics for a Free Choice by the Robert Sterling Clark Foundation: $457,000.

Compton Foundation
545 Middlefield Road, Suite 178
Menlo Park, California 94025
Telephone: (650) 328-0101
FAX: (650) 328-0171
Web address: http://www.comptonfoundation.org
Assets: $118,001,253 (December 31, 1999)

* **2000:** $60,000 "for Catholic Voices: An International Forum" [Compton Foundation Web site at http://www.comptonfoundation.org].

* **1999:** $60,000 "for Catholic Voices: International Forum on Population and Development" [Compton Foundation Web site at http://www.comptonfoundation.org].

* **1998:** $40,000 "for Catholics for Contraception" [*FGI*, 2001, page 278; *TFR*, 2002, page 218].

* **1997:** $40,000 "for Catholics for Contraception" [*FGI*, 2000, page 268].

* **1996:** $40,000 [*FGI*, 1999, page 235].

* **1994:** $40,000 [*FGI*, 1997, page 205].

* **1992:** $30,000 "for New Constituencies/New Approaches Project" [*FGI*, 1995, page 191].

Total donations to Catholics for a Free Choice by the Compton Foundation: $310,000.

S.H. Cowell Foundation
120 Montgomery Street, Suite 2570

San Francisco, California 94104
Telephone: (415) 397-0285
Web address: http://www.shcowell.org/
Assets: $195,452,445 (December 31, 1999)

* **1995:** $25,000 "for population program" [*FGI*, 1998, page 214].
* **1994:** $10,000 [*FGI*, 1997, page 205].

Total donations to Catholics for a Free Choice by the S.H. Cowell Foundation: $35,000.

C.S. Fund
469 Bohemian Highway
Freestone, California 95472
Telephone: (707) 874-2942
FAX: (707) 874-1734
E-mail: kathyk@csfund.org
Assets: $2,070,214 (October 31, 2000)

* **1984:** $10,000 "for general support of programs of public education and technical assistance on reproductive rights issues" [*FGI*, 1986, page 28].

Nathan Cummings Foundation
475 Tenth Avenue, 14th Floor
New York, New York 10018
Telephone: (212) 787-7300
FAX: (212) 787-7377
E-mail: info@cummings.ncf.org
Web address: http://www.ncf.org
Assets: $414,947,042 (December 31, 2000)

* **1993:** $55,000 "for Latina Initiative, to increase participation of national Hispanic organizations in the reproductive health debate" [Nathan Cummings Foundation Web site at http://www.ncf.org; *FGI*, 1996, page 219].
* **1992:** $45,000 "to increase participation of national Hispanic organizations in the reproductive health debate" [Foundation Center DIALOG search by Mr. Bruce Gumm requested by Human Life International dated September 10, 2001].
* **1992:** $34,000 "to explore strategies for moderating abortion debate by developing middle-ground solutions" [*FGI*, 1995, page 205].
* **1991:** $39,500 "to encourage Hispanic organizations to develop reproductive health positions which support health of their constituents" [*FGI*, 1994, page 798].

Total donations to Catholics for a Free Choice by the Nathan Cummings Foundation: $173,500.

Alida Rockefeller Dayton Fund

* **1981:** $9,947 [CFFC's 1981 Federal income tax return].

Geraldine R. Dodge Foundation
Post Office Box 1239
Morristown, New Jersey 07962-1239
Telephone: (973) 540-8442
E-mail: info@grdodge.org
Web address: http://www.grdodge.org
Assets: $337,658,000 (December 31, 2000)

* **1998:** $50,000 "to mobilize Catholics in support for family planning, for Lifting Up Catholic Voices: Family Planning at Home and Abroad, which seeks to involve U.S. Catholics in activities to make pro-family planning position known" [*FGI*, 2001, page 1,071].

Dyson Foundation
25 Halcyon Road
Millbrook, New York 12545-9611
Telephone: (845) 677-0644
FAX: (845) 677-0650
E-mail: info@dyson.org
Web address: http://www.dysonfoundation.org
Assets: $323,870,389 (December 31, 2000)

* **1995:** $10,000 "for public education and research to monitor access to reproductive health care services in changing health care environment" [*FGI*, 1998, page 231].

Educational Foundation of America
35 Church Lane
Westport, Connecticut 06880-3515
Telephone: (203) 226-6498
Web address: http://www.efaw.org
Assets: $283,387,124 (December 31, 1999)
Notes: The Educational Foundation of America was established in New York in 1959 with funds donated by the late Richard Prentice Ettinger, the founder of the Prentice-Hall publishing company. EFA has funded many pro-abortion and population control organizations. It has given money to the Alan Guttmacher Institute, Planned Parenthood affiliates, and various abortion mills [Educational Foundation of America's 1993 *Annual Report*, pages 23 to 25].

* **1998:** $200,000 (2 years) "for educating and reaching out to religious community" [Educational Foundation of America Web site at http://www.efaw.org; *FGI*, 2001, page 284].

186

*   **1995:** $225,000 (3 years) "for educating and reaching out to religious community" [*FGI*, 1997; *TFR*, 2002, page 313].

*   **1993:** $50,000 "for communications project" [*FGI*, 1995, page 194].

*   **1992:** $57,900 (2 years) "for Hispanic Outreach Project" [*FGI*, 1994, page 186].

*   **1991:** $50,000 (2 years) "for grassroots organizing and Hispanic outreach projects" [*FGI*, 1993, page 182].

*   **1990:** $80,000 "for education and communications program" [*FGI*, 1992, page 173].

*   **1988:** $80,000 "for education and communications programs to further national dialogue on ethical questions related to human reproduction and implementation of sound public policy related to family planning" [*FGI*, 1990/1991, page 94].

*   **1985:** $20,000 "for Spanish publications dissemination program" [*FGI*, 1986, page 106].

*   **1983:** $25,000 "to educate the community about the issues of reproductive choice and advance public debate about abortion" [*FGI*, 1985, page 95; *TFR*, 1985, page 175].

*   **1982:** $50,000 "to further develop Catholic involvement in reproductive rights through an intensive program of public education, publications and publication dissemination, and media visibility" [*FGI*, 1984, page 88]; "education: materials, media and outreach" [*TFR*, 1984, page 174].

*   **1981:** $50,000 [CFFC's 1981 Federal income tax return].

Total donations to Catholics for a Free Choice by the Educational Foundation of America: $887,900.

Field Foundation
15306 South Carmenita Road
Santa Fe Springs, California 90670
Assets: $212,530 (December 31, 2000)

*   **1980:** $15,000 "for defense of reproductive rights of women" [*TFR*, 1982, page 193; *FGI*, 1982, page 209].

Leland Fikes Foundation
500 North Akard
Dallas, Texas 75201
Telephone: (214) 754-0144
Assets: $75,579,043 (December 31, 1999)

*   **1998:** $25,000 "for projects in Latin America" [*FGI*, 2001, page 316; *TFR*, 2002, page 335].

*   **1998:** $10,000 "for prochoice activities in Mexico" [*FGI*, 2001, page 316; *TFR*, 2002, page 335].

*   **1996:** $20,000 "for projects in Central/South America — reproductive

rights" [IRS form 990-PF, "Return of Private Foundation," Leland Fikes Foundation, 1996; *FGI*, 1999, page 263].
* **1995:** $20,000 "for projects in Latin America" [*FGI*, 1998, page 243].
* **1994:** $20,000 "for general support" [*FGI*, 1997, page 232].
* **1993:** $20,000 "for projects in Latin America" [*FGI*, 1996, page 231].
* **1992:** $30,000 "for general support" [*FGI*, 1995, page 216].
* **1991:** $30,000 "for projects in Mexico and general support" [*FGI*, 1994, page 209].
* **1990:** $25,000 "for general support" [*FGI*, 1993, page 203].
* **1989:** $25,000 [*TFR*, 1992, page 259].
* **1988:** $15,000 "for general support" [*FGI*, 1990/1991, page 695].
* **1985:** $10,000 "for general support" [*FGI*, 1987, page 630].

Total donations to Catholics for a Free Choice by the Leland Fikes Foundation: $250,000.

Ford Foundation
320 East 43rd Street
New York, New York 10017
Telephone: (212) 573-5000
Web site: http://www.fordfound.org
Assets: $14,659,683,000 (September 30, 2000)
Notes: Although the Ford Foundation was originally funded with hundreds of millions of dollars of Ford Motor Company stock, it has completely divested itself of all Ford Company holdings. Today the Ford foundation has no ties whatsoever to the Ford family or the Ford Motor Company.

* **1999:** $1,200,000 "for research, education and advocacy work in issues of sexual and reproductive health and rights" [Ford Foundation Web site at: http://www.fordfound.org/grants_db/view_grant_detail.cfm?grant_counter=522; *FGI*, 2001, page 301; *TFR*, 2002, page 3].
* **1999:** $100,000 "for conference "Catholic Voices: An International Forum on Population and Development"" [Ford Foundation Web site at : http://www.fordfound.org/grants_db/view_grant_detail.cfm?grant_counter=515; *FGI*, 2001, page 301].
* **1998:** $218,000 (2-year grant) to CFFC-Uruguay "For continued support to consolidate pro-choice Catholic groups and promote public discussion on sexual and reproductive health."
* **1998:** $200,000 (2-year grant) to *CDD*-Mexico "for continued support for public education and dissemination of Catholic pro-choice values."
* **1998:** $190,000 to *CDD*-Mexico "for preparatory activities for International Conference on Population and Development (ICPD) Plus 5."
* **1998:** $100,000 (2-year grant) to *CDD*-Mexico "for working group of senior developing country ethicists in reproductive health."
* **1998:** $67,000 to *CDD*-Mexico "to promote public discussion among Catholics in Mexico on sexual and reproductive health."

* **1997:** $50,000 to CFFC-Uruguay "for Latin American Regional Conference for Catholics for the Right to Decide Network."

* **1996:** $1,300,000 "for general support" [*FGI*, 1998, page 231].

* **1996:** $150,000 to *CDD*-Brazil "for public education and dissemination of Catholic pro-choice values."

* **1996:** $100,000 to CFFC-Uruguay "for consolidation of pro-choice Catholic groups in four Latin American countries: Argentina, Chile, Colombia and Peru."

* **1996:** $73,000 to *CDD*-Mexico "to promote public discussion among Catholics in Mexico on sexual and reproductive health."

* **1995:** $30,000 "for general support" [*FGI*, 1997, page 221; Ford Foundation 1995 *Annual Report*, page 89].

* **1995:** $42,000 "for participants from developing countries to attend Kennedy Institute of Ethics' advanced course on feminist perspective on bioethics" [*FGI*, 1997, page 833; Ford Foundation 1995 *Annual Report*, page 86].

* **1995:** $45,000 "to consolidate pro-choice Catholic groups in four countries."

* **1994:** $770,000 "for general support" [*FGI*, 1996, page 221; Ford Foundation 1994 *Annual Report*, page 83].

* **1994:** $210,000 (18-month grant) "to consolidate a Latin American network on women's reproductive health and rights."

* **1994:** $46,200 to *CDD*/Brazil "for ethics, law, and policy analysis" [Ford Foundation 1994 *Annual Report*, page 87].

* **1994:** $50,000 to CFFC-Uruguay "for community involvement" [Ford Foundation 1994 *Annual Report*, page 86].

* **1993:** $210,000 "for international program, institutional evaluation and convening religious consultation on population and reproductive health" [*FGI*, 1995, page 206].

* **1992:** $100,000 (18-month grant) "for participants from developing countries to attend Kennedy Institute of Ethics' advanced course on feminist perspective on bioethics."

* **1992:** $100,000 "toward consolidation of Latin American Women's Reproductive Health and Rights Network" [*FGI*, 1994, page 800].

* **1991:** $150,000 "for family planning and reproductive health program in developing countries" [*FGI*, 1993, page 740].

* **1991:** $50,000 "for education on reproductive health and rights in Latin America" [*FGI*, 1993, page 193].

* **1991:** $300,000 (2-1/2 year grant) "for supplement for public policy and education programs on reproductive choice in U.S." [*FGI*, 1993, page 193].

* **1990:** $200,000 (2 year grant) "for supplement for research and education on reproductive rights in U.S." [*FGI*, 1992, page 183].

* **1988:** $120,000 (2 year grant) "for public education on issues related to reproductive choice" [*FGI*, 1989, page 426].

* **1987:** $90,000 "for public education and policy analysis in area of reproductive choice" [*FGI*, 1988, page 400].

* **1985:** $50,000 "to expand distribution of organization's publications, which explore religious, ethical and policy issues related to abortion" [*FGI*, 1986, page 361].

* **1984:** $25,000 [CFFC's 1984 Federal Income Tax Return].

* **1983:** $25,000 "for fellowship program in journalism and moral theology dealing with theme of Catholics and abortion" [*FGI*, 1984, page 291].

* **1982:** $19,560 "for study of effects of religious upbringing and religious attitudes on decision to have abortion" [*FGI*, 1983, page 249].

Total donations to Catholics for a Free Choice by the Ford Foundation: $6,380,760.

General Service Foundation
557 North Mill Street, Suite 201
Aspen, Colorado 81611-1513
Telephone: (970) 920-6834
FAX: (970) 920-4578
E-mail: info@generalservice.org
Web address: http://www.generalservice.org
Assets: $82,597,242 (December 31, 1999)
Notes: Beginning in 1970, world population control became — and has remained — a major concern of the General Service Foundation. A 1981 Foundation publication commemorating its first 35 years of operation disclosed that the GSF has "worked closely over twenty years with ... Planned Parenthood, American Friends Service Committee, Population Council, Population Crisis Committee, Columbia University, and others" to cope with the "awesome ... consequences of unrestricted population growth" [Foundation booklet entitled *General Service Foundation 1946 to 1981*, pages 2 and 6]. In 1979 and 1980, GSF made population control its main area of concentration, with "up to two-thirds of the Foundation's income" during that period designated for such activity. Accordingly, "a major contribution [was made] to the Population Council in support of its [population programs] in Latin America and the Caribbean, with emphasis on Mexico." Thanks to GSF funding, the Population Council was able to expand "similar activities ... [in] Brazil, Colombia, the Dominican Republic, Peru, and El Salvador." In recent years, GSF has funded International Projects Assistance Services (IPAS), a manufacturer of manual vacuum aspiration (MVA) abortion machines, for the purpose of placing its devices and training physicians in their use in Ecuador (1988 and 1990, $25,000 each year), Nicaragua (1989, $28,000; 1990 and 1991, $20,000 each year), and Mexico (1992-1993, $40,000) [*TFR*, 1990, page 238; *TFR*, 1992, page 305; General Service Foundation *Annual Reports*, 1989 (page 10), 1990 (page 11), 1991 (page 11) and 1992/1993 (unnumbered).

Interestingly, James Patrick Shannon sat on the Board of Directors of the General Service Foundation for many years. Shannon, a defrocked Roman Catholic priest, was formerly auxiliary bishop of the Archdiocese of Saint Paul from 1965 to 1968. In November 1968, Shannon abandoned the priesthood and married outside the Church. He grumbled that "In my pastoral experience I have found that this rigid teaching (*Humanae Vitae*) is simply impossible of observance [sic] by many faithful and generous spouses, and I cannot believe that God binds men to impossible standards" [Megan Hartman. "*Humanae Vitae*: Thirty Years of Discord and Dissent." *Conscience*, Autumn 1998].

* **2000:** $8,335 "to cover the costs of three Mexican participants from *Católicas por el Derecho a Decidir*/Mexico to attend the Beijing+5 meetings" [General Service Foundation Web site at http://www.generalservice.org/pages/00RHRGrantees.htm].

* **2000:** $65,000 "for general support of CDD's efforts to ensure the exercise of reproductive and sexual rights in Mexico, including access to adequate services and the ultimate goal of ensuring safe, legal abortion" [General Service Foundation Web site at http://www.generalservice.org/pages/00RHRGrantees.htm].

* **1999:** $100,000 (2 years) "to raise awareness of Catholic support for reproductive health care and to counter the Catholic Church's attempts to undermine reproductive freedom" [General Service Foundation Web site at http://www.generalservice.org].

* **1998:** $20,000 "to *CDD* to develop educational publications used to support the organization's activities to strengthen the voices of prochoice Catholics in Mexico" [General Service Foundation Web site at http://www.generalservice.org].

* **1997:** $80,000 (2 years) "for general support of CFFC's core domestic programs" [General Service Foundation Web site at http://www.generalservice.org; *FGI*, 2000, page 272].

* **1995:** $80,000 (2 years) "toward educating and building networks of pro-choice Catholics at state, local and national levels as participants in public debate over sexuality and reproductive providers" [*FGI*, 1998, page 218].

* **1995:** $10,000 "for work with organizations and coalition in Latin America to help implement International Conference on Population and Development Program of Action in region" [*FGI*, 1998, page 830].

* **1993:** $90,000 (2 years) "for Latin America Program which seeks to educate and mobilize Latin American citizens on important reproductive health and population issues in the region" [*FGI*, 1996, page 206].

* **1992:** $4,800 "to support the International Network of Feminists Interested in Reproductive Health and Ethics (IN/FIRE)" [*FGIQ*, September 1994, page 18].

* **1991:** $80,000 (2 years) "for general program support to provide analysis, education and advocacy on reproductive health issues from a religious and ethical perspective" [*FGI*, 1994, page 186].

* **1990:** $32,000 "for general program support" [*FGI*, 1993, page 182].

* **1989:** $32,500 "for general support of this organization which provides analysis, education and advocacy on reproductive health issues from a religious and ethical perspective for a domestic and international audience" [1989

General Service Foundation *Annual Report*, page 9].

* **1988:** $28,000 "for organization's work to counter efforts of Roman Catholic Church to limit legal access to reproductive health care" [*FGI*, 1990/1991, page 88].

* **1987:** $31,500 "to support Latin American Program which utilizes ethical and theological perspectives and service-oriented methods to assist Latin American Catholics with issue of reproductive choice" [*FGI*, 1989, page 88].

* **1986:** $7,500 "to disseminate radio documentary to members of Congress which provides expert scientific information on fetal brain development to counter assumptions put forth in film, *The Silent Scream*" [*FGI*, 1988, page 94].

* **1986:** $23,000 to CFFC International Program: Latin America "to support Latin American component of organization's 1986 conference, Ethical Issues in Reproductive Health: Religious Perspectives, and to support their Latin American program in 1987" [*FGI*, 1988, page 94].

Total donations to Catholics for a Free Choice by the General Service Foundation: $692,635.

Wallace Alexander Gerbode Foundation
470 Columbus Avenue, Suite 209
San Francisco, California 94133-3930
Telephone: (415) 391-0911
FAX: (415) 391-4587
E-mail: maildesk@gerbode.org
Web address: http://fdncenter.org/grantmaker/gerbode/
Assets: $84,888,021 (December 31, 1999)

* **1999:** $150,000 (3 years) "for support of its work in the area of reproductive rights and health" [Gerbode Foundation Center Web site at http://fdncenter.org/grantmaker/gerbode/grcomm99.html].

* **1997:** $15,000 "for support of its work to advance sexual and reproductive rights" [Gerbode Foundation Center Web site at http://fdncenter.org/grantmaker/gerbode/grcomm97.html].

* **1996:** $30,000 "for support of its work to advance sexual and reproductive rights" [Gerbode Foundation Center Web site at http://fdncenter.org/grantmaker/gerbode/grcomm96.html].

* **1995:** $15,000 "for support of its work to advance sexual and reproductive rights" [Gerbode Foundation Center Web site at http://fdncenter.org/grantmaker/gerbode/grcomm95.html].

* **1994:** $90,000 "for work to advance sexual and reproductive rights" [*FGI*, 1996, page 204].

* **1991:** $25,000 for "support of its family planning and abortion rights work" [*TFR*, 1994, page 491].

* **1989:** $75,000 (3 years) "for family planning and abortion rights work" [*FGI*, 1990/1991, page 31].

192

Total donations to Catholics for a Free Choice by the Wallace Alexander Gerbode Foundation: $400,000.

Global Fund for Women
1375 Sutter Street, Suite 400
San Francisco, California 94109
Telephone: (415) 202-7640
FAX: (415) 202-8604
Web address: http://www.globalfundforwomen.org

* **1999:** $15,000 to *CDD* "to build grassroots mobilization, increase leg islative support and improve availability of services to make abortion safe and legal in Mexico" [Global Fund for Women Web site at http://www.globalfundforwomen.org/].

Richard & Rhoda Goldman Fund
One Lombard Street, Suite 303
San Francisco, California 94111
Telephone: (415) 788-1090
FAX: (415) 788-7890
E-mail: info@goldmanfund.org
Web address: http://www.goldmanfund.org
Assets: $430,000,000 (December 31, 2000)

* **1998:** $200,000 (2 years) "for the Catholics for Contraception Campaign" [Goldman Fund Web site at: http://www.goldmanfund.org/grantslist/population.html; *FGI*, 2001, page 279].
* **1997:** $50,000 "for general support" [*FGI*, 2000, page 269].
* **1996:** $50,000 "for general support" [*FGI*, 1999, page 236].
* **1995:** $25,000 "for final payment of grant for Catholic Health Care System and Health Reform Study, to examine Catholic health care system, its role in national health care reform and implications for reproductive health care delivery in U.S." [*FGI*, 1998, page 816].
* **1994:** $25,000 "for Catholic Health Care System and Health Reform study, to examine Catholic health care system, its role in national health care reform and implications for reproductive health care delivery in U.S." [*FGI*, 1997, page 768].

Total donations to Catholics for a Free Choice by the Richard & Rhoda Goldman Fund: $350,000.

George Gund Foundation
45 Prospect Avenue West.
Cleveland, Ohio 44115-1018
Telephone: (216) 241-3114

FAX: (216) 241-6560
Web address: http://www.gundfdn.org
Assets: $447,324,123 (December 31, 1999)
Notes: George Gund's fortune began with the purchase of a decaffeinated coffee firm which became Sanka coffee under Kellogg's and General Foods' auspices. The Gund Foundation has long been a funder of abortion and population control groups, including Frances Kissling's old outfit, the National Abortion Federation, and the Pre-Term abortion mill in Cleveland [Gund Foundation's 1993 *Annual Report*, page 26].

* **1999:** $100,000 (2 years) "for operating support" [*FGI*, 2001, page 314].
* **1998:** $100,000 (2 years) "for operating support" [Gund Foundation Web site at http://www.gundfdn.org/; *FGI*, 2000, page 301].
* **1996:** $100,000 (2 years) "for operating support" [*FGI*, 1998, page 241].
* **1994:** $90,000 (2 years) "for operating support" [*FGI*, 1996, page 229].
* **1993:** $30,000 "for retreat for pro-choice leadership" [*FGI*, 1995, page 215; *TFR*, 1996, page 550. **NOTE:** That must have been *some* retreat!]
* **1992:** $85,000 (2 years) "for operating support" [*FGI*, 1994, page 207].
* **1991:** $41,708 "for operating support" [*FGI*, 1993, page 201].
* **1990:** $30,000 "for reproductive rights activities" [*FGI*, 1992, page 190].
* **1989:** $12,500 "for operating support for CFFC's advocacy and public education programs related to abortion rights" [CFFC's 1989 Federal income tax return].
* **1988:** $50,000 "for operating support for advocacy and public education programs related to abortion rights" [*FGI*, 1990/1991, page 595].
* **1987:** $25,000 "for continued operating support for public education and advocacy efforts supporting Catholic dissent on issue of abortion" [*FGI*, 1989, page 589].
* **1986:** $25,000 "toward general operating expenses and for such activities as expanded publication distribution effort, conference on Ethical Issues in Reproductive Health Care, and continued public educative activities" [*FGI*, 1987, page 539].
* **1985:** $15,000 "for operating assistance for national membership organization dedicated to preserving reproductive freedom and upholding separation of church and state" [*FGI*, 1986, page 522].
* **1984:** $17,000 "for operating support for national membership organization dedicated to preserving reproductive rights and upholding separation of church and state" [*FGI*, 1985, page 459].
* **1983:** $20,000 "for third year operating assistance for national membership organization dedicated to preserving reproductive rights and upholding principle of separation of church and state" [*FGI*, 1984, page 427].
* **1982:** $20,000 "for projects aimed at increasing public understanding of issues related to reproductive freedom" [*FGI*, 1983, page 357].

*   **1981:** $20,000 "for operating support for organization dedicated to pre serving reproductive freedom and upholding principle of church and state separation" [*FGI*, 1982, page 336].

Total donations to Catholics for a Free Choice by the George Gund Foundation: $781,208.

William & Flora Hewlett Foundation
525 Middlefield Road, Suite 200
Menlo Park, CA 94025
Telephone: (650) 329-1070
FAX: (650) 329-9342
Web site: http://www.hewlett.org
Assets: $2,738,945,087 (December 31, 1999)

*   **1998:** $600,000 (3 years) "for general support, with focus on international programs" [*FGI*, 2000, page 269].
*   **1995:** $450,000 "for general support" [*FGI*, 1997, page 206].

Total donations to Catholics for a Free Choice by the William & Flora Hewlett Foundation: $1,050,000.

Huber Foundation
Post Office Box 277
Rumson, New Jersey 07760
Telephone: (732) 933-7700
Assets: $48,965,140 (December 31, 2000).
Notes: The secretive Huber Foundation was established in 1949 by members of the Huber family, owners of the 1.2 billion-dollar J.M. Huber Corporation. In the mid-1970s, the Huber Foundation "stepped into the spotlight ... to announce that all future grants would promote 'reproductive freedom.'" The foundation then "slipped back into the obscurity that had shrouded it since its creation ..." One article reported that "[m]embers of the Huber family are wary about discussing their philanthropy" and ignored "repeated calls to the foundation." Indeed, so secretive is the foundation that its official annual reports simply list the organizations receiving Huber grants without disclosing the amounts each was awarded. A review of the foundation's Internal Revenue 900 tax forms was required to ascertain that information. True to its earlier declaration, the Foundation's *Annual Report* states that the Huber foundation "focuses its grant-making on the issues of Reproductive Health, Population Education and Family planning ... Only organizations that make a substantial commitment of time and resources to these issues will be considered for funding." The Huber Foundation gives large grants to radical pro-abortion groups, including the Alan Guttmacher Institute, the Association for Voluntary Sterilization (AVS), the National Abortion Federation (NAF), the National Abortion and Reproductive Rights Action League (NARRAL), the Planned Parenthood Federation of America (PPFA) and

its affiliates, the Population Crisis Committee (PCC), the Religious Coalition for Reproductive Choice (RCRC) and Zero Population growth (ZPG) [*The Record* [Hackensack, New Jersey], February 10, 1991; *Taft Foundation Reporter*, 1995, page 639].

* **1999:** $50,000 "for general support" [IRS form 990-PF, "Return of Private Foundation," Huber Foundation, 1999; *FGI*, 2001, page 298].
* **1998:** $120,000 "for general support" [IRS form 990-PF, "Return of Private Foundation," Huber Foundation, 1998].
* **1997:** $30,000 "for general support" [*FGI*, 2000, page 286].
* **1996:** $40,000 "for general support" [*FGI*, 1999, page 249].
* **1995:** $30,000 "for general support" [*FGI*, 1997, page 218].
* **1993:** $30,000 [*FGI*, 1996, page 217].
* **1992:** $40,000 [*FGI*, 1995, page 203].
* **1991:** $25,000 [*TFR*, 1994, page 657].
* **1990:** $55,000 [*TFR*, 1993, page 446].
* **1989:** $30,000 [*TFR*, 1992, page 403].
* **1988:** $20,000 [*FGI*, 1990/1991, page 338].
* **1987:** $20,000 [*TFR*, 1990, page 320].
* **1985:** $20,000 [*TFR*, 1987, page 303].
* **1983:** $20,000 [*TFR*, 1986, page 315].
* **1982:** $15,000 [*TFR*, 1984, page 288].

Total donations to Catholics for a Free Choice by the Huber Foundation: $545,000.

Alfred Jurzykowski Foundation
15 East 65th Street
New York, New York 10021
Telephone: (212) 535-8930
Assets: $45,524,040 (December 31, 1999)

* **1998:** $25,000 "to support the prochoice movement in Poland" [IRS form 990-PF, "Return of Private Foundation," Alfred Jurzykowski Foundation, 1998].
* **1998:** $40,000 "in support of their Brazil project" [IRS form 990-PF, "Return of Private Foundation," Alfred Jurzykowski Foundation, 1998; *TFR*, 2002, page 594].
* **1993:** $30,000 "in support of their program activities in Brazil" [*TFR*, 1996, page 739].
* **1992:** $20,000 "for programs to further reproductive rights in Brazil" [*FGI*, 1995, page 209].

Total donations to Catholics for a Free Choice by the Alfred Jurzykowski Foundation: $115,000.

Esther A. & Joseph Klingenstein Fund
787 Seventh Avenue, 6th Floor
New York, New York 10019-6016
Telephone: (212) 492-6181
FAX: (212) 492-7007
Assets: $165,394,681 (September 30, 2000)

* **1996:** $25,000 "for family planning and teenage pregnancy programs" [*FGI*, 1999, page 972].
* **1995:** $25,000 "for family planning and teenage pregnancy programs" [*FGI*, 1998, page 897].
* **1994:** $25,000 [*FGI*, 1997, page 224].

Total donations to Catholics for a Free Choice by the Esther A. & Joseph Klingenstein Fund: $75,000.

Albert A. List Foundation
180 West 80th Street, Suite 213
New York, New York 10024-6301
Telephone: (212) 799-1090
FAX: (212) 799-1160
Web address: http://fdncenter.org/grantmaker/listfdn/
Assets: $15,463,161 (December 31, 1999)

* **1999:** $20,000 "for Challenging the Religious Right: Focus on Gender, Sexuality and Reproduction" [Foundation Center DIALOG search by Mr. Bruce Gumm requested by Human Life International dated September 10, 2001].
* **1998:** $30,000 "for Challenging the Religious Right: Focus on Gender, Sexuality and Reproduction" [*FGI*, 2001, page 306].
* **1997:** $60,000 [*FGI*, 2000, page 294].
* **1996:** $75,000 [*FGI*, 1999, page 255].
* **1995:** $33,850 [*FGI*, 1998, page 235; *TFR*, 1998, page 763].
* **1993:** $30,000 for ""Freedom of Choice" area grant" [*TFR*, 1995, page 820].

Total donations to Catholics for a Free Choice by the Albert A. List Foundation: $248,850.

J. Roderick MacArthur Foundation
9333 North Milwaukee Avenue
Niles, Illinois 60714
Assets: $37,677,606 (December 31, 1999)

* **1983:** $10,000 [CFFC's 1983 Federal income tax return].

John D. & Catherine T. MacArthur Foundation
140 South Dearborn Street, Suite 1100
Chicago, Illinois 60603-5285
Telephone: (312) 726-8000
FAX: (312) 920-6258, TDD: (312) 920-6285
E-mail: 4answers@macfdn.org
Web address: http://www.macfdn.org
Assets: $4,629,518,668 (December 31, 1999)
Note: The MacArthur Foundation gives millions of dollars every year to extreme pro-abortion groups, including the Boston Women's Health Collective, the Global Fund for Women, the Population Council, the Program for Appropriate Technology in Health (PATH) and the Center for Population Options, the vast majority of which is used in Latin America. It also gives tens of thousands of dollars to Latin American researchers for such purposes as "To support investigation of ideology and activities of conservative, pro-life groups in Mexico" [The John D. and Catherine T. MacArthur Foundation 1993 *Report on Activities*, pages 152 to 166].

* **1999:** $650,000 (3 years) "for reproductive rights work in Latin America" [MacArthur Foundation Web site at http://www.macfdn.org; *FGI*, 2001, page 296].
* **1996:** $600,000 (3 years) "for research, seminars and publications in Latin America" [*FGI*, 1999, page 243; *TFR*, 2002, page 687].
* **1995:** $49,500 "for activities related to Fourth World Conference on Women in Beijing, China" [*FGI*, 1998, page 1,271].
* **1993:** $525,000 (3 years) "in support of the organization's Latin America program. Catholics for a Free Choice is an international educational organization dedicated to supporting the right for reproductive health care, especially family planning and abortion. The organization also works to reduce the incidence of abortion and to increase women's choices in childbearing and child-rearing through advocacy of social and economic programs for women, families, and children. This grant will support efforts to deepen public dialogue and raise awareness of reproductive health issues in Latin America by publishing educational materials in English, Spanish, and Portuguese and by strengthening the group's regional programs in Uruguay, Brazil, and Mexico" [The John D. and Catherine T. MacArthur Foundation 1993 *Report on Activities*, page 157; *FGI*, 1996, page 211].
* **1991:** $375,000 (3 years) "for Latin American programs" [*FGI*, 1994, page 766].

Total donations to Catholics for a Free Choice by the John D. & Catherine T. MacArthur Foundation: $2,199,500.

John Merck Fund
11 Beacon Street, Suite 1230

Boston, Massachusetts 02108
Telephone: (617) 723-2932
FAX: (617) 523-6029
E-mail: info@jmfund.org
Assets: $211,668,907 (December 31, 1999)

* **1995:** $50,000 "for Constituency Building Project, to enlarge base of active support among Catholics for reproductive freedom" [*FGI*, 1998, page 223].
* **1994:** $50,000 "to promote reproductive rights and health in Catholic countries in Central America, South America and Europe" [*FGI*, 1997, page 214].
* **1994:** $35,000 "To analyze and publicize role and impact of Catholic hospitals and medical facilities in providing health care in U.S." [*FGI*, 1997, page 214].
* **1991:** $83,775 "to assist local activists in responding to recent legal challenges to reproductive rights in Poland and Germany and to maintain branch office in Uruguay for promoting reproductive rights in Latin America, and to expand reproductive rights advocacy in Mexico" [*FGI*, 1994, page 193].
* **1990:** $30,000 "for Latin American program" [*FGI*, 1993, page 188].
* **1989:** $20,000 "to support a program based in Uruguay that promotes access to family planning and the full range of reproductive health care for Latin American women and men" [*FGI*, 1992, page 179; foundation's 1989 *Annual Report*, page 8].

Total donations to Catholics for a Free Choice by the John Merck Fund: $268,775.

Moriah Fund
1634 I Street NW, Suite 1000
Washington, DC 20006
Telephone: (202) 783-8488
FAX: (202) 783-8499
Assets: $218,722,432 (December 31, 2000)

* **1999:** $30,000 "for general support" [IRS form 990-PF, "Return of Private Foundation," Moriah Fund, 1999; *FGI*, 2001, page 285].
* **1998:** $30,000 "for general support" [*FGI*, 2000, page 275].
* **1996:** $30,000 "for general support" [*FGI*, 1999, page 240].
* **1994:** $30,000 "for reproductive rights education in Latin America and Eastern Europe" [*FGI*, 1997, page 214].
* **1993:** $35,000 "for reproductive rights and health program in Latin America and Eastern Europe" [*FGI*, 1996, page 212].
* **1992:** $35,000 "for reproductive rights and health program in Latin America and Eastern Europe" [*FGI*, 1995, page 199].

Total donations to Catholics for a Free Choice by the Moriah Fund: **$190,000.**

Ruth Mott Fund
111 East Court Street, Suite 3C
Flint, Michigan 48502-1649
Telephone: (810) 233-0170
FAX: (810) 767-1207
E-mail: susanp@mfo.com
Assets: $54,961,728 (December 31, 1999)

* **1989:** $24,625 "for conference component on reproductive health ethical and policy perspectives" [*FGI*, 1992, page 686].

Ms. Foundation

* **1980:** $2,500 "to publish booklets in Spanish for dissemination in the Hispanic community" [CFFC's 1980/1981 Federal income tax return].
* **1979:** $13,000 [Ms. Foundation's 1979 *Annual Report*].

Total donations to Catholics for a Free Choice by the Ms. Foundation: **$15,500.**

Norman Foundation

* **1981:** $10,000 [CFFC's 1981 Federal income tax return].
* **1980:** $10,000 "for general support of educational activities aimed at articulating and airing the pro-choice position of many Catholics on abortion" [*FGI*, 1982, page 279].
* **1979:** $7,500 to CFFC Education Fund "to support educational activities aimed at articulating and airing the pro-choice position of many Catholics on the subject of abortion" [*FGI*, 1980, page 262; *TFR*, 1982, page 469].

Total donations to Catholics for a Free Choice by the Norman Foundation: **$27,500.**

North Shore Unitarian Veatch Program

* **1983:** $5,000 [Veatch Program's 1983-1984 *Annual Report*, page 49].
* **1981:** $10,000 [CFFC's 1981 Federal income tax return].
* **1980:** $22,500 "small group providing a forum for dissenting Catholics and is a member of the Religious Coalition for Abortion Rights" [Veatch Program's 1979-1980 *Annual Report*, pages 20 and 44].
* **1979:** $45,000 [Veatch Program's 1979-1980 *Annual Report*, pages 20

and 44].

Total donations to Catholics for a Free Choice by the North Shore Unitarian Veatch Program: $82,500.

Jessie Smith Noyes Foundation
Six East 39th Street, 12th Floor
New York, New York 10016-0112
Telephone: (212) 684-6577
FAX: (212) 689-6549
E-mail: noyes@noyes.org
Web address: http://www.noyes.org
Assets: $88,504,809 (December 31, 1999)

* **1992:** $20,000 "to support education, advocacy and outreach initiatives designed to further dialogue and policymaking, and to forge consensus around important reproductive health issues in Latin America" [*FGI*, 1994, page 203].
* **1991:** $20,000 "for *Católicas por el Derecho a Decidir* (Uruguay)" [1991 Noyes Foundation *Annual Report*, pages 52 and 55].
* **1990:** $40,000 "to build grassroots support for reproductive rights in targeted states and regions, and to provide outreach and technical assistance to Hispanic organizations concerning this issue" [*FGI*, 1992, page 187].
* **1989:** $15,000 "for *Católicas por el Derecho a Decidir* (Uruguay), for initial support for newly formed organization dealing with population and reproduction rights" ["Family Planning & Reproductive Health," 1990/1991, card #42].

Total donations to Catholics for a Free Choice by the Jessie Smith Noyes Foundation: $95,000.

Open Society Institute
400 West 59th Street, 4th Floor
New York, New York 10019
Telephone: (212) 548-0600
FAX: (212) 548-4679
Web address: http://www.soros.org
Assets: $449,765,934 (December 31, 1999)

* **1999:** $150,000 "for general support" [Foundation Center DIALOG search by Mr. Bruce Gumm requested by Human Life International dated September 10, 2001].
* **1998:** $100,000 "for general support" [*FGI*, 2001, page 308].

Total donations to Catholics for a Free Choice by the Open Society Institute: $250,000.

Louise L. Ottinger Foundation
80 Broad Street, 17th Floor
New York, New York 10004
Telephone: (212) 764-3878
FAX: (212) 764-4298
Web address: http://www.ottingerfoundation.org
Assets: $7,971,507 (December 31, 1999)

* **1980:** $5,000 to CFFC Education Fund "for educational program about history and practices of Catholic Church on reproductive matters" [*FGI*, 1982, page 282].

David & Lucile Packard Foundation
300 Second Street, Suite 200
Los Altos, California 94022
Telephone: (650) 948-7658
Web address: http://www.packfound.org
Assets: $9,375,053,138 (December 31, 2000)
Notes: The Packard Foundation was started in 1964 by David Packard, co-founder of the Hewlett-Packard Company, and his wife, the late Lucile Salter Packard. Hewlett-Packard is an acknowledged leader in a wide variety of computer products, including HP Laser Jet and DeskJet printers. Besides its long-time support of Catholics for a Free Choice, the Packard Foundation has been an enthusiastic supporter of world population control measures. In 1993, the Packard Foundation gave $20,000 to the Rockefeller-allied Population Council to "prepare and plan for the introduction of RU-486 in the United States," $80,000 to the National Abortion Federation, and $75,000 to the National Abortion Rights Action League (NARAL).

* **2000:** $2,000,000 "for initiative, Securing Reproductive Rights in Latin America" [Foundation Center DIALOG search by Mr. Bruce Gumm requested by Human Life International dated September 10, 2001].
* **1999:** $655,000 "to *CDD* to support two components of a collaborative reproductive rights initiative focusing on Catholic communities in Mexico" [Packard Foundation Web site at http://www.packfound.org].
* **1999:** $360,000 "to *CDD* for the implementation of five major goals" [Packard Foundation Web site at http://www.packfound.org].
* **1998:** $1,000,000 (3 years) "for general support" [Packard Foundation Web site at http://www.packfound.org; *FGI*, 2000, page 270].
* **1998:** $150,000 "to *CDD*, Mexico City, Mexico, for work to strength en voice of pro-choice Catholics in Mexico and to train primary school teachers to implement sex education programs in Mexico" [*FGI*, 2000, page 270].
* **1998:** $20,800 "to improve paper and electronic data management" [*FGI*, 2000, page 270].

* **1997:** $200,000 "for continued general support" [*FGI*, 1999, page 237].
* **1996:** $100,000 "for general support" [*FGI*, 1998, page 216].
* **1995:** $75,000 "for general support of domestic programs" [*FGI*, 1997, page 207].
* **1994:** $80,000 "for Mexico program and for general support for domestic program" [*FGI*, 1996, page 205].
* **1993:** $40,000 "for general support of domestic programs" [*FGI*, 1995, page 192].
* **1993:** $40,000 "to expand Mexican program" [*FGI*, 1995, page 192].
* **1993:** $65,000 "nonlegislative publications and outreach programs and preparation for the North South Dialogue in Mexico City" [*TFR*, 1995, page 1,045].
* **1992:** $40,000 "for non-legislative publications and outreach programs" [*FGI*, 1994, page 184].
* **1992:** $25,000 "for preparation costs for North South Dialogue in Mexico City" [*FGI*, 1994, page 184].
* **1991:** $30,000 "for U.S. and Latin American programs" [*FGI*, 1993, page 180].
* **1990:** $35,000 "for general support" [*FGI*, 1992, page 172].
* **1990:** $10,000 "to print and distribute copies of publication, Guide for Pro-Choice Catholics: The Church, the State, and Abortion Politics" [*FGI*, 1992, page 172].
* **1988:** $45,000 "for general support" [*FGI*, 1990/1991, page 61].
* **1987:** $40,000 "for general support" [*FGI*, 1989, page 55].
* **1986:** $25,000 "for general educational effort to help Catholics consider reproductive options and ethics" [*FGI*, 1988, page 52].
* **1986:** $5,000 "for two educational briefings on population issues for Catholic members of Congress and their staffs" [*TFR*, 1988, page 538].
* **1985:** $40,000 "for general support and translating and disseminating Spanish publications" [*FGI*, 1987, page 53].
* **1983:** $10,000 "for general support" [*FGI*, 1985, page 59].
* **1982:** $5,000 "for community contact program" [*FGI*, 1984, page 50].

Total donations to Catholics for a Free Choice by the David & Lucile Packard Foundation: $5,095,800.

Playboy Foundation

* **1983:** $10,000 [Playboy Foundation's 1983 *Annual Report*, page 8].
* **1982:** $10,000 "for reproductive freedom programs" [*FGI*, 1983, page 114].

Total donations to Catholics for a Free Choice by the Playboy Foundation: $20,000.

Prospect Hill Foundation
99 Park Avenue, Suite 2220
New York, New York 10016-1601
Telephone: (212) 370-1165
FAX: (212) 599-6282
Web address: http://fdncenter.org/grantmaker/prospecthill/
Assets: $85,629,626 (June 30, 2000)

* **1994:** $7,000 "for meeting in Latin America on ethical issues of abortion" [Jim Miller's personal communication with foundation spokesperson, December 8, 1994].
* **1993:** $2,500 "to promote reproductive choice in Latin America" [*Foundation 1000* 1994/1995, page 2,097].
* **1992:** $12,500 "for International Program's activities in Central and South America" [*FGI*, 1994, page 204].
* **1991:** $17,500 "to promote reproductive choice in Latin America" [*TFR*, 1991, page 1,109].
* **1990:** $20,000 "to promote reproductive choice in Latin America" [*FGI*, 1992, page 187].
* **1988:** $20,000 "for international program that enhances family planning efforts of health and religious workers in Latin American countries by making available supportive information prepared by Catholic scholars" [*FGI*, 1990/1991, page 529].
* **1987:** $15,000 "for international program that enhances family planning efforts of health and religious workers in Latin American countries by making available supportive information prepared by leading Catholic scholars" [*FGI*, 1989, page 521].

Total donations to Catholics for a Free Choice by the Prospect Hill Foundation: $94,500.

Public Welfare Foundation
1200 U Street NW
Washington, D.C. 20009-4443
Telephone: (202) 965-1800
Web site: http://www.publicwelfare.org/
Notes: The PWF has funded 15 different Planned Parenthood abortion and population programs run by a dozen different Planned Parenthood affiliates, and, through Planned Parenthood affiliates in New York City and London, has funded Planned Parenthood activities in Upper Guinea, Colombia, Mexico, Thailand, Bangladesh and Vietnam. The PWF has also been very generous to Population Services International (PSI), funding its programs to distribute condoms in the United States, Benin, Central African Republic, Zaire and Rwanda (while Rwanda was in the midst of a savage civil war and severe famine, Public Welfare Foundation and Planned Parenthood donated not food, not clean drinking water, not shelter — but thousands of condoms). The PWF has also funded

International Projects Assistance Service (IPAS) to send its abortion machines to Eastern and Southern Africa. Altogether, PWF donated nearly $3,000,000 in 1993 alone for the promotion of abortion, sterilization and population control, almost entirely in developing nations [Foundation's *Annual Report*, 1992-1993, pages 38 to 41].

* **1996:** $160,000 [*TFR*, 1998, page 1,028].
* **1996:** $70,000 "for general support for work supporting the right to legal and accessible reproductive health care, including family planning and abortion" [Public Welfare Foundation Web site at http://www.publicwelfare.org/; *FGI*, 1998, page 220].
* **1995:** $70,000 "for general support of this organization that supports the right to legal and accessible reproductive-health care, including family planning and abortion" [Public Welfare Foundation Web site at http://www.publicwelfare.org/; *FGI*, 1997, page 210].
* **1994:** $80,000 "for its work to secure the right to legal and accessible reproductive health care, including family-planning and abortion services" [Public Welfare Foundation Web site at http://www.publicwelfare.org/]; "for general support for international educational organization dedicated to supporting right to legal and accessible reproductive health care, including family planning and abortion" [*FGI*, 1996, page 208].
* **1993:** $80,000 "for continued general operating support" [*FGI*, 1995, page 195].
* **1992:** $80,000 "for continued general operating support for international educational organization, supporting right to legal reproductive health care, especially family planning and abortion" [*FGI*, 1994, page 187].
* **1991:** $50,000 "for general support for work to reduce incidence of abortion and to increase women's choices in child-bearing and child-rearing through advocacy of social and economic programs for women, families and children" [*FGI*, 1993, page 183].

Total donations to Catholics for a Free Choice by the Public Welfare Foundation: $590,000.

Rockefeller Foundation
420 Fifth Avenue
New York, New York 10018-2702
Telephone: (212) 869-8500
Web site: http://www.rockfound.org
Assets: $3,837,542,000 (December 31, 1999)

* **1994:** $60,000 "for public education project concerning role religious organizations played in setting agenda for 1994 United Nations International conference on Population and Development" [*FGI*, 1996, page 852].

Scherman Foundation
16 East 52nd Street, Suite 601
New York, New York 10022-5306
Telephone: (212) 832-3086
Assets: $110,088,080 (December 31, 2000)
Notes: The Scherman Foundation was established in 1941 by Harry Scherman, founder of the Book-of-the-Month Club. "Family planning" is one of the "main interests of the Scherman Foundation." Among the radical population control and pro-abortion groups it has funded are the American Civil Liberties Union's Reproductive Freedom Project, Association for Voluntary Sterilization (AVS), International Projects Assistance Services (IPAS), Planned Parenthood affiliates, Population Action International (PAI), and the Religious Coalition for Reproductive Choice (RCRC) [Scherman Foundation 1993 *Annual Report*, pages 3 and 4].

* **1998:** $20,000 "for 25th anniversary gift" [*FGI*, 2000, page 299].
* **1998:** $60,000 (2 years) "for general support" [*FGI*, 2000, page 299; *TFR*, 2002, page 966].
* **1996:** $50,000 (2 years) "for general support" [*FGI*, 1999, page 260].
* **1995:** $50,000 [*TFR*, 1998, page 1,111].
* **1994:** $50,000 "for general support" [*FGI*, 1997, page 229].
* **1992:** $50,000 (2 years) "for general support" [*FGI*, 1995, page 213].
* **1990:** $50,000 (2 years) "for general support" [*FGI*, 1993, page 200].
* **1988:** $40,000 (2 years) "for general support" [*FGI*, 1990/1991, page 553].
* **1986:** $35,000 (2 years) "for general support" [*FGI*, 1988, page 534].
* **1984:** $30,000 (2 years) "for general support" [*FGI*, 1986, page 475].
* **1982:** $25,000 [*TFR*, 1984, page 555].
* **1981:** $75,000 [CFFC's 1981 Federal income tax return].

Total donations to Catholics for a Free Choice by the Scherman Foundation: $535,000.

Summit Charitable Foundation
2099 Pennsylvania Avenue NW, Suite 1000
Washington, DC 20006
Telephone: (202) 912-2900
FAX: (202) 912-2901
E-mail: info@summitfdn.org
Assets: $162,000,784 (December 31, 1999)

* **1999:** $50,000 "for public education and policy outreach targeting International Conference on Population and Development (ICPD) Plus Five process" [*FGI*, 2001, page 286].

Sunnen Foundation
7910 Manchester Avenue
St. Louis, Missouri 63143
Assets: $15,654,722 (December 31, 2000)
Notes: Sunnen is a manufacturer of high precision tools and gauges, including honing machines, abrasive supplies, auto engine rebuilding equipment, and precision hole gauges. The Sunnen Products Company produced Emko contraceptive foam as a sideline business before selling it off to the Johnson and Johnson Company.

* **1993:** $25,000 [*TFR*, 1995, page 1,302].
* **1992:** $50,000 [Jim Miller's personal communication with Foundation spokesperson, December 6, 1994].
* **1991:** $100,000 [*TFR*, 1994, page 1,315].
* **1990:** $100,000 [*TFR*, 1993, page 889].
* **1989:** $75,000 [*TFR*, 1992, page 797].
* **1988:** $100,000 [*TFR*, 1990, page 634].
* **1987:** $126,700 [*TFR*, 1989, page 642].
* **1986:** $75,000 [*TFR*, 1988, page 676].
* **1985:** $100,000 [*TFR*, 1987, page 637].
* **1984:** $100,000 [*TFR*, 1986, page 676].
* **1983:** $70,000 [*TFR*, 1985, page 639].
* **1982:** $63,500 [*TFR*, 1984, page 605].
* **1981:** $6,500 [CFFC's 1981 Federal income tax return].
* **1980:** $75,000 [*TFR*, 1982, page 614].

Total donations to Catholics for a Free Choice by the Sunnen Foundation: $1,066,700.

Tides Foundation
Post Office Box 29903
San Francisco, California 94129-0903

* **1997:** $15,000 [IRS form 990-PF, "Return of Private Foundation," Tides Foundation, 1997].
* **1993:** $20,000 "for general program support" [Tide Foundation's 1993 *Annual Report*].
* **1992:** $15,000 "for general program support" [Tide Foundation's 1992 *Annual Report*].

Total donations to Catholics for a Free Choice by the Tides Foundation: $50,000.

Turner Foundation
1 CNN Center, Suite 1090, South Tower
Atlanta, Georgia 30303
Telephone: (404) 681-9900

FAX: (404) 681-0172
E-mail: turnerfi@mindspring.com
Web address: http://www.turnerfoundation.org
Assets: $327,261,232 (December 31, 1999)

* **1998:** $60,000 [*FGI*, 2001, page 288].
* **1997:** $35,000 [*FGI*, 2000, page 277].
* **1996:** $25,000 [*FGI*, 1999, page 242].

Total donations to Catholics for a Free Choice by the Turner Foundation: $110,000.

Wallace Global Fund
1990 M Street NW, Suite 250
Washington, DC 20036
Telephone: (202) 452-1530
FAX: (202) 452-0922
E-mail: tkroll@wgf.org
URL: http://www.wgf.org
Assets: $135,544,196 (December 31, 2000)

* **1998:** $250,000 (2 years) "for support of CFFC's efforts to protect and expand access to family planning and to safe, legal abortion around the world. CFFC's work in constituency building, publications, communications and educational programs is designed to articulate sound ethical arguments in favor of family planning and choice, and to mobilize Catholics to speak out in favor of such policies" [Wallace Global Fund Web site at http://www.wgf.org/; *FGI*, 2001, page 286].

Weeden Foundation
747 Third Avenue 34th Floor
New York, New York 10017
Telephone: (212) 888-1672
Web site: http://www.weedenfdn.org
Assets: $37,334,744 (June 30, 2000)

* **2000:** $25,000 "general support for work with their Latin American partners - *Católicas por el Derecho a Decidir*. CFFC is the leading Catholic-based critic of the Church's contraception and abortion positions. Funds will help them maintain a strong media presence in Mexico, counter the efforts of Human Life International in Bolivia, and support their publications and technical assistance services" [Weeden Foundation Web site at http://www.weedenfdn.org].
* **1999:** $25,000 "in support of special activities in Mexico and their general operations in Latin America. CFFC is focusing on strengthening

their Mexican partners so they may be better equipped to counter the Catholic Church's mass media campaign against legalizing abortion. They are expanding their Spanish-language publications program, and will continue to offer technical assistance, an information clearing house, and a trilingual Web site to assist partner groups in Brazil, Bolivia, and Argentina" [Weeden Foundation Web site at http://www.weedenfdn.org].

* **1998:** $15,000 "funding for their 1998 efforts to build a pro-choice, pro family planning Catholic voice in Latin America. CFFC's Latin American network includes groups in Bolivia, Peru, Colombia, Argentina, Brazil, Mexico, and Chile. CFFC will continue to publish and translate materials, offer networking and outreach services, research policy, hold workshops, and provide technical assistance to these groups" [Weeden Foundation Web site at http://www.weedenfdn.org; *FGI*, 2000, page 300].

* **1996:** $30,000 "for Latin America program and global initiative on population policy" [*FGI*, 1998, page 240].

* **1995:** $15,000 "for continued support for Latin America program" [*FGI*, 1997, page 1,005].

* **1994:** $15,000 "for education for women in Latin America who are seeking reproductive health services" [*FGI*, 1996, page 1,222].

* **1993:** $10,000 "to promote awareness of reproductive health issues in Latin America" [*FGI*, 1995, page 816].

* **1991:** $5,000 "an unrestricted grant in support of this organization's educational efforts" [1991 Weeden Foundation *Annual Report*].

Total donations to Catholics for a Free Choice by the Weeden Foundation: $140,000.

Endnotes

1   Sun Tzu, c. 500 B.C. *The Art of War*. New York: Oxford University Press, 1973.
2   In the United States, approximately 0.36% of all abortions are performed to preserve the life or health of the mother, 0.09% for rape and incest, and 0.24% for fetal birth defects (eugenics), for a total of 0.69% of all abortions. This means that 99.31% of all abortions performed in the United States are for social reasons, or to "save the lifestyle of the mother." For detailed calculations and documentation, see Brian Clowes. *The Facts of Life* [2nd Edition]. Front Royal: Human Life International. Chapter 13, "United States Abortion Statistics."
3   The Population Institute. *The Population Activist's Handbook*. New York: MacMillan, 1974. Pages 4 and 22.
4   Cicero, quoted in "Worth Repeating." *The New American*, May 12, 1997, page 30.
5   National Conference of Catholic Bishops. "Catholics for a Free Choice Not a Catholic Group." November 4, 1993 Statement of the NCCB, Washington, D.C. This complete statement is contained in Appendix A.
6   Magaly Llaguno. "'Catholics for a Free Choice:' A Dossier." *Vida Humana Internacional*, December 1994, page 2.
7   Pamela J. Maraldo. "Misogyny That Will Pass." *Conscience*, Winter 1993/1994, page 38; "More on Maraldo." *National STOPP News*, January 20, 1993, page 1.
8   Richard Doerflinger. "Who are Catholics for a Free Choice?" *America*, November 16, 1985, pages 312 and 313.
9   Mary Meehan. "Foundation Power." *Human Life Review*, Fall 1984, pages 42 to 60.
10 See Table 2 in the text.
11 Doerflinger, *op. cit.*
12 Ellen Kirby, Assistant General Secretary, Section of Christian Social Relations, Women's Division of the United Methodist Church, in a March 1986 letter to the National Federation for Decency. "United Methodist Women's Division Representative Clarifies Support of Abortion Rights Group." National Federation for Decency *Journal*, April 1986, page 6; Mary Meehan. "Foundation Power." *Human Life Review*, Fall 1984, pages 42 to 60.
13 "*Playboy* Funds Pro-Abortion Group." National Federation for Decency *Journal*, February 1985, page 16.
14 Frances Kissling, quoted in "CFFC Notebook." *Conscience*, Winter 1993/1994, pages 50 to 52.
15 Doerflinger, *op. cit.*
16 Sunnen Foundation, 1979 letter to Michael Schwartz of the Catholic League for Religious and Civil Rights.
17 Doerflinger, *op. cit.*
18 *Ibid.*
19 *Ibid.*
20 *Advertising Age*, December 24, 1984.
21 Doerflinger, *op. cit.*
22 *Ibid.*

23   *Ibid.*

24   *Ibid.*

25   *Declaración de Preocupación* ["Statement of Concern"]. *Conciencia Latinoamericana*, April/May/June 1993, page 8.

26   Magaly Llaguno. "Catholics for a Free Choice Unmasked." Presentation at Human Life International's 16th World conference in Minneapolis-St. Paul, Minnesota, April 1997.

27   Cristina Grela. *"Transitamos un camino común."* *Revista de la Red de Salud/Isis Internacional* [Magazine of the Health Network/Isis International, Santiago, Chile], April/September 1994, page 57.

28   "CFFC Notebook: Pop Culture." *Conscience*, Autumn 1993, page 48.

29   "CFFC Notebook: Faith, Hope and ~~Charity~~." *Conscience*, Winter 1996/1997, page 34; "Editorial: The Vatican's Cheap Shot at UNICEF." *Conscience*, Winter 1996/1997, pages 36 and 37.

30   Frances Kissling. "The Vatican's Cheap Shot at UNICEF." *Conscience*, Winter 1996/1997, pages 36 and 37.

31   Daniel C. Maguire. "The Splendor of Control: A Commentary on *Veritatis Splendor* and the Elephant in the Living Room." *Conscience*, Winter 1993/1994, pages 26 to 29.

32   "We Are (.06 Percent of the) Church." *This Rock*, January 1998, pages 8 to 10.

33   Frances Kissling in a BBC Television interview. Quote downloaded from the CFFC Web site at http://www.cath4choice.org/media/francis.htm on July 23, 2001.

34   Austin Ruse. "They Want the Vatican Nixed. Why?" *National Catholic Register*, December 12-18, 1999.

35   Domenico Bettinelli, Jr. "No "See Change"." *Catholic World Report*, April 2000.

36   John Mallon. "Evangelicals, Rabbi Support Vatican at UN." *Inside the Vatican*, April 2000.

37   Bettinelli, *op. cit.*

38   See the "See Change" Web site at http://www.seechange.org/.

39   See the "Holy See Campaign" signatory list at the C-FAM Web site, http://www.cfam.org/HolySee/index.html.

40   Bettinelli, *op. cit.*

41   Weekly Roundup, Catholic News Service, July 12, 2000.

42   "Pro-Abortion Groups Compare Holy See's UN Status to the Soviet Politburo." *National Catholic Register*, February 6-12, 2000.

43   Frances Kissling, quoted in Patricia Miller. "Religion, Reproductive Health and Access to Services." *Conscience*, Summer 2000, pages 2 to 8

44   Margot Patterson. "Bishops' Conference Approves Directives." *National Catholic Reporter*, June 29, 2001; "Editor's Note: Voices from Around the Globe." *Conscience*, Summer 2000.

45   Martin Haskell, from the *Sixty Minutes* episode of June 2, 1996 entitled "Partial Birth Abortion Ban;" Robert W. Lee. "The Partial-Birth "Choice"." *New American*, April 15, 1996, pages 4 to 8.

46   "CFFC Notebook: Reproductive Health." *Conscience*, Autumn 1996, page 43.

47   *Conscience*, July/August 1988, page 13.

48   "CFFC Notebook." *Conscience*, Winter 1993/1994, pages 50 to 52; "CFFC in the News." *Conscience*, May/June 1988, page 19.

49   *Conscience*, July/August 1988, page 13; Margaret Conway. "Public Funding: CFFC Makes Waves in Michigan Abortion Rights Battle." *Conscience*, May/June 1988, pages

12-16; "Religious Involvement Heats Up in Michigan." *Conscience*, July/August 1988, page 20.

50   CFFC press release dated May 11, 2001, at http://www.catholics4choice.org.

51   February 7, 2001 letter to Mr. Poul Nielson, Commissioner, Development European Union Humanitarian Aid Office. This letter was signed by 22 pro-abortion NGOs, including the American Humanist Association, Americans for Religious Liberty, Catholics for a Free Choice, the National Abortion Federation, the National Abortion and Reproductive Rights Action League, the Planned Parenthood Federation of America, Population Action International, the Population Institute, and the Religious Coalition for Reproductive Choice.

52   Charles Chaput, O.F.M. Cap. Archbishop of Denver. "The Evil of Embryo Destruction." Zenit News Agency, July 28, 2001.

53   "Catholics for the Right to Decide in Latin America." *Conscience*, Summer 2001, page 27.

54   Maggie Hume. "Editor's Note: The Joy of ..." *Conscience*, Winter 1993/1994, inside front cover.

55   *Conscience*, Summer 1997, page 31.

56   "Kissling Takes Debate to London: Challenging the Vatican on Abortion." *Conscience*, May/June 1988, page 24.

57   *Ibid.*

58   "Catholic Group Favours Liberal Abortion Option." *The Irish Times*, December 14, 1999.

59   *The Irish Times*, July, 13, 2000.

60   "CFFC Notebook: In Brief." *Conscience*, Autumn 1993, page 49.

61   Frances Kissling's July 1996 letter. WEDO *News & Views*, June-July 1996.

62   "CFFC Notebook: In Brief." *Conscience*, Spring 1996, page 33.

63   *Revista de la Red de Salud*, Isis International, Chile, April 1992.

64   "Announcement: New Network." *Conscience*, January/February 1991, page 21.

65   Adelle-Marie Stan, "A Decade of Dissent." *Conscience*, September-December 1987, pages 24 to 26.

66   "Catholics for the Right to Decide in Latin America." *Conscience*, Summer 2001, pages 24 to 27.

67   *Ibid.*

68   *Ibid.*

69   *Conciencia*, January/July 1997, pages 3 to 5.

70   *Ibid.*

71   Alejandra Folgarait. *"Mujeres Católicas Por el Derecho a Elegir"* (Catholic Women for the Right To Choose). *Página 12* (Buenos Aires, Argentina), June 16, 1994, page 3.

72   "Mexican Feminism: An Interview With Sylvia Marcos." *Conscience*, January/February 1991, pages 16 and 17.

73   Ana María Portugal [Editor]. *Mujeres e Iglesia: Sexualidad y Aborto en América Latina* [*"Women and the Church: Sexuality and Abortion in Latin America"*]. México, D.F.: Distribuciones Fontamara, S.A., 1989, pages vii, 21, 23, 58, 59, 76, 77, 97 and 118,

74   Margaret Sanger (editor). *The Woman Rebel*, March 1914 [Volume I, Number 1]. "On Picket Duty." Page 3. "The Margaret Sanger Papers" Web site at http://mep.cla.sc.edu/ms/ms-table.html has all issues of *The Women Rebel* on line.

75   Portugal, *op. cit.*

76   "Mexican Feminism: An Interview With Sylvia Marcos." *Conscience*, January/February

1991, pages 16 and 17; Rosemary Radford Ruether. "Lessons from Chiapas." *Conscience*, Spring 1996, pages 36 and 37. In the "Letters" section of the June 1997 *Catholic World Report*, Bishop García stated that he had never met Mejías, and wanted it made perfectly clear that he and the other bishops of Chiapas vigorously opposed CFFC's efforts in their state.

77   Akua Furlow. Manuscript entitled "The Tuskegee Conspiracy." Book to be published by Human Life International in 2002.

78   Claudia López Muñiz. "Dear Readers" and "Catholics for a Free Choice - Hispanic Project." *Instantes 1*, August 16, 1992, page 2.

79   Ivan Roman. "*Plan de abortos a pobres recibe apoyo Hispano*" ["Abortion Planning for Poor Receives Hispanic Support]. *El Nuevo Herald*, April 2, 1993.

80   Católicas por el Derecho a Decidir. "*Y María fue consultada para ser Madre de Dios*" ["And Mary Was Consulted To Be God's Mother"]. México, D.F.: Centro Nacional Pro Maternidad Voluntaria, Despenalización y Legalización del Aborto.

81   Magaly Llaguno. Research paper "'Catholics for a Free Choice:' A Dossier by *Vida Humana Internacional*." December 1994, page 9.

82   *Conscience*, September/October 1988.

83   *Associacao Nacional Pró-vida e Pró-Familia* ["Pro-Life and Pro-Family Association"]. *Boletin Informativo* [Newsletter] Number 08, July/August 1994, page 6.

84   "Gazette." *Conscience*, May/June 1988, page 18.

85   Reuters, November 13, 1991; December 30, 1991 letter of Dr. Geraldo Hideu Osanai, President, *Associacao Pro-Vida de Brasilia*, to Andrew M. Nibley and Thomas D. Thompson of the Reuters News Agency in New York City.

86   *Boletim Informativo*, July/August 1994, *op. cit.*

87   *Southern Nebraska Register*, March 22, 1996.

88   Marjorie Reiley Maguire (former member of the CFFC Board of Directors). "Not Catholic." *National Catholic Reporter*, April 21, 1995, page 18.

89   "Kissling Takes Debate to London: Challenging the Vatican on Abortion." *Conscience*, May/June 1988, story beginning on back cover. This article was also printed in the March 31, 1988 edition of *The Irish Times*.

90   Ron Brackin. "'Sister' Frances Kissling: Cardinal of Death." *Liberty Report*, January 1987.

91   *Ibid.*

92   C. Joseph Doyle. "Agent of Influence." *Catholic World Report*, January 1994, pages 44 and 45.

93   Mary Meehan. "Kissling Speaks Frankly about Past Activism." *National Catholic Register*, September 7, 1986, page 1.

94   "Kissling Takes Debate to London: Challenging the Vatican on Abortion." *Conscience*, May/June 1988, story beginning on back cover.

95   Mary Meehan. "Kissling Speaks Frankly about Past Activism." *National Catholic Register*, September 7, 1986, page 1.

96   *Ibid.*

97   Pope John Paul II. "Be Faithful in Expounding the *Whole* Ministry of Christ!" Discourse to American Bishops from Iowa, Kansas, Missouri and Nebraska during their *ad limina* visit, May 28, 1993.

98   Donna Steichen. *Ungodly Rage: The Hidden Face of Catholic Feminism.* San Francisco: Ignatius Press, 1991, pages 32, 156 and 304.

99   Kenneth L. Woodward. "Feminism and the Churches." *Newsweek* Magazine, February 13, 1989, page 60.

100 Rosemary Radford Ruether. *Women-Church: Theology and Practice of Feminist Liturgical Communities*. San Francisco: Harper & Row, 1985, pages 15 to 23, cited by Steichen, page 165.

101 Molly O'Neill, "Roman Catholic Rebel Becomes a Cause Célèbre." *The New York Times,* March 17, 1993, page C1.

102 Rosemary Radford Ruether (member of the CFFC Board of Directors). *Womanguides: Readings Toward a Feminist Theology.* Beacon Press, 1985.

103 Kenneth L. Woodward. "Feminism and the Churches." *Newsweek* Magazine, February 13, 1989, page 60.

104 Rosemary Radford Ruether (member of the CFFC Board of Directors). Quoted in C. Powell Sykes. "Rosemary Radford Ruether gives 1998 Sprunt Lectures; Says 'Flesh became Word not Word became Flesh'." *The Presbyterian Layman*, March/April 1998. Downloaded from
http://www.layman.org/layman/the-layman/1998/march-april/ruether.html.

105 Diann Neu, pamphlet entitled "Liturgy of Affirmation for Making a Difficult Decision." At the bottom of this pamphlet, it says "Liturgies by Diann Neu, feminist liberation theologian and co-director of WATER, the Women's Alliance for Theology, Ethics and Ritual in Silver Spring, MD."

     In CFFC's publication *Conscience*, Neu also describes a "rite" she made up as a "mourning ceremony" for women who have had an abortion. In order to celebrate this ritual, the woman must ask the abortionist to give her the remains of her aborted baby, and then she gathers her sexual 'partner' and her friends. Together they say prayers such as: "Blessed are you, Holy One, mother and father, that you have given us the power of choice. We are saddened that the life circumstances of (name of woman) and (name of man) are such that the choice to bring this pregnancy to completion is not a life-giving one for all involved. Such a choice is never simple; it's filled with pain and hurt, with anger and questions. Our beloved sister has made a very hard choice. We promise to con tinue to stand with her in her ongoing life. Blessed are you, Holy One, for your presence with her." Then when the woman who aborted explains why she made that decision, she opens a hole in the backyard, with the help of her mate, and both say the following prayer while they bury their unborn baby: "O Mother Earth, we lay this spirit to rest in your bosom." Neu suggests that this "rite" and other similar ones be used to bring "healing," and she says that they "celebrate women's spirituality" [Diann Neu. "Affirming Our Work, Creating Our Community." *Conscience*, January/February 1989, page 12.

106 Verbatim transcript of the talk given by Diann Neu during the 1996 Call to Action National Conference in Detroit.

107 "Wisdom" is the female personification of God's wisdom in Proverbs, Chapters 7 through 10, a purely literary device used by the author to enhance the importance of wisdom for right conduct in daily life. In the New Testament the personification is seen as pointing to Christ, in whom God's wisdom took flesh. Quotes are from *The Re-Imagining Conference: A Report*. American Family Association, April, 1994.

108 *Ibid.*

109 Steichen, *op. cit.*, page 162.

110 Radford, *Womanguides, op. cit.*

111 Thomas Marron. "Songs for the Angels. Three: Gabriel Considers His Horn."

Conscience, Spring 1994, page 20.

112 The "Ten Voluntary Initiatives" are listed in Charles Trueheart. "Ted Turner Updates Moses: Cable Mogul Delivers Ten Commandments." The *Washington Post*, October 31, 1989, pages C1 and C6; Ted Turner, quoted in Thomas Goetz. "Billionaire Boy's Cause: Can Three of the World's Richest Men Put Overpopulation Back on the Public Agenda?" Downloaded from *The Village Voice* Online, October 1, 1997, http://www.villagevoice.com:80/ink/news/40goetz.shtml.

113 Daniel C. Maguire, quoted in Janice Hughes. "The Catholic Constituency: What Church Leaders Don't Tell Congress." *Conscience*, May/June 1988, pages 2 and 10.

114 The Bible condemns child sacrifice in Leviticus 20:2-5; Leviticus 18:21; 2 Kings 23:10; and Jeremiah 32:35.

115 See especially Deuteronomy 27:25 and 30:19; Amos 1:13; Jeremiah 7:6 and 22:17; Psalm 106:37-38; Proverbs 6:16-19; Isaiah 53:6; Luke 17:2; and Matthew 18:10,14.

116 See especially Psalm 139:13-16; Isaiah 44:24 and 64:8; and Jeremiah 1:5. Additionally, St. Paul rejoices that God "... set me apart before I was born ..." [Galatians 1:15].

117 Martin Luther. *Luther's Works*. St. Louis, Concordia Publishing, Volume VII, page 21.

118 See specifically Genesis 29:31; 30:2,22; 49:25; 1 Samuel 1:5; Job 31:15; Psalm 139:13; Isaiah 44:2,24; 49:1,5; 66:9; Jeremiah 1:5; Luke 1:15;41-44; Wisdom 7:1; and Sirach 49:7.

119 An undated CFFC pamphlet entitled "Did You Know that Most Catholics Believe in Reproductive Freedom?" claims that "We believe that women should not be the victims of random fertility" [This sounds as if pregnancy bears no relation whatever to sexual activity]. ... "The Catholic hierarchy is trapped in an outdated authoritarianism which denies full equality to women and regards sex as evil." Marjorie Reiley Maguire has said that "The voice of the officers of the Catholic Church on reproductive matters speaks to me of a materialistic God ... whose greatest joy comes from playing cruel reproductive tricks on women and watching them squirm" [Marjorie Maguire, quoted in Phyllis Zagano. "The Limits of Choice." *National Catholic Register*, October 12, 1986].

120 **Homosexual activity:** See Deuteronomy 23:17; 1 Kings 14:24, 15:12, 22:46; and 2 Kings 23:7. **Divorce:** See Matthew 5:31-32, 19:3-9; Luke 16:18; and 1 Corinthians 7:10-15. **Fornication:** See 2 Chronicles 21:11; Isaiah 23:17; Ezekiel 16:26,29; Matthew 5:32, 19:9; John 8:41; Acts 15:20,29, 21:25; Romans 1:29; 1 Corinthians 5:1, 6:13,18, 7:2, 10:8; 2 Corinthians 12:21; Galatians 5:19; Ephesians 5:3; Colossians 3:5; 1 Thessalonians 4:3; Jude 1:7; and Revelation 2:14,20-21, 9:21, 14:8, 17:2,4, 18:3,9, and 19:2. **Adultery:** See Exodus 20:14; Leviticus 18:20, 19:20, 20:10-12; Deuteronomy 5:18, 22:13-29, 27:20, 27:23; Proverbs 6:26, 6:29, 6:32; Matthew 5:27,28,32, 15:19, 19:9,18; Mark 7:21, 10:11-12,19; Luke 16:18, 18:20; John 8:4-11, Romans 7:3, 13:9, 1 Corinthians 6:9; Galatians 5:19; Ephesians 5:5; and Hebrews 13:4.

121 Frances Kissling. "Divine Ecstasy: Sin, Asceticism and Sexuality in the Catholic Tradition." Nerve.com's March 30, 1999 interview of cultural critic Camille Paglia, ex-priests Robert Francouer and Thomas Moore, religion professor Elaine Pagels, and Frances Kissling. Downloaded from http://www.nerve.com/Dispatches/voicebox/religion on May 17, 2001.

122 Frances Kissling during a CNN interview. Quote downloaded from the CFFC Web site at http://www.cath4choice.org/media/francis.htm on July 23, 2001.

123 Steve Askin. "Challenging the Right." *Conscience*, Spring 1994, pages 65 and 66; "Abortion and Catholic Thought: The Little-Known History." *Conscience*, Autumn

1996, pages 2 to 5.

124 Marjorie Reiley Maguire and Daniel C. Maguire. "Abortion: A Guide to Making Ethical Choices." Washington, DC: Catholics For a Free Choice, 1983; also see "What is Conscience?" *Conscience*, Spring/Summer 1993, page 61. Note that the Maguires say that four influences must be brought to bear on the situation. One is "the feelings of our heart" — this while the woman is being pressured by abortion mill "counselors" to abort. Another is "the standards of moral behavior we have learned from society" — once again, what standards are the women going to hear about in the waiting room of an abortion mill? Finally, notice that the last of the four influences is "religious teachings" — but, of course, only "when appropriate."

125 Christine E. Gudorf. "To Make a Seamless Garment, Use a Single Piece of Cloth." *Conscience*, Autumn 1996, pages 10 to 21.

126 Steve Askin. "Challenging the Right." *Conscience*, Spring 1994, pages 65 and 66.

127 *Paquette v. Regal Art Press, Inc.* [656 A.2d 209 (Vt. 1994)]. *Atlantic Reporter*, 2d Series, pages 209-211; "Pro-Life Printers Wage Battle of Conscience." Free Speech Advocates newsletter, January 1991, pages 2 and 3; "Vermont Printers Win Three-Year Fight." *Catalyst* [Journal of the Catholic League for Religious and Civil Rights], April 1994, pages 1 and 12. The Bible contains many references to the human conscience. It describes the fate of someone who does not guard or "keep" his conscience [Hebrews 9:14 and 1 Peter 3:16], and who allows his conscience to become "seared" [1 Timothy 4:2]. The Bible also speaks of a "weak conscience" [1 Corinthians 8:7], a "wounded conscience" (1 Corinthians 8:12), a "good" and "perfect" conscience (Hebrews 9:9 and 13:18; 1 Peter 3:21; and 1 Timothy 1:5,19]; a "clear" (blameless) conscience [Acts 24:16 and 1 Timothy 3:9], and a conscience that is "evil" or defiled [Titus 1:15].

128 "Spotlight on Marie Baldwin." *Conscience*, September/October 1990, pages 18 to 20.

129 Daniel C. Maguire. "Where There's Doubt, There's Freedom." *Conscience*, Spring/Summer 1993, page 15; Daniel C. Maguire. "The Splendor of Control: A Commentary on *Veritatis Splendor* and the Elephant in the Living Room." *Conscience*, Winter 1993/1994, pages 26 to 29. Frances Kissling incorrectly describes probabilism this way: "And the important thing is that there is a long tradition in the Roman Catholic Church called **probabilism**. And probabilism holds that an individual may engage in an activity that is considered factually or legally doubtful if the individual can find a couple of respectable authorities to assert the opinion in a cogent way and in a way that continues to be respectful of the Catholic tradition" [Frances Kissling's talk during the conference entitled "Antiprogestin Drugs: Ethical, Legal and Medical Issues," held at the Hyatt Regency Crystal City in Arlington, Virginia, December 6-7, 1991, session entitled "Diverse Perspectives: Feminism, Anthropology and Theology"]. Kissling has also said that "The principle of probabilism in Roman Catholicism holds that where the church can not speak definitively on a matter of fact (in this case, on the personhood of the fetus), the consciences of individual Catholics must be primary and respected" [Frances Kissling. "Abortion: Articulating a Moral View." *Conscience*, Summer 2000, pages 21, 22 and 27].

130 Daniel C. Maguire. "Where There's Doubt, There's Freedom." *Conscience*, Spring/Summer 1993, page 15.

131 This prohibition on the use of probabilism when a prohibiting law is certain has been constant through the ages. The 1917 *Catholic Encyclopedia* stated that "When a prohibiting law is certain, the subjects of the law are bound to abstain from performing the action which the law forbids, unless they are excused by one of the ordinary exempting causes"

[the complete discussion of probabilism in the 1917 *Catholic Encyclopedia* is available at http://www.newadvent.org/cathen/12441a.htm]. The defenders of probabilism "require a person reasonably to seek direct certainty regarding the moral problem before seeking indirect certainty through the use of reflex principles. ... for if it [the opinion for liberty] is only slightly probable it has no value against the opinion for law" [*New Catholic Encyclopedia*. Washington, D.C.: The Catholic University of America, 1967. Volume 11, pages 814 and 815.

132 Fr. Peter M.J. Stravinkas, Ph.D., S.T.L. [Editor]. *Our Sunday Visitor's Catholic Encyclopedia*. Huntington, Indiana: Our Sunday Visitor Press, 1991, page 786.

133 National Council of Catholic Bishops Committee on Doctrine. "Abortion and "Free Choice:" The Catholic Church Teaches Direct Abortion is Never a Moral Good," November 1984. See Appendix A for the full text of this document.

134 The complete discussion of probabilism in the 1917 *Catholic Encyclopedia* is available at http://www.newadvent.org/cathen/12441a.htm.

135 *Ibid.*

136 Patty Crowley. "Galileo All Over Again." *Conscience*, Winter 1993/1994, pages 30 and 31. This article is part of the commentary "Tarnished Silver Anniversary: Reflections on *Humanae Vitae*."

137 "Tarnished Silver Anniversary: Reflections on *Humanae Vitae*." *Conscience*, Winter 1993/1994. Most of this issue is consumed with complaints about *Humanae Vitae*. Another example of this double standard is contained in Rosemary Radford Ruether. "Women, Sexuality, Ecology, and the Church." *Conscience*, Spring/Summer 1993, pages 6 to 11.

138 Fr. Peter M.J. Stravinkas, Ph.D., S.T.L. [Editor]. *Our Sunday Visitor's Catholic Encyclopedia*. Huntington, Indiana: Our Sunday Visitor Press, 1991, page 786.

139 Alberto Munera, S.J. "Catalyst for Moral Thinking." *Conscience*, Winter 1993/1994, page 38. This article is part of the commentary "Tarnished Silver Anniversary: Reflections on *Humanae Vitae*."

140 "News: United States: Doctor, Escort Killed." *Conscience*, Autumn 1994, pages 48 and 49.

141 Undated CFFC flyer entitled "CFFC is the Voice of the 77% of American Catholics Who Believe in Abortion Rights."

142 Frances Kissling, in "CFFC Notebook: A Mouse that Roars Turns 20." *Conscience*, Spring/Summer 1993, page 54.

143 Father John Courtney Murray, S.J., principle author of Vatican II's *Declaration on Religious Freedom*, quoted in Russell Shaw. "Answers." *National Catholic Register*, September 13, 1992, page 4.

144 Frances Kissling. "The Vatican and Politics of Reproductive Health: A Speech to a Study Group of the British Parliament." *Conscience*, Winter 1996/1997, pages 25 to 29.

145 Munera, *op. cit.*

146 Frances Kissling. "Abortion: Taking on the Hard Questions." *Conscience*, Autumn 1999, pages 2 to 12 [this statement directly contradicts an earlier one by Kissling, when she said that "Church leaders imply — or say outright — that fetuses are persons, entitled to an absolute right to life; abortion therefore is murder" (Frances Kissling. "Latin American Feminists Speak Out." *Conscience*, July/August 1989, pages 21 to 23)].

147 *Ibid.*

148 Tertullian [*Apologeticus*, cap. 9, n. 8; Migne, *Patrologiae Cursus Completus*, Series

217

Latina, 221 vols., Parisii, 1858-1864]; Hippolytus [*Refutatio Omnium Haeresium*, edit. Wendland (also known as *Philosophoumena*), lib. IX, cap. 12, n. 25]; and St. John Chrysostom [*Commentariis in Epistolam ad Romanos*, Homilia XXIV, n. 4; MPG, LX, 626].

149 Frances Kissling. "Abortion: Taking on the Hard Questions." *Conscience*, Autumn 1999, pages 2 to 12.

150 Marjorie Reiley Maguire and Daniel C. Maguire. "Abortion: A Guide to Making Ethical Decisions." CFFC, September 1983.

151 Frances Kissling. "Abortion: Taking on the Hard Questions." *Conscience*, Autumn 1999, pages 2 to 12.

152 Marjorie Reiley Maguire, quoted in *Conscience*, March/April 1984, and in Mary Meehan. "The Maguires Bring Abortion Issue to a Turbulent Boil." *National Catholic Register*, May 27, 1984, pages 1 and 7.

153 "Abortion and Catholic Thought: The Little-Known History." *Conscience*, Autumn 1996, pages 2 to 5.

154 See also *The Catechism of the Catholic Church*, ¶496-507.

155 Monsignor William Smith, "*Humanae Vitae*, Dissent, and Infallibility." Presentation at Human Life International's "Conference on Love, Life, and the Family," held in Santa Barbara, California in March of 1991. This talk answers all of the difficult questions that may be posed by pro-abortionists on Catholic teaching regarding abortion and artificial contraception. The tape of Msgr. Smith's talk would be very useful as a part of catechism classes and natural family planning presentations, and can be ordered from Human Life International, 4 Family Life, Front Royal, VA 22630, USA, telephone: 1-(800) 549-LIFE.

156 Rosemary Radford Ruether. "Catholics and Abortion: Authority vs. Dissent." *Conscience*, November/December 1985, pages 9 to 11.

157 "Against Incapacitation — for an Open Catholicism" [the Cologne Declaration], published in *Conscience*, March/April 1989, pages 5 to 7.

158 *Ibid.*

159 Maurice Hamington. "Like a Virgin ... The Sexual Paradox of Mary." *Conscience*, Spring 1998, pages 15 to 19.

160 *Ibid.*

161 Daniel C. Maguire. "The Splendor of Control: A Commentary on *Veritatis Splendor* and the Elephant in the Living Room." *Conscience*, Winter 1993/1994, pages 26 to 29.

162 "News: Hierarchy Tries to Clamp Down." *Conscience*, Winter 1995/1996, page 33.

163 Excerpts from Frances Kissling's input to Annie Lally Milhaven's book *Inside Stories:*

13 *Valiant Women Challenging the Church. Conscience*, September-December 1987, pages 29 to 37.

164 Maryknoll Sister Rose Dominic Trapasso, quoted in "*Otras Voces*: Latina Feminists and the Church." *Conscience*, July/August 1986, page 13.

165 "The Editors Interview Rosemary Radford Ruether." *U.S. Catholic*, April 1985, page 19.

166 Christine E. Gudorf. "Sexism Enshrined." *Conscience*, Spring/Summer 1995, pages 11 to 17.

167 Rosemary Radford Ruether. *Womanguides: Readings Toward a Feminist Theology*. Beacon Press, 1985, page 104.

168 Mary E. Hunt and Frances Kissling. "The *New York Times* Ad." *Conscience*, Spring/Summer 1993, pages 16 to 23.

169 Adelle-Marie Stan. "A Decade of Dissent." *Conscience*, September-December 1987,

pages 24 to 26.

170 Mary E. Hunt (former member of the CFFC Board of Directors). "Abortion in a Just Society." *Conscience*, July/August 1988, pages 9 to 12 [emphasis in original].

171 "Noted feminist sociologist" Sister Marie Augusta Neal, quoted in Frances Kissling. "Editorial." *Conscience*, November/December 1988, page 2.

172 Hunt, "Abortion in a Just Society," *op. cit.*

173 Mary E. Hunt. "Lovingly Lesbian: Toward a Feminist Theology of Friendship." In James B. Nelson and Sandra P. Longfellow [editors]. *Sexuality and the Sacred: Sources for Theological Reflection.* Westminster: John Knox Press, 1994.

174 Mary Hunt, quoted in *The Re-Imagining Conference: A Report.* American Family Association, April, 1994.

175 CFFC Press Release dated November 13, 2000, at http://www.cath4choice.org.

176 Women-Church Convergence. "Equal is as Equal Does: From the Women-Church Convergence, a Catholic Feminist Commentary on the Report of the Holy See in Preparation for the Fourth World Conference on Women." *Conscience*, Spring/Summer 1995, pages 3, 4, 6, 8 and 9.

177 Steve Askin. "Challenging the Right." *Conscience*, Spring 1994, pages 65 and 66.

178 Mary E. Hunt. "Abortion in a Just Society." *Conscience*, July/August 1988, pages 9 to 12.

179 Rosemary Radford Ruether. "The Church and the Ordination of Women." *Conscience*, September-December 1987, page 12.

180 Mary E. Hunt. "Limited Partners." *Conscience*, May/June 1988, pages 6 to 10.

181 Adelle-Marie Stan. "A Decade of Dissent." *Conscience*, September-December 1987, pages 24 to 26.

182 Doreen Ercolano. "Hunt Speaks on 21st Century Catholic Church." *Record* [Troy, New York], April 25, 1988; Tim O'Brien. "Catholics Protest Theologian's Views." *Times Union* [Albany, New York], April 25, 1988; for a full history of the scandal of Hunt's presentation, see Donna Steichen. *Ungodly Rage: The Hidden Face of Catholic Feminism.* San Francisco: Ignatius Press, 1992. Pages 108 to 111.

183 Excerpts from Frances Kissling's input to Annie Lally Milhaven's book *Inside Stories: 13 Valiant Women Challenging the Church. Conscience*, September-December 1987, pages 29 to 37.

184 For the teachings of the churches on abortion: (1) "Organizations That Have Taken a Position on Abortion Rights," Congressional Research Service, The Library of Congress, HQ 780, October 22, 1985; and (2) T.J. Bosgra. "Abortion, the Bible, and the Church." Booklet from Hawaii Right to Life Education Foundation, Post Office Box 10129, Honolulu, Hawaii 96816. For church membership statistics: (1) Bureau of the Census, United States Department of Commerce. National Data Book and Guide to Sources, *Statistical Abstract of the United States.* 1997 (117th Edition). Washington, DC: United States Government Printing Office. Table 85, "Religious Bodies — Selected Data." (2). Eileen W. Lindner [editor]. *Yearbook of American & Canadian Churches 2001: Considering Charitable Choice.* Nashville: Abingdon Press, 2001. Table 2, "Membership Statistics in the United States," pages 345 to 357.

185 *Ibid.*

186 For methodology and summary of the statistics on this study, see Brian Clowes. *Call to Action or Call to Apostasy?: How Dissenters Plan to Remake the Catholic Church in Their Own Image.* Front Royal, Virginia: Human Life International, 1997.

187 "Statement of Barbara Ferraro and Patricia Hussey." *Conscience*, May/June 1988, page 4.

188 Frances Kissling. "The Catholic Church's Achilles' Heel." *Conscience*, Winter 1999/2000.

189 Barbara Ferraro and Patricia Hussey. "... A Response." *Conscience*, July/August 1986, page 11.

190 Frances Kissling, quoted in Ron Brackin. "'Sister' Frances Kissling: Cardinal of Death." *Liberty Report*, January 1987.

191 Steve Askin. "Challenging the Right." *Conscience*, Spring 1994, pages 65 and 66.

192 Bene E. Madunagu. "Moving Forward." *Conscience*, Summer 1999.

193 Janet Wallach. "The Cardinal of Choice: Frances Kissling's Crusade to Change the Church." *The Washington Post Magazine*, August 24, 1986 cover story; Excerpts from Frances Kissling's input to Annie Lally Milhaven's book *Inside Stories: 13 Valiant Women Challenging the Church. Conscience*, September-December 1987, pages 29 to 37.

194 John Giles Milhaven (former member of the CFFC Board of Directors). "In What Are Women Equal to Men?: Finding Words for What We Know by Intuition." *Conscience*, Winter 1995/1996, pages 2 to 6.

195 Emily Erwin Culpepper. "She Who Creates Values." *Conscience*, Summer 1992, pages 14 to 18 [emphasis in original].

196 *Ibid.*

197 Frances Kissling says that "We believed this [abortion] right was so fundamental that it protected even decisions that others considered wrong, morally reprehensible or irre sponsible."

198 Marcia Gillespie, Editor-in-Chief of *Ms.* Magazine. "Gotta Be Bolder." *Conscience*, Winter 1997/1998, pages 22 to 25.

199 The *Conn v. Conn* case was the first pure `father's rights' litigation brought to the attention of the Supreme Court of the United States, and decisively demonstrated that fathers have no rights whatever regarding their preborn children. In this court case, Erin Andrew Conn of Elkhart, Indiana, won a court order in June 1988 barring his wife from having an abortion. She defied the court injunction and the wishes of the father of her unborn child and obtained an abortion with the help of the American Civil Liberties Union. Her lawyer, Richard A. Waples of the Indiana ACLU, stated in legal papers that "she did what she had to do to protect both her physical and emotional health." Sounds like a pretty seri ous reason to get an abortion, doesn't it? In reality, court documents showed that she had the abortion because she had planned a trip to the beach and wanted to look good in her new bathing suit! [*In re* Unborn Baby H., No. 84C01 8804JP185, slip opinion at 1-2 (Vigo County, Indiana Circuit Court, April 8, 1988). Also see "Woman Defies Court, Father, Aborts Child." *Washington Times*, April 15, 1988.

200 Frances Kissling. "Defining Personhood/Developmental Views." *Conscience*, Spring 1992, page 25; also repeated in Steve Askin. "Challenging the Right." *Conscience*, Spring 1994, page 66.

201 Patricia Wilson-Kastner and Beatrice Blair. "Biblical Views on Abortion: An Episcopal Perspective." *Conscience*, November/December 1985, pages 4 to 8.

202 Excerpts from Frances Kissling's input to Annie Lally Milhaven's book *Inside Stories: 13 Valiant Women Challenging the Church. Conscience*, September-December 1987, pages 29 to 37.

203 Mary Jean Wolch. "An Open Letter From a Catholic Birth Mother." *Conscience*, Autumn

1996, pages 25 to 28; Daniel C. Maguire. "Reflections of a Catholic Theologian on Visiting an Abortion Clinic." *Conscience*, Autumn 1996, pages 29 to 34.

204 *Paquette v. Regal Art Press, Inc.* [656 A.2d 209 (Vt. 1994)]. *Atlantic Reporter*, 2d Series, pages 209-211; "Pro-Life Printers Wage Battle of Conscience." Free Speech Advocates newsletter, January 1991, pages 2 and 3; "Vermont Printers Win Three-Year Fight." *Catalyst* [Journal of the Catholic League for Religious and Civil Rights], April 1994, pages 1 and 12.

205 Ethel Klein. "Whose Health — Catholic Hospitals'? Or Women's?" *Conscience*, Spring/Summer 1995, pages 29 to 36; Patricia Miller. "Religion, Reproductive Health and Access to Services." *Conscience*, Summer 2000, pages 2 to 8; and "Respecting Conscience." *Conscience*, Summer 2000, page 9.

206 Christine E. Gudorf. "Earth's Inhabitants." *Conscience*, Winter 1997/1998, page 25.

207 Diann Neu, pamphlet entitled "Liturgy of Affirmation for Making a Difficult Decision." At the bottom of this pamphlet, it says "Liturgies by Diann Neu, feminist liberation theologian and co-director of WATER, the Women's Alliance for Theology, Ethics and Ritual in Silver Spring, MD."

208 Marcia Gillespie, Editor-in-Chief of *Ms.* Magazine. "Gotta Be Bolder." *Conscience*, Winter 1997/1998, pages 22 to 25.

209 Frances Kissling. "Abortion: Articulating a Moral View." *Conscience*, Summer 2000, pages 21, 22 and 27.

210 Author's conversation with researchers at the NRA's Institute for Legal Action, May 1, 2001.

211 In the United States, 99.31% of all abortions performed in the United States are for social reasons, or to "save the lifestyle of the mother." For detailed calculations and documentation, see Brian Clowes. *The Facts of Life* [2nd Edition]. Front Royal: Human Life International, 2001. Chapter 13, "United States Abortion Statistics."

212 Two examples are *Conscience*, Winter 1996/1997, pages 18-19, and Summer 1996, pages 9 to 11.

213 Daniel C. Maguire. "Reflections of a Catholic Theologian on Visiting an Abortion Clinic." *Conscience*, Autumn 1996, pages 29 to 34.

214 Brian Clowes. *The Facts of Life* [2nd Edition]. Front Royal: Human Life International, 2001. Chapter 13, "United States Abortion Statistics."

215 Rev. Edward J. Hayes, *et.al. Catholicism and Ethics*. Norwood, Massachusetts: C.R. Publications, 1997. Pages 54 to 57.

216 For example, at the 1980 national convention of the National Abortion Federation (NAF), abortionist Lise Fortier said that "Each and every pregnancy threatens a woman's life. From a strict medical viewpoint, every pregnancy should be aborted" [Andrew Scholberg. "The Abortionists and Planned Parenthood: Familiar Bedfellows." *International Review of Natural Family Planning*, Winter 1980, page 308].

One of the most ridiculous pro-abortion abuses of the "double effect" was committed by John M. Swomley of the Religious Coalition for Abortion Rights (now RCRC), of which CFFC is a member organization. Swomley claimed that "The Roman church argues that although the death of the fetus is foreseen, it is not intended because the intention is to preserve the health and life of the woman. Isn't it just as reasonable to assert that the intention of most women is the separation of the fetus from the woman, not the killing of the fetus, though its death may be foreseen?" [June 1987 propaganda pamphlet by RCAR entitled "Six Ethical Questions"].

217 Willard Cates Jr., M.D., *et al*. "Abortion as a Treatment for Unwanted Pregnancy: The Number Two Sexually-Transmitted Condition." Address presented to the Association of Planned Parenthood Physicians Conference, Miami Beach, Florida, November 11-12, 1976.

218 Barbara H. Roberts, M.D. "Abortion Laws Murder Women." Essay in a Women's National Abortion Action Coalition booklet entitled "Abortion is a Woman's Right: March on Washington, DC and San Francisco, November 20 [1972]."

219 Warren Hern. "Is Pregnancy Really Normal?" Alan Guttmacher Institute's *Family Planning Perspectives*, January 1971, page 9; Warren Hern. *Abortion Practice*. Philadelphia: J.B. Lippincott Company, 1984.

220 In some countries there currently exist advanced techniques that can save both the mother and her preborn child even in the extreme case of a tubal pregnancy. Abdominal pregnancies present a less difficult scenario insofar as saving both mother and child, because less advanced technology is required than in the case of tubal pregnancies.

   In the case where the particular medical facility does not have such technology available to save *tubal* babies, competent moralists and doctors affirm that with the present medical technology we can diagnose such pregnancies earlier than before, and we can also accompany expectantly (ready to act but without intervening) a woman pregnant with a tubal preborn baby until we can attempt to save him (if that is indeed possible) or until we know the tubal baby has unfortunately died, in order to then remove him or her without damage to the mother. This way of acting is more respectful towards the preborn baby and the one to be followed, and we should set aside utilitarian considerations about costs, etc. [Niceto Blázquez. *Bioética Fundamental*. Madrid: Biblioteca de Autores Cristianos, 1996].

   Of course, where none of the above techniques are available, the doctors will do the best they can to save both mother and child or at least one of them under the principle of the double effect.

   We must also clarify that many times doctors, when faced with what they think is a tubal pregnancy, immediately rush to intervene without the proper diagnosis. And when they *do* intervene, they use drugs or other means to kill the tubal baby and then remove him or her. This is gravely immoral and does not constitute a correct use of the principle of double effect but a direct abortion.

   Every effort should be made to obtain those techniques to save mother and preborn child and also to prevent ectopic pregnancies, since not enough is being done in this area. Let us keep in mind that many ectopic pregnancies are caused by promiscuity, which can result in sexually transmitted diseases (STDs) and/or the use of the intrauterine device (IUD), which is also abortifacient [see Brian Clowes *The Facts of Life*. Front Royal, Virginia: Human Life International, 2001 (2nd Edition). Chapter 3, "Abortifacients"].

   The case of the cancerous uterus in a pregnant woman no longer presents a problem in saving both mother and preborn child. Therefore the principle of the double effect can not be invoked any longer in this case to justify an intervention that results in the death of the preborn baby [Blázquez, *op. cit.*].

221 Pope Paul VI, *Humanae Vitae* (¶14), July 25, 1968, and Pope Pius XII, "Allocution to Midwives," (¶27), October 29, 1951.

222 Pete Sheehan. "'Pro-Choice Catholics:' What Do They Want?" *Catholic Twin Circle*, June 25, 1989, pages 4 to 9; Lou Jacquet. "Director: Planned Parenthood Not Involved in Ad." *Our Sunday Visitor*, February 24, 1985, page 21.

223 Mary C. Segers. "Catholics and Pluralistic Society." *Conscience*, Spring/Summer 1993, page 24.

224 Full-page CFFC ad, displayed in *Conscience*, Spring/Summer 1993, page 41.

225 Beryl Benderly in her book *Thinking About Abortion*, said that "The Supreme Court placed the decision to end a pregnancy, like that to remove a wart or straighten a nose, in the hands of the patient and her doctor." Quoted in Leslie Bond. "Pre-Natal Program Funds Used for Abortion." *National Right to Life News*, May 1, 1986, page 9.

226 Frances Kissling. "The Abortion Debate — Moving Forward." *Conscience*, January/February 1991, pages 1 and 3.

227 Rosemary Radford Ruether. "Women, Sexuality, Ecology and the Church." *Conscience*, Spring/Summer 1993, pages 6 to 11.

228 Stanley K. Henshaw and Jennifer Van Vort. "Abortion Patients in 1994-1995: Characteristics and Contraceptive Use." *Family Planning Perspectives* [Alan Guttmacher Institute], July/August 1996, pages 140 to 148.

229 Bureau of the Census, United States Department of Commerce. National Data Book and Guide to Sources, *Statistical Abstract of the United States*, 1990 (110th Edition). Table 99, "Contraceptive Use By Women, 15-44 Years Old, By Age, Race, Marital Status, and Method of Contraception: 1982."

230 Robert A. Hatcher, *et. al. Contraceptive Technology* (17th Revised Edition). New York: Ardent Media, Inc., 1998. Table 31-1, "Percentage of Women Experiencing an Unintended Pregnancy During the First Year of Typical Use and the First Year of Perfect Use of Contraception and the Percentage Continuing Use at the End of the First Year: United States," page 800; Robert A. Hatcher. *Contraceptive Technology, 1986-1987* (13th Revised Edition). New York: Irvington Publishers, 1986, page 139. Also see Kim Painter. "'Disturbing' Data on Birth Control Failure." *USA Today*, July 13, 1989, page 1D.

231 Accumulated failure rates can be calculated with the formula $1-(1-f)n$, where f equals the failure rate and n equals the number of years.

232 *Report of the House Select Committee on Children, Youth and Families*. "Teen Pregnancy: What is Being Done? A State-By-State Look." Washington, D.C. U.S. Government Printing Office, December 1985, pages 378 and 385.

233 C. Tietze, J. Bongaarts, and B. Schearer. "Mortality Associated with the Control of Fertility." *Family Planning Perspectives*, January-February 1976, pages 6 to 14.

234 For figures on the number of contraceptive users: Bureau of the Census, United States Department of Commerce. National Data Book and Guide to Sources, *Statistical Abstract of the United States*, 1990 (110th Edition). Table 99, "Contraceptive Use By Women, 15-44 Years Old, By Age, Race, Marital Status, and Method of Contraception: 1982." For figures on contraceptive failure rates: William R. Grady, Mark D. Hayward, and Junichi Yagi. "Contraceptive Failure in the United States: Estimates for the 1982 National Survey of Family Growth." Alan Guttmacher Institute's *Family Planning Perspectives*, September/October 1986, page 204.

235 Henshaw and Van Vort, *op. cit.*

236 Maria Romero, quoted in Janice Perrone. "Controversial Abortion Approach." *American Medical News*, January 12, 1990, pages 9, 18, and 19.

237 Kristin Luker. *Taking Chances: Abortion and the Decision Not to Contracept*. Berkeley: University of California Press, 1975. Inside front dust jacket cover.

238 Leslie Savan. "Abortion Chic: The Attraction of 'Wanted-Unwanted Pregnancies'," *The*

Village Voice, February 4, 1981, pages 10 to 13.

239 Marilyn Buckham, director of the Buffalo GYN Womenservices Clinic abortion mill, quoted in the Revolutionary Communist Party's *Revolutionary Worker*, March 6, 1989.

240 Henshaw and Van Vort, *op. cit.*

241 Aida Torres and Jacqueline Darroch Forrest. "Why Do Women Have Abortions?" *Family Planning Perspectives* [Alan Guttmacher Institute], July/August 1988, pages 169 to 176, Table 1. In 1998, the AGI published the results of studies showing that "lifestyle" reasons also predominate among aborting women all over the world. Its summary of surveys per formed in 27 countries including the United States showed that the primary reasons for aborting given by the 62,658 women interviewed were: "I want no (more) children" (30.9%); "I want to postpone childbearing" (21.1%); "Having a child will disrupt my education or job" (19.9%) "My mental health is at risk" (9.8%); "I can't afford a baby now" (6.6%); "I have a problem with my relationship or my partner does not want this pregnancy" (4.4%); "There is a risk to fetal health" (negative eugenics) (3.1%); "I am too young; my parent(s) or other(s) object to my pregnancy" (1.5%); "My physical health is at risk" (1.1%); and other reasons (1.6%) [Akinrinola Bankole, Susheela Singh and Tayl Haas. "Reasons Why Women Have Induced Abortions: Evidence from 27 Countries." *International Family Planning Perspectives*, August 1998. Table 2, "Percentage Distribution of Women Who Had an Abortion, by Main Reason Given for Seeking Abortion, Various Countries and Years"].

242 Frances Kissling, quoted in "Late-Term Abortion: Speaking Frankly." *Ms.* Magazine, May/June 1997, pages 67 to 71.

243 "Are Young People Different Today?" *Population Reports* [Series J], October 1995, page 13. Johns Hopkins School of Public Health.

244 United States Department of Commerce, Bureau of the Census. Reference Data Book and Guide to Sources, *Statistical Abstract of the United States*. Washington, DC: United States Government Printing Office. 1999 (119th Edition). Table 123, "Abortions — Number, Rate, and Ratio, by Race: 1975 to 1996."

245 Human Life International has documented the deaths of 245 women who were all victims of so-called "safe and legal" abortion. The races of 166 of these women could be positively identified. They included 81 Blacks, 29 Latinas, 4 Asians, one Native American and 51 Whites. This means that *69 percent* of the identifiable legal abortion deaths have occurred among minority women. By comparison, minority women obtain 35 percent of all abortions. This means that the death rate among minority women who abort is *more than four times higher* than that of White women who abort. Planned Parenthood con firms this figure by admitting that the risks of abortion for Black women *are more than three times as high as for White women.* Planned Parenthood says that the death rates for second-trimester abortions for Black and White women respectively are 24.8 and 6.8 deaths per 100,000 abortions [John Benditt. "Special Report: Second-Trimester Abortions in the United States." *Family Planning Perspectives*, November/December 1979, page 359]. For further details, see Brian Clowes. *The Facts of Life* [2nd Edition]. Front Royal: Human Life International, 2001. Chapter 13, "United States Abortion Statistics," Question 135.

246 Lynn Phillips. *Everywoman.* January 22, 1971, pages 17 and 18. Reprinted from the December 14, 1970 *Liberated Guardian.*

247 Henshaw and Van Vort, *op. cit.*

248 Copy Editor Carolyn Hax of the *Washington Post*, quoted in Stephen Settle. "There's No

Middle Ground." *National Catholic Register*, April 25, 1993, page 5.

249 Christopher Durang. "Natural Law and Disorder." *Conscience*, Spring/Summer 1995, pages 7 and 8.

250 Marie Baldwin. "Ardently Prochoice." *Conscience*, Winter 1997/1998, pages 15 and 16.

251 Margaret Conway. "Public Funding: CFFC Makes Waves in Michigan Abortion Rights Battle." *Conscience*, May/June 1988, pages 12 to 16; and Mary E. Hunt. "Limited Partners." *Conscience*, May/June 1988, page 7.

252 "Kissling Takes Debate to London: Challenging the Vatican on Abortion." *Conscience*, May/June 1988, story beginning on back cover. This article was also printed in the March 31, 1988 edition of *The Irish Times*.

253 Rosemary Radford Ruether. "The Catholic Bishops' Pastoral on Women: A Flawed Effort." *Conscience*, May/June 1988, pages 5 and 6.

254 Mike Royko, quoted in "The Late Mike Royko Answers Feminist Attack." *The Life Advocate* [Foundation for Life, Houston], September/October 1998, page 11.

255 Jane Hurst. "Abortion in Good Faith: The History of Abortion in the Catholic Church: The Untold Story." *Conscience*, March/April 1991, pages 1 and 3 to 17 [italics in the original].

256 See Endnote 120 for a list of bible quotations condemning homosexual activity, adultery, fornication and divorce.

257 Canon 63 of the Council of Elvira states "If a woman shall have conceived in adultery while her husband was absent, and afterwards shall have killed the conceptus (child conceived), she shall not be given communion even at death, because she did this twofold wicked deed" [J.D. Mansi, *Sacrorum Conciliorum Nova et Amplissima Collectio*, 2,16].

258 Canon 21 of the Council of Chalcedon, *Conciliorum Oecumenicorum Decreta*. Alberigo, Joannou, Leonardi and Prodi [editors]. Friburg: Herder Press, 1962 page 63.

259 Frances Kissling's talk during the National Abortion Federation (NAF) 16th Annual Meeting, theme: "Abortion: Moral Choice and Medical Imperative," April 12-15, 1992, in San Diego, California, closing session entitled "Cooperation and Competition."

260 Donald DeMarco. *In My Mother's Womb: The Catholic Church's Defense of Natural Life*. Manassas, Virginia: Trinity Communications, 1987. Pages 7 through 25 include an excellent and detailed account of the teaching of the Catholic Church on abortion.
Additionally, for an excellent summary of the history of Church teaching on abortion, see Most Reverend Rene H. Gracida, D.D., Bishop of Corpus Christi, Pastoral Letter on Abortion and Excommunication, "Choose Life, Not Death!" September 8, 1990, Appendix A, "An Historical Review of Law Relating to Abortion." You can access this document at http://www.priestsforlife.org/magisterium/gracida.htm.

261 Lucius Farraris, *Bibliotheca Iuridica Moralis Theologica*. Roma: 1885, I, pages 36 to 38.

262 Paolo Zacchia, Physician-General of the Vatican State. *Quaestiones Medico-Legales*. Lyons: 1701. Library 6, Title 1, Questions 7 and 16.

263 Denzinger-Schoenmetzer. *Enchiridion Symbolorum*. Rome: Herder, 1965. Pages 2,134 to 2,135.

264 *Codicus Iuris Canonici Fontes*. 9 Volumes. Rome, 1923 to 1939, specification number 552.

265 Thomas A. Shannon and Patricia Beattie Jung [editors]. *Abortion and Catholicism: The American Debate* (1988), page 6. Excerpted in Lisa M. Hisel. "Abortion: A Reader's Guide." *Conscience*, Autumn 1996, page 40.

266 See Genesis 9:5-6; Jeremiah 7:5-6; Isaiah 1:10-17, and 29:13; Proverbs 24:11-12; and

Matthew 25:34-40.

267 Garry Wills. "Mario Cuomo's Trouble with Abortion." *Conscience*, September/October 1990, pages 1, 4-9, 16, 17 and 20.

268 Ellen Carton, New York executive director of the National Abortion Rights Action League (NARAL), quoted in "Gazette." *Conscience*, May/June 1988, page 17.

269 Annie Lally Milhaven. "Fatherly Fanaticism." *Conscience*, July/August 1988, page 6.

270 Ellen Carton, New York executive director of the National Abortion Rights Action League (NARAL), says that " ... commotion outside a clinic increases stress and affects the performance of medical personnel." Quoted in "Gazette." *Conscience*, May/June 1988, page 17.

271 Frances Kissling has said that "Protesting or praying outside women's health centers by cardinals and other church leaders, no matter how non-violent it appears, offends and hurts women." Quoted in Cathleen Falsani. "Abortion Foes Gather to Pray: Cardinal Bernardin Leads Mass at Chicago Clinic." *Daily Southtown*, June 27, 1999, pages 1 and 10 [NOTE: Falsani, the "religion writer" for this newspaper, could not even get the name of the Cardinal right in her article. It was Cardinal George who let the Mass at the abortion mill, not Cardinal Bernardin, who died more than a year earlier]. CFFC also boasted that "In June, we held a press conference to criticize Cardinal John O'Connor's "prayer picket" in front of a New York City abortion clinic" ["CFFC Notebook." *Conscience*, Summer 1992, pages 38 and 39].

272 Richard Doerflinger. "Who are Catholics for a Free Choice?" *America*, November 16, 1985, page 313.

273 Mary Jean Wolch. "An Open Letter From a Catholic Birth Mother." *Conscience*, Autumn 1996, pages 25 to 28.

274 "Gazette." *Conscience*, May/June 1988, page 17.

275 Letter by Rev. E.L. O'Hickey, *Conscience*, May/June 1988, page 19.

276 Margaret Conway. "State Updates." *Conscience*, July/August 1989, pages 16 and 17.

277 "In the News: Not in My Building, You Don't." *Conscience*, January/February 1991, page 22.

278 "In Brief." *Conscience*, Spring/Summer 1995, page 57 ["If religious leaders sincerely want to deter the terrorists, they must disavow one premise, ... that there is no significant difference between the human life of the unborn and human life of the born human being"].

279 Frances Kissling. "The Vatican's Cheap Shot at UNICEF." *Conscience*, Winter 1996/1997, pages 36 and 37.

280 Excerpts from Frances Kissling's input to Annie Lally Milhaven's book *Inside Stories: 13 Valiant Women Challenging the Church. Conscience*, September-December 1987, pages 29 to 37.

281 Various pro-abortionists, interviewed by Lisa M. Hisel and Patricia Miller. "Bribery or Benevolence: Prochoice Leaders Examine the Generosity of a Scottish Cardinal." *Conscience*, Winter 1999/2000.

282 Marjorie Reiley Maguire (former member of the CFFC Board of Directors). "Not Catholic." Letter published by the *National Catholic Reporter*, April 21, 1995, page 18.

283 Christine E. Gudorf. "To Make a Seamless Garment, Use a Single Piece of Cloth." *Conscience*, Autumn 1996, pages 10 to 21.

284 Letter from Thomas J. Gumbleton, Auxiliary Bishop of Detroit, to *Conscience*, Autumn 1996, page 45.

226

285 Rosemary Radford Ruether. "The Mantra of "Anti-Catholicism:" What is Bigotry?" *Conscience*, Autumn 2000.

286 Valerie J. Stroud, United Kingdom liaison for the dissenting group International Movement We Are Church. "Where We Go From Here: What *Ad Tuendam Fidem* — "To Defend the Faith" — Means for Progressive Catholics." *Conscience*, Autumn 1998, pages 2 and 3.

287 Robin Tolmach Lakoff. "Radical Cheek: The Evolution of a Revolutionary Word." *Conscience*, Autumn 1997, pages 21 to 24.

288 "Mean" [Frances Kissling, on John Cardinal O'Connor. Quoted in E. Bumiller. "As Pope's Important Ally, Cardinal Shines High in Hierarchy." *New York Times*, October 8, 1995, page 41]; "terrible" [Frances Kissling's talk during the National Abortion Federation (NAF) 16th Annual Meeting, theme: "Abortion: Moral Choice and Medical Imperative," April 12-15, 1992, in San Diego, California, closing session: "Cooperation and Competition"]. The following are all from *Conscience* Magazine: "Absolutist" [Winter 1996/1997, page 5]; "angry," "dogmatic," "harsh" and "unkind" [Winter 1996/1997, pages 14 and 17]; "angry," "dogmatic," "hard-hearted," "harsh" and "unkind" [Winter 1996/1997, pages 14 to 17]; "arrogant" [Winter 1993/1994, page 27]; "betrayers of Christ" and "the seed of Satan" [Spring 1997, page 4]; "blind" and "hard-hearted" [September-December 1987, page 8]; "bullies" [Spring 1996, page 32]; "callous" and "coercive" [Summer 1999]; "confused" and "narrow-minded" [January/February 1996, page 9]; "cruel," "ruthless," "vehement," "anti-woman," "slippery, a clerical Barbie Doll" [referring to Bernard Cardinal Law], and "rigid" [September-December 1987, pages 40 and 41]; "dangerous" and "nasty" [Summer 2000, pages 10 to 13]; "dumb" and "hypo critical" [September-December 1987, pages 29 to 37]; "embarrassing," "misogynist" and "pernicious" [Winter 1993/1994, page 38]; "fanatical" [September-December 1987, pages 22 and 23]; "harsh" [Winter 1996/1997, page 24]; "illogical," "loony," "pig-headed" and "tyrannical" [Spring/Summer 1995, pages 7 and 8]; "imperialistic" [Winter 1996/1997, inside front cover]; "irresponsible" [September-December 1987, page 27]; "liars" [Winter 1995/1996, page 8]; "Luddites" and "reactionaries" [Spring 2001, page 7]; "manipula-tive" and "unethical" [Winter 1999/2000]; "mean" [Spring 1996, page 32]; "obsessive" [Winter 1996/1997, page 5]; "obstructive" [Winter 1995/1996, page 12]; "pathological" [Winter 1993/1994, page 32]; "prattlers" [September/October 1989, page 3]; "ranting" [speech given at the candlelight vigil of the Religious Coalition for Abortion Rights by Rosemary Stasek of California CFFC, January 19, 1992]; "self-righteous" and "sancti-monious" [Autumn 1996, pages 29 to 34]; "simplistic" [Spring/Summer 1993, page 9]; "totalitarian" [Autumn 1998, page 3]; "unhinged" [September/October 1990, page 9] "unjust" [Spring/Summer 1993, page 18]; "vehement" [Spring/Summer 1995, page 27]; "virulent" [Spring/Summer 1993, page 16, and Winter 1999/2000]; and "vituperative" [July/August 1989, page 8, and January/February 1996, page 5].

289 Barbara Ferraro and Patricia Hussey. "... A Response." *Conscience*, July/August 1986, page 11.

290 Mary E. Hunt. "Limited Partners." *Conscience*, May/June 1988, pages 6 to 10.

291 Frances Kissling, quoted in a fundraising pitch on page 17 of *Conscience*, September-December 1987.

292 Excerpts from Frances Kissling's input to Annie Lally Milhaven's book *Inside Stories: 13 Valiant Women Challenging the Church. Conscience*, September-December 1987, pages 29 to 37.

293 Magaly Llaguno. "'Catholics for a Free Choice:' A Dossier." *Vida Humana Internacional*, December 1994, page 2.

294 Lisa Desposito. "High Hopes — Quickly Dashed." *Conscience*, September-December 1987, pages 6 and 7; *Conscience*, September-December 1987, page 18.

295 *Ibid.*

296 Mary M. Sullivan. "Defying Tradition: One Irish Woman's Struggle for the Right to Choose." *Conscience*, September-December 1987, pages 20 and 21.

297 Frances Kissling. "Holy Role Models: The Vatican's Beatifications Send a Message to Girls." *Conscience*, Autumn 1994, pages 41 and 42; Frances Kissling. "Latin American Feminists Speak Out." *Conscience*, July/August 1989, pages 21 to 23.

298 Janet L. Parker. "Religious, "Right," and Heterosexist." *Conscience*, Spring 1996, pages 3 to 14.

299 CFFC board member Rosemary Radford Ruether. "Women, Sexuality, Ecology, and the Church." *Conscience*, Spring/Summer 1993,, pages 6 to 11.

300 Robin Tolmach Lakoff. "The Rhetoric of Reproduction." *Conscience*, Summer 1992, pages 4 to 12; Frances Kissling and Denise Shannon. "Who's Right?" *Conscience*, Spring 1994, page 4; Annie Lally Milhaven. "Fatherly Fanaticism." *Conscience*, July/August 1988, page 6; Frances Kissling. "Summer Releases: Four 'Must' Reads." *Conscience*, July/August 1988, pages 19 and 20. Rabbi Balfour Brickner. "Matters Sexual." *Conscience*, Winter 1997/1998, pages 18 and 19; Frances Kissling and Denise Shannon. "Who's Right?" *Conscience*, Spring 1994, page 3.

301 Malcolm Potts, President, Family Health International [FHI]. "Religious Liberty." *Conscience*, Winter 1997/1998, page 35.

Index

Notes